JOHN JAKES

JOHN
JAKES

A Critical Companion

Mary Ellen Jones

CRITICAL COMPANIONS TO POPULAR CONTEMPORARY WRITERS
Kathleen Gregory Klein, Series Editor

Greenwood Press
Westport, Connecticut • London

Library of Congress Cataloging-in-Publication Data

Jones, Mary Ellen, 1937–
    John Jakes : a critical companion / Mary Ellen Jones.
    p.   cm.—(Critical companions to popular contemporary
writers, ISSN 1082–4979)
    Includes bibliographical references and index.
    ISBN 0–313–29530–1 (alk. paper)
    1. Jakes, John, 1932–   —Criticism and interpretation.
I. Title. II. Series.
PS3560.A37Z73   1996
813'.54—dc20   96–18205

British Library Cataloguing in Publication Data is available.

Library of Congress Catalog Card Number: 96–18205
ISBN: 0–313–29530–1
ISSN: 1082–4979

First published in 1996

Greenwood Press, 88 Post Road West, Westport, CT 06881
An imprint of Greenwood Publishing Group, Inc.

Printed in the United States of America

The paper used in this book complies with the
Permanent Paper Standard issued by the National
Information Standards Organization (Z39.48–1984).

10 9 8 7 6 5 4 3 2 1

For
Charles A. Dominick,
who saved my life

Contents

PART III: NEW BEGINNINGS

Series Foreword

The authors who appear in the series Critical Companions to Popular Contemporary Writers are all best-selling writers. They do not have only one successful novel, but a string of them. Fans, critics, and specialist readers eagerly anticipate their next book. For some, high cash advances and breakthrough sales figures are automatic; movie deals often follow. Some writers become household names, recognized by almost everyone.

But novels are read one by one. Each reader chooses to start and, more importantly, to finish a book because of what she or he finds there. The real test of a novel is in the satisfaction its readers experience. This series acknowledges the extraordinary involvement of readers and writers in creating a best-seller.

The authors included in this series were chosen by an Advisory Board composed of high school English teachers and high school and public librarians. They ranked a list of best-selling writers according to their popularity among different groups of readers. Writers in the top-ranked group who had not received book-length, academic literary analysis (or none in at least the past ten years) were chosen for the series. Because of this selection method, Critical Companions to Popular Contemporary Writers meets a need that is not addressed elsewhere.

The volumes in the series are written by scholars with particular expertise in analyzing popular fiction. These specialists add an academic focus to the popular success that the best-selling writers already enjoy.

The series is designed to appeal to a wide range of readers. The general reading public will find explanations for the appeal of these well-known writers. Fans will find biographical and fictional questions answered. Students will find literary analysis, discussions of fictional genres, carefully organized introductions to new ways of reading the novels, and bibliographies for additional research. Students will also be able to apply what they have learned from this book to their readings of future novels by these best-selling writers.

Each volume begins with a biographical chapter drawing on published information, and biographies or memoirs, prior interviews, and, in some cases, interviews given especially for this series. A chapter on literary history and genres describes how the author's work fits into a larger literary content. The following chapters analyze the writer's most important, most popular, and most recent novels in detail. Each chapter focuses on a single novel. This approach, suggested by the Advisory Board as the most useful to student research, allows for an in-depth analysis of the writer's fiction. Close and careful readings with numerous examples show readers exactly how the novels work. These chapters are organized around three central elements: plot development (how the story line moves forward), character development (what the reader knows about the important figures), and theme (the significant ideas of the novel). Chapters may also include sections on generic conventions (how the novel is similar to or different from others in its same category of science fiction, fantasy, thriller, etc.), narrative point of view (who tells the story and how), symbols and literary language, and historical or social context. Each chapter ends with an "alternative reading" of the novel. The volume concludes with a primary and secondary bibliography, including reviews.

The Alternative Readings are a unique feature of this series. By demonstrating a particular way of reading each novel, they provide a clear example of how a specific perspective can reveal important aspects of the book. In each alternative reading section, one contemporary literary theory—such as feminist criticism, Marxism, new historicism, deconstruction, or Jungian psychological critique—is defined in brief, easily comprehensible language. That definition is then applied to the novel to highlight specific features that might go unnoticed or be understood differently in a more general reading of the novel. Each volume defines two or three specific theories, making them part of the reader's understanding of how diverse meanings may be constructed from a single novel.

Taken collectively, the volumes in the Critical Companions to Popular

Contemporary Writers series provide a wide-ranging investigation of the complexities of current best-selling fiction. By treating these novels seriously as both literary works and publishing successes, the series demonstrates the potential of popular literature in contemporary culture.

Kathleen Gregory Klein
Southern Connecticut State University

Acknowledgments

"Many traps are set in this wilderness. You were caught in the cruelest of all. Trust."

John Jakes, "Manitow and Ironhand."

As Ironhand discovered, however, one cannot survive without trust. My sincere thanks, thus, to all who held out your knives, handle first.

Thanks to Barbara Brannon, of the University of South Carolina, for your assistance in compiling the bibliography. To Lori Judy, of Wittenberg University, thanks for rounding up copies of all but two of Jakes' books.

To friends—most especially Esther and Harvey Damaser, Sandy Freshour and Ron Grosh—thanks for your constancy, your common sense, your humor, and your help in fending off the bad guys. And to Bob Fricke, thanks for being there—as always.

Finally, my deepest thanks belongs to John Jakes—who has offered far more than a lifetime of good stories. For what you've taught me about the writer's craft, for your generous and hospitable responses to all my questions, and, ultimately, for your model of human decency, your faith in the good in a world where absolute evil exists—thanks for being one of the "better angels."

PART I

BIOGRAPHY AND GENRES

1

"The People's Author":
The Life of John Jakes

John Jakes: "godfather of the historical novel," "the people's author," "America's history teacher." The "acknowledged contemporary master of the family saga, John Jakes is the creator of the legendary eight-volume *Kent Family Chronicles*, the Main and Hazard families of the *North and South Trilogy*, James and Nellie Chance of *California Gold*, and now the Crowns of Chicago, German-Americans whose stories interweave the history of the twentieth century in *Homeland* and subsequent novels" (unpublished biography).

John Jakes is so prolific that rumors circulated that no such individual truly existed, but that he was, rather, a team of writers and researchers. He is so popular that more than 50 million copies of his works are currently in print. His first blockbuster, *The Bastard*, is in its fifty-ninth printing with 4.6 million copies in print (letter to the author, 16 August 1995). None of the Kent Family Chronicles sold fewer than 3.5 million copies (Dahlin, "John Jakes," 99). In 1985, with *The Rebels*, *The Seekers*, and *The Furies*, Jakes became the first author to have three *New York Times* best-sellers in a single year. Six of his major novels have been filmed as miniseries, and the first *North and South* production (ABC, David L. Wolper Productions) was one of television's ten highest Nielson rated miniseries. *Homeland* is Jakes' thirteenth consecutive *New York Times* best-seller; optioned by David L. Wolper six months before publication, it was named by the *Times* as one of its notable books of 1993.

Jakes is the recipient of honorary degrees from Wright State University (1976), DePauw University, his alma mater (1977), Winthrop College, the University of South Carolina (1993) and Ohio State University (1996). He has spent a term as writer-in-residence at DePauw University and has been, since 1989, a research fellow in the department of history at the University of South Carolina. In 1995 alone he received the Ohio State University College of Humanities Alumni Award; the citizen and celebrity award for library advocacy from the White House Conference on Libraries and Information Systems Task Force; and the Western Heritage Award at the National Cowboy Hall of Fame for the best western short story of 1994. From December 1993 through January 1994 he was the subject of an exhibition at the Thomas Cooper Library at the University of South Carolina entitled "John Jakes: The People's Author."

With so many accomplishments and such recognition, with a wife of forty-four years whom he credits with providing support through good times and bad, with four grown children, successful in their own right, and with homes in Hilton Head, South Carolina, and Greenwich, Connecticut, it would seem that John Jakes has it all. In reality, he is a man who has earned his success, having paid his dues several times over. He experimented in a variety of genres, writing over seventy books before achieving "instant" success with *The Bastard* in 1974; several times in his career he has been beset by doubt and depression. Persevering, he is a man who, in many ways, lives the American values so often personified in his characters.

John Jakes was born 31 March 1932 in Chicago, the son of John Adrian and Bertha Retz Jakes. As an only child of parents who were in their forties when he was born, the young Jakes shared many of their "adult" recreational activities, especially reading and Saturday visits to the movies or to legitimate theater. These influenced him deeply.

He frequently notes that his early inspiration came from "the swashbuckling adventure films of the 1930s and 1940s. . . . I have this gigantic cinemascope screen in my head. . . . I always see what I'm writing about in terms of the colors of the clothes, the weather, the sky," (*Contemporary Authors*, NRS 43: 229). One critic, Mel Watkins, comments on Jakes' narrative style in *North and South*: "The narrative shifts cinematically from scene to scene—North to South, plantation to industrial town—and each new scene or mini-drama adds a bit more detail to the author's overall portrait of a country splitting in two and the social dynamics that escalate its impending conflict" (Watkins, 24). In his introduction to the Pinnacle Edition of *King's Crusader* Jakes acknowledged his debt quite specifically: "This book was written in the 1960s as a tribute to a major influence on the imagination of a would-be writer growing up in the streets and movie palaces of Chicago, ... a string of great adventure films loosely based on historical subjects and produced in the late thirties and forties by Warner Brothers ... *The Adventures of Robin Hood. Dodge City. They Died with Their Boots On. Charge of the Light Brigade.* And more. They had in common not only their origin in a single studio but also an impossibly dashing leading man, Errol Flynn, and a style of music scoring which fairly shouted '*Derring do!*' " Jakes recognizes that these films often lacked plausible character motivation. "But such flaws are forgivable because those movies offered so many other good things. Opulence. Spectacle. Romance. Nonstop excitement salted with tantalizing historical names and events. After seeing such a picture, I usually whizzed to the Chicago Public Library to find out more about Custer or Balaklava" (*King's Crusader*, xi-xii). Such early awareness of the conventions of nonprint media may make Jakes more comfortable with the television miniseries adaptations of his works. Unlike some other authors, he does not rail at producers' modifications of his text. "An adaptation is never a truthful rendering of the book. So I've been reasonably happy. . . . I understand the system and how it works" (Czura, 60).

Not only did the young Jakes rush to the library to "find out more about Custer and Balaklava," he also got hooked on the mysteries that his parents were reading. Unfortunately, he couldn't take adult fiction from the Chicago Public Library with a juvenile card. He discovered, however, that if you worked for the library, you could have all the adult fiction you wanted. So, "at 13 or 14 I became a page, shelving books at a branch on North Broadway. I joyfully brought home armloads of thrillers" (Jakes, "There's Always a Book," 12). Jakes is today a passionate library advocate, aware of his own debt to the Chicago Public Library and to his parents. "If I did not have the library habit—which is passed on by families—I certainly couldn't research and write the first chapter of a historical novel" (Jakes, "There's Always a Book," 12-13). Nonetheless, he does not condemn television; rather, he believes that adaptations of books to TV may well drive viewers to the library to read the original of the miniseries they loved. That more can do so, Jakes has been active in Hilton Head, serving on the Cultural Council in its drive for a performing arts center and advocating a larger library facility with an expanded collection.

This dual civic responsibility also reflects his third early influence— the theater. At one time, he dreamed of being an actor. In high school, he was part of a comedy team that performed at dances and amateur shows. But when he sold his first story—about a diabolical toaster which took over its owner's body—to the *Magazine of Fantasy and Science Fiction*, his career took a turn. Already he'd grown from the boy who had begun reading science fiction at eleven or twelve: "It took me a couple of years just to discover that you weren't supposed to send manuscripts to magazines written in pencil on two sides of sheets of notebook paper" (*Tiros: Weather Eye in Space*, end matter). "I became convinced that it was easier to go to the corner mailbox and make a little money than it was to go to Broadway. . . . [W]hen I got that twenty-five dollar check . . . that was when I really turned the corner. . . . It's a good thing . . . because I've never been that good an actor" (*Contemporary Authors*, NRS 10: 224). He did, however, have a bit part in the miniseries adaptation of *The Seekers* and *The Furies*. "I made my film debut as the lawyer, Elphinstone. George Hamilton as Stovall disposed of me" (letter to the author, 5 August 1995). Jakes has written several plays as well as the book or lyrics for musical comedies; his adaptation of *A Christmas Carol* has been performed at a number of regional theaters. Although his theater projects are now mainly avocational, he feels that "theater work has practical benefits for novel writing . . . it gives you a much better ear for dialogue" (*Something About the Author*, 62: 87).

Jakes graduated from the creative writing program at DePauw University (1953). Even during college, his ferocious work habits were evident. During his sophomore year, he moved out of his fraternity house to one of the annexes—a privilege usually reserved for seniors—because he was writing fiction as well as carrying a full academic load and he needed more quiet. It was at the end of his sophomore year, on June 15, 1951, that he and Rachel Anne Payne, who had been his zoology lab instructor, married. He then earned an M.A. in American literature from Ohio State (1954) but left the Ph.D. program to meet the demands of a growing family. His first job was with Abbott Laboratories (1954-1960), where he began as copywriter and became product promotion manager. From then until 1971 he worked at a number of advertising agencies in Rochester, New York, and Dayton, Ohio; among the accounts he worked on were Eastman Kodak, Frigidaire Division of General Motors, Winters National Bank (Bank One), and RCA Consumer Electronics. His theater interest had an outlet in a specialty he developed—writing annual sales meetings for corporations. Executives are not encouraged to "wing it—presentations are tightly scripted, with all audio-visuals (films, slides) prepared ahead of time. Sometimes these meetings are quite lavish—

songs, special lyrics, orchestra, professional cast" (letter to the author, 19 August 1995). This multimedia, cooperative creative expertise shows up later, most especially in his collaboration on *Susanna of the Alamo* with Paul Bacon (who designed the jackets for *California Gold* and all three books in the North and South series). "[Paul and I] planned it page by page, in storyboard form, before I ever wrote a word of text" (letter to the author, 9 July 1995). They storyboarded the book much as a film is created, planning how the plot might be handled visually, considering camera angles and settling on the movie technique of "showing sinister figures or grisly happenings as oversized silhouettes; shadows on a wall" as a solution to the problem of portraying violence in a children's book (*Something About the Author*, 62: 89).

During his advertising years, Jakes wrote at least sixty books, probably more; for awhile he kept a running total of the number. "At 78, I lost count," he says (Czura 12). Many of these were written under pseudonyms—Alan Payne, Rachel Anne Payne, and Jay Scotland. His editor for the original edition of *I, Barbarian*, Jakes' first historical novel, was dead set against using the name John Jakes on the cover. "Sounds like a piece of machinery, unfit for big-scale stuff with a lot of action and romance." Only with the Kent Family Chronicles could Jakes reclaim his name as a writer of historical fiction. " 'Jakes' wrote a good deal of science fiction; evidently a clanking, clattering name is all right for science fiction" (*I, Barbarian*, Pinnacle Edition, ix). The lack of autonomy Jakes experienced during this early period is further demonstrated by the fact that, although he wanted to write historical novels with American themes, his publishers told him that "those guys in three-cornered hats don't sell." And in those days, he wrote to sell. Besides any author's drive to create, he had a financial motive. "We had four children. . . . Virtually everything that I made from my writing went into their college education" (*Something About the Author*, 62: 85). He wrote at night, squeezing in a regular three sessions a week in addition to his day job and his family responsibilities. He and Rachel certainly fulfilled their dream for their children. All four are now married, with children. Andrea has a Ph.D. in clinical psychology from the University of Florida; Ellen, a Ph.D. in communications from Northwestern; Michael, a J.D. from Georgetown Law School; and Victoria, an M.A. in journalism from the University of South Carolina.

Jakes realizes that he did not write his best during this period. "Though I fulfilled the goal in fine style, I have a certain amount of regret about the hasty writing during this period. 'More,' not 'better' was the watchword for too long" (letter to the author, 22 June 1995). During this early period, Jakes wrote in a variety of genres: science fiction, mystery/suspense, fantasy, a detective series; short stories and novels; children's fiction and nonfiction.

The nadir of his writing career came in 1973 when he accepted a flat fee of $1,500 to novelize *Conquest of the Planet of the Apes*. Jakes recently mused: "When that *Planet of the Apes* thing came along, I said to Rachel, 'I've been wasting the last 20 years.' I finally began to think I couldn't cut it as a writer" (Dahlin, "John Jakes," 99). It was during this period, too, that Jakes developed a conviction that evil truly exists in the world. "In Rochester, New York (1960-65) I went through one of several very dark periods of doubt and despair—about my work, and everything in general. . . . Sometime in this period I came to the conclusion that, yes, absolute evil (in human form) does exist—with no redeeming 'causes,' excuses, or other ameliorating aspects. It may be relatively rare, but I believe it's with us. Look at the pathological Nazis for an obvious example" (letter, 7/9/95). Despite Jakes' fundamental optimism, some of this philosophical blackness is present in his writings to this day.

The bleakness could be professional as well as personal. "On reflection," he recently wrote, "I've concluded that there are two relatively clear periods in my writing." During the first, into the 1970s, his books were primarily plot-driven; his purpose "solely to entertain." Though Jakes believes that "without hooking (i.e. entertaining) the reader *first*, you can't accomplish any other goals, . . . I felt I fell short . . . didn't do enough. . . . My success came in the second period, when I fused my dedication to entertaining a reader with a desire to provide solid historical content—I guess you could say 'teach' if that isn't too pretentious" (letter, 7/9/95).

The breakthrough came when Jakes was approached by Lyle Kenyon Engel, creator of a frankly commercial publishing idea, a series of historical novels, timed to coincide with the American Bicentennial. Don Moffit, with whom Jakes had worked in an ad agency in Rochester, was first asked to do the job, but he was busy with a series of spy novels and so recommended Jakes. "So really I was the second-choice writer. . . . [T]here's a lot of luck and timing involved in success" (*Contemporary Authors*, NRS 10: 244-45).

The Kent Family Chronicles, originally planned for five novels to bring the Kent family to 1976, grew to eight and was still some ninety years short when Jakes begged off doing any more. Not only was he tired (eight blockbuster books in six years), but he believes in the theater principle of "leaving the audience wanting more, rather than taking the television route where the story drags on and on week after week" (Dahlin, "John Jakes," 99).

Jakes has analyzed the reasons for the success of the Kent Family Chronicles. First of all, he says, he tries to tell good stories. Second, the time was ripe for a rebirth of the family saga. But, perhaps most important, his writing reflected recent history and thus resonated with the reading public of the 1970s. Despite the national disillusionment of the "Viet Nam-Johnson-Nixon-Watergate years—the terrible years," Jakes believed that "there was a great deal good about this country that we had forgotten. I set out to state some of those positive things. . . . I didn't try to gloss over the slavery question or the stealing of Indian lands, but nevertheless there's a good deal about this country and what it stands for that we had kind of lost sight of in that really crappy time that we went through. I think this played through strongly in the books" (*Dictionary of Literary Biography Yearbook*, 265).

With subsequent novels—*North and South, Love and War, Heaven and Hell, California Gold*, and *Homeland*—he continues to demonstrate those beliefs. Though he does not think it wise to insert "messages" into his fiction, he does believe that historical fiction "permits you to comment on the past, and, by indirection, the present" (Jakes, "The Historical Family Saga," 46).

Jakes is aware of his responsibility to his readers, aware that for many, he is their only source of history. Thus he spends about 50 percent of the time on any novel doing research. He usually starts with a good general work of the period before deciding which events his characters will participate in and which historical figures they'll encounter. Next he moves on to biographies and social histories. Then he'll read diaries of the period for details of what clothes women wore, what songs were popular, what camp life was like for a soldier (*Something About the Author*, 62: 86). Once, in an almost fanatic search for accuracy, Jakes waded through twelve books before determining exactly which of Jefferson Davis' eyes was bad. "That's the sort of thing that drives a writer crazy. . . . It was the left eye" (*Contemporary Authors*, 10: 244).

Jakes is a self-confessed workaholic. Though he has slowed from the furious pace demanded by the Kent Family Chronicles, he's at the computer by 8 A.M., having mentally set himself the task of writing a certain amount of material, whether it's a scene or half a chapter, usually 2,000 to 4,000 words each day. Although in his early career he used to stay up all night writing, he no longer does so. "I found long ago that much more than six hours of really hard work is not productive." Usually he works five days a week, but "when I get excited," or toward the end of a project, his work week becomes seven days (Czura, 37). Sometimes, after thorough research and hard work, he lets the subconscious solve creative problems. "Often, before going to bed, I'll briefly think over the scene or section to be written the next day. Not in detail; just quickly. In the morning, many times when I'm in the shower, the dialogue starts unreeling in my head—requiring a lurch from the shower dripping wet, to the pad and pen kept ready . . . the material just spills out. It needs to be re-worked, polished, of course; but it's there in rough form" (letter to the author, 29 September 1994).

Jakes is aware of one of the dangers of success—writing the same book over and over again, in part because the public demands it. Such writers "exhibit very little growth or change in a body of work over a period of years. Maybe I'm jealous—for I've always thought that my efforts to change from book to book—not write the same novel twice (though consciously or unconsciously I do use and re-use some of the *devices* I've developed)—has been done to my detriment. Readers who stick with a writer through book after book want 'the same thing only different.' But I take heart when I look at my idol, Mr. Dickens, who wrote his greatest crowd-pleasers early in his career, and followed them with masterpieces—and darkening visions—such as 'Bleak House.' . . . I do like and admire my colleague Steve King because he *has* made the effort to change—grow—expand and test the limits of his talent in different kinds of work" (letter to the author, 18 July 1995).

For relaxation, Jakes swims a lot in the summer, loves tennis, and, with his wife Rachel, makes several trips each year to New York to see new plays. Most recently, he has acquired a nineteen-foot boat which is anchored in the Calibogue Sound behind his Hilton Head home.

But writing remains his focus. Despite a heart attack in August 1994 as well as some creative disagreement with his publisher, he is now hard at work on the second volume of *Homeland*. It can't come too soon.

2

From Apprentice to Master Craftsman: The Many Genres of John Jakes

Even a quick examination of Chapter 1 reveals John Jakes as a person in love with words and a master craftsman in using them—from the thirteen-year-old who became a page at the Chicago Public Library so he could borrow adult books, to the advertising executive conscious of every word's value in a thirty-second radio commercial or the precisely evocative copy headline, to, finally, the best-selling novelist whose new title can be expected to sell at least 3 million copies. Over the years, he has written voluminously—over 70 books, 200 short stories, and occasional articles. Not only has he been incredibly prolific, but he has also been incredibly versatile, having written mystery/suspense, science fiction, fantasy, juvenile works—both fiction and nonfiction—and musical comedy in addition to the historical fiction for which he is most well known.

This diversity may create an uneven body of work. Jakes is aware of potential problems. He wrote in 1977, "I like to do too many kinds of things, and I think that's always been one of my troubles. I never really specialized enough" (Polking, 23). Moreover, some of the early work was done quickly, especially before he became a full-time writer. Even later, contract demands—as with the Kent Family Chronicles—required a relentless pace. Critics thus sometimes attack him for his very speed—implying a corresponding shallowness—or ponder the rumor that John Jakes was the "corporate name for a whole team of writers and researchers that churned the stuff out to the precise specifications of the publisher" (Cook, "They Went Thataway," E3). The truth, as we have seen, is that Jakes is a terribly hard-working author, one whose "lesser" genres reveal his developing skills as a writer, establish some of his ongoing themes, and separate him from the academic writer, often satirized as learning more and more about less and less. For Jakes enjoys experimentation, and his appetite for learning is voracious. This chapter will examine how Jakes served a kind of apprenticeship as he worked in his "lesser" genres before he achieved his great success in historical fiction, especially the continuing family saga. Unfortunately, many of these early works, published in paperback, are now difficult to find in libraries. The books discussed in Chapters 3-12 are currently available; moreover, they are Jakes' most mature novels.

One may see in his earlier works many embryonic techniques and themes that he developed through the rest of his career. Already in *Gonzaga's Woman* (1953) his ability to develop a compelling plot line kept his reader turning pages; moreover, he occasionally introduced striking images and had already begun to make use of external detail, especially nature, to convey characters' emotions. In *A Night for Treason* (1956) Jakes was experimenting with simultaneous events from different plot lines to sharpen the contrast between forces of good and evil. In *The Seventh Man* (1958) he makes frequent use of literary allusions; this familiarity with the literary canon becomes integral to his explication of theme when, in *Time Gate* and especially in his blockbuster novels, he makes use of the epigraph to underscore the central ideas of the novel. In *The Devil Has Four Faces* (1958) Jakes uses a detective's report to clarify expository details which would otherwise be difficult to provide in a fast-paced narrative; a similar device in the North and South series is his use of characters' journals. And, in *The Impostor* (1959), Jakes tries for the first time the structural device so common in his big historical books, the separation of the narrative into distinct sections, a technique often useful in achieving economy.

We see Jakes experimenting not only with techniques in his early works, but also with genre. The initiation novel, best illustrated by *Homeland*, is foreshadowed by the earlier juvenile novels *The Texans Ride North*, *The Secrets of Stardeep*, and *Time Gate*. In addition, he experiments early on with the continuing family saga. In three of his science fiction novels, members of different generations of the Dragonard family serve as protagonists: Robin in *The Planet Wizard*, Wolf in *Tonight We Steal the Stars*, and Maxmillion in *When the Star Kings Die*.

Furthermore, it is fascinating to see how Jakes interweaves continuing research into different books. Stephen Crane and Richard Harding Davis were two journalists profiled in *Great War Correspondents*; they later appear covering the Spanish-American War in *Homeland*. Similarly, it is intriguing to compare Jakes' treatment of Susanna Dickinson, a survivor of the Alamo, in the charming children's biography *Susanna of the Alamo* and in *The Furies*, Volume 4 of the Kent Family Chronicles.

Finally, Jakes early on addresses some of his ongoing themes. The theme of the Other, including the conflict between different cultures, is central to the musical comedy *Pardon Me, Is This Planet Taken?* Later we will see it in virtually all of Jakes' westerns as well as in *Homeland*. As early as in *A Night for Treason*, Jakes affirms the necessity for ethical behavior, decency, morality, and love. In all of his science fiction novels, Jakes suggests that although science can dispel fear and superstition, it can also be perverted in the pursuit of wealth and power rather than used to benefit society. He also often questions the nature of humanity. His answer seems to be that, although intelligence is more important than brute strength (the Johnny Havoc series), it is not enough without love, courage, and an absence of greed (*The Planet Wizard*).

Most important, Jakes explores American values throughout his career. Contrasting the United States with Nazi Germany in *The Devil Has Four Faces*, Jakes points toward that affirmation so central to the big historical novels, which will follow: that the United States, and the principles upon which it was founded, are unique and precious. They can, however, be undermined by those who, in the name of protecting society, subvert its principles. Jakes creates, in *The Impostor*, the first of many policemen-as-bad-guys, a category of villain especially evil for their combined power and hypocrisy. Jakes seems to argue that we must be on guard against those who emphasize order over freedom. Another danger to American democracy is the perversion of the belief that, in America, one who works hard can succeed; generally this is true, but when external economic forces intervene, resulting in the fragmentation of society into the haves and the have-nots (*The Impostor, When the Star Kings Die, Black in Time*), the fabric of society is seriously threatened. Often, in such situations, the individual seems impotent. As early as *The Hybrid* (1969), Jakes raises the age-old question in a democracy: What difference can one man make? Unless one tries, the book argues, the forces of despotism will succeed.

Despite periods of personal bleakness, often reflecting crises in the national conscience, Jakes' central theme through his entire career is an optimistic affirmation of America and its principles.

HISTORICAL FICTION

Despite his success with five other genres, John Jakes is best known for his historical fiction. In his first six historical novels, Jakes makes his own the genre established in 1814 by Sir Walter Scott with *Waverley* and subsequently practiced by authors such as Leo Tolstoy (*War and Peace*), Robert Graves (*I, Claudius*), Erich Maria Remarque (*All Quiet on the Western Front*), and Ernest Hemingway (*For Whom the Bell Tolls*). "The historical novel not only takes its setting and some characters and events from history, but makes the historical events and issues crucial for the central characters and narrative. Some of the greatest historical novels also use the protagonists and actions to reveal what the author regards as the deep forces that impel the historical process" (Abrams, 133). Some authors of historical fiction, such as James Alexander Thom (*Panther in the Sky*), take great pride in including *only* historical figures in their novels. Most, however, like Jakes, interweave historical and created characters, thus gaining creative freedom while maintaining historical verisimilitude.

Even if one discounts his early *The Texans Ride North*, Jakes had written six quite effective historical novels by 1963. Of these, even though he had "a notion about writing a book on the American Revolution, or perhaps the French and Indian War" (*The Man from Cannae*, xi), only one had an American setting. The editor he had approached, conscious of marketing trends in publishing, told Jakes in no uncertain terms that stories about "guys in three-cornered hats don't make it" (*Cannae* xi). Now he's become, for many Americans, a major source of their own history. A reader of Jakes' novels can do respectably well in the American History category on *Jeopardy!* As Nick Salvatore and Ann Sullivan put it, "The themes Jakes presents constitute an important and influential source of public history in modern American culture" (Salvatore and Sullivan, 142).

Moreover, Jakes has clearly thought about the historical novel, writing theoretical material in introductions to revised versions of his six early historical novels, in the introduction to the collection of his western short stories (*In the Big Country*, 1993), and in "The Historical Family Saga," an article published in *The Writer*. Though he would never use so pompous a term, Jakes has become something of a theoretician—as well as a practitioner—of historical fiction. The following pages will explore his early historical novels and his attention to the Western as a distinct genre; they will conclude with his analysis of the historical family saga as an introduction to the discussion of those books for which he's best known.

JAKES' EARLY HISTORICAL NOVELS

I, Barbarian (1976), originally published in 1959 under the Jay Scotland pseudonym, was John Jakes' first historical novel. Set in the thirteenth century High Asia of Ghengis Khan, the novel is based on considerable research. Jakes explains:

> I wanted to make the world of Ghengis Khan a real world. I dislike the historical novels in which a character takes "a drink" and wears "clothes." I want to know *what* he drank and *what* he wore; not to the point of boredom, but I want to get something of the feel and flavor of a period. I think readers do too. (xi)

From the very beginning Jakes indicates that the novel's conflicts are not merely those of palace intrigues, war, and conquest, but also those between value systems, religions, and established laws. The conflict is internal, too, for, when we first meet him, the protagonist, James Frankistan, has a divided identity. The son of a Frank who had gone on the Third Crusade and who probably had served under Richard Lion-Heart, the blond James was raised after his father's death by the Mongol Kajin. Thus he can be seen as the outsider, a man in search of his identity.

In this novel, Jakes introduces two motifs, religion and justice, which will run through many later books. He asks fundamental questions: Is man meant for happiness—or is his destiny more somber? He introduces the father-son motif (James and his two fathers; Ghengis Khan and his two sons). Also in this novel, Jakes introduces the eye motif. In many of his books he uses the eyes as a mirror of a character's soul. Equally often he elicits an atavistic horror from the reader through the maiming of a character's eyes. Here one character is blinded by blazing torches; another suffers the "death of retribution"—melted silver is poured into her eyes and ears. Jakes, early on, was already a master of horror and gore.

Finally, in this book Jakes seems to affirm a new professional direction. In a scene reminiscent of *The Arabian Nights*, he has the ragged, battered, starving James and Bela meet up with an old Arab trader/camel driver. A deal is struck: in return for food and drink and weapons, James will provide another kind of sustenance. The old trader "want[s] to know all you know about [the city of] Mirv's fall." James bargains, " 'This story will take at least two nights to relate. But it's full of thrilling and frightening descriptions.' . . . I hadn't reckoned on the depth of his hunger for news and companionship. I suddenly wished I had promised a tale of *four* nights' duration" (249).

The scene becomes almost a metaphor of the writer's life. Early in his career, at the point he first tries a historical novel, John Jakes declares the value of storytelling. A good story, in the camel driver's camp, is an article of trade, the sharing of information, and the fulfilling of human hunger for news and companionship. James "settled down comfortably and began narrating our adventures" (249).

Jakes did so too.

Having completed research for *I, Barbarian*, John Jakes "became sufficiently interested in events at the other end of the known world" to do a novel about them too (*I, Barbarian*, xi). That book is *King's Crusader*, originally published under the Jay Scotland pseudonym as *Sir Scoundrel* and revised by Jakes in 1977. The central event is the Third Crusade, led by Richard Lion-Heart. The novel is told from the point of view of Blondel de Nisle, minstrel at Richard's court and a close friend from childhood. In the book's introduction, Jakes points out that, though most of the characters—Richard, Saladin, Berengaria of Navarre, Hubert Walter—actually existed, Blondel is a character of legend. Though stories of his wanderings in search of his imprisoned king persist, no evidence exists to authenticate him. Thus we see Jakes consciously blending historical and created characters in his fictional treatment of history.

The close friendship between the minstrel and the king is sneered at by other characters due to Richard's probable homosexuality. It is significant that Richard confesses this tendency to a priest—and renounces it, before his marriage to Berengaria. For Richard is virtually the only homosexual character in Jakes' works who receives positive treatment. Elsewhere, a hint of homosexuality or sexual deviancy almost always signals a villain. Consider, for example, the evil Tarn in *Master of the Dark Gate*, who practices both pedophilia and incest. Consider Vondamm in *Tonight We Steal the Stars*, with his "effeminate hands . . . folded at the waist"; when shot by Dragonard with a blastergun, " Vondamm sobbed like a woman" (109, 113-14). Or consider, most especially, the almost archetypally evil Elkanah Bent of *North and South*. About these, Jakes has recently written, "Giving a villain homosexual traits was regrettable. Especially when hints of menacing a young male were involved, it was a cheap and easy way to establish a villain. . . . I would never do this now; I learn slowly, but I learn" (letter, 6/22/95).

In *The Veils of Salome* Jakes concentrated on the juxtaposition between the cultures of Rome and the Holy Land. He "deliberately plotted this book so as to be able to suggest a few of the social, political, and religious differences between the two" (4). There's a vivid portrait of the Rome of Tiberius Claudius Nero in decadence: a society of sharp class differences, of slavery, of little value placed on the individual, of sexual license and depravity, of political conniving. In contrast, the Holy Land, under Roman dominance, is witnessing the rise of the Sicarii, dagger-wielding advocates of freedom from foreign domination, as well as the "religious nonsense"—as Herod Antipas calls it—of John the Essene and Jesus of Nazareth. The juxtaposition, so dramatic here, is a tool Jakes will continue to use to delineate plot, character, and thematic concepts.

For Jakes, this novel was something of an experiment—to see if he could write a first-person narrative from the point of view of a woman. This he does, giving Salome, known to most simply as the rather salacious dancer who demanded John the Baptist's head on a platter, dimensions not often seen: a victim of her conniving mother, separated from the man she loves, the physician Marcus, and granted previously unknown strengths, as well as absolution, from Jesus. She thus becomes, along with her almost unremittingly evil mother Herodias, the first of a string of strong women who will people Jakes' later novels.

The Man from Cannae (1977), originally published in 1963 by Jay Scotland as *Traitor's Legion*, is an illustration of John Jakes' ability to write a novel on demand. Although by 1962 Jakes wanted to do a book either on the American Revolution or the French and Indian War, the publishing trend then was novels on Rome; since Jakes had already published *The Veils of Salome*, he and his publisher agreed on another novel with that setting. *The Man from Cannae* deals with the period 216 to 211 B.C., the period of the Second Punic War between Carthage and Rome. The plot intertwines the strands of love and war, as Jakes will do so often in his major novels, not least of which is the second volume of the North and South series, *Love and War*. Moreover, Jakes emphasizes ongoing themes in *The Man from Cannae*; among them are his absolute faith in good, despite evidence to the contrary; the resolution of class conflict in favor of democracy; and the admiration of protagonists who are not only adept at fighting but who can use their brains.

Thus, although *The Man from Cannae* was written on assignment, in response to a publisher's analysis of "what sells," it demonstrates an early Jakes, already a storyteller, mastering his craft and working with thematic ideas he has pursued through much of his career.

Arena (1963) is virtually unavailable today in public libraries. It is the adventure of a gladiator in Nero's Rome during the early Christian era. Jakes says it's the "best of JS [Jay Scotland] historicals, in my opinion" (letter, 6/22/95).

Also written under the Jay Scotland pseudonym, *Strike the Black Flag* (1961) begins in 1718 during the last days of pirates terrorizing merchant ships in the Windward Passage from North Carolina to the Caribbean.

In *Strike the Black Flag* Jakes experiments with many of the genre's conventions, which he will develop more fully in the Kent Family Chronicles and in the North and South series. Jakes provides the reader with all the action one might expect. There are sword fights, sea battles, and shark attacks; the Spanish out of Havana attack the English outpost; Blackbeard meets an end no less brutal than his life: shot, stabbed, gored with a pike, one ear hacked off, the legend finally fell to the deck, his head lopped off by a British naval lieutenant who raised the gory trophy to the sun. With so much to set in motion, Jakes uses a technique he's quite fond of, beginning *in medias res* (in the middle of things): "In the great dark of the hold I awoke all at once, a dagger-point pressing my throat" (5).

Perhaps the device most similar to those of his big books is Jakes' creation of a plot that allows actual historical people to interact with those he has created. In the author's note, Jakes explains the process:

> In this tale of the close of the great days of piracy on the Spanish Main, certain historical materials have been incorporated intact, others have been compressed or changed in minor detail, while still others have been used solely as models for characters or happenings that must be counted mainly the author's invention. . . . A novel, after all, is not a text of history.

Consciously adopted in 1961, this blending of fact and fiction becomes a Jakes staple in those later books for which he is most noted. He does not, of course, invent the historical novel, but he seems comfortable working within the genre, relishing its richness and adapting to its limitations. One obvious requirement of this genre is verisimilitude; not only must central historical events be treated with integrity, but the author must create accuracy of period and character. This Jakes does with thorough research, providing the reader with a sense of social history.

And, perhaps most important leading toward the Kent Family Chronicles, there's a strong current of Americanism here. The initial conflict between the pirates of New Providence and Governor Rogers becomes a conflict between Americans and the dandified English. Principles which will be crucial in *The Rebels* are introduced here, especially the issue of the source of governmental power and the relation between the individual and those by whom he is ruled.

THE WEST AND WESTERNS

For over forty years, John Jakes has written westerns. As a young unknown, Jakes contributed stories to such western pulp magazines as *Ranch Romances, Max Brand's Western, .44 Western,* and *Big-Book Western.* His first book, *The Texans Ride North* (1952), was a coming of age novel for young people, set on the great Texas cattle drives. He most recently published *New Trails: 23 Original Stories of the West* (1994), a collection of original short stories by members of the Western Writers of America which he co-edited with Martin H. Greenberg. It contains an extraordinary new Jakes story, "Manitow and Ironhand," for which—as well as for a lifetime of achievement in the western—Jakes received the Western Heritage Award from the National Cowboy Hall of Fame in March 1995.

One of Jakes' first adult novels, *Wear a Fast Gun* (1956), is an action-packed western in which the protagonist, a newly hired sheriff, is virtually indistinguishable from the gunslingers he has been hired to oppose. Yet Jakes also gives Fallon many of the traits of the prototypical cowboy hero, Owen Wister's Virginian. As always, Jakes introduces satisfying violence—from gunfights to eye-gouging, crotch-kicking fistfights. As always, Jakes draws villains the reader can love to hate. Jakes also draws on a literary tradition common since James Fenimore Cooper's Leatherstocking Tales, the tradition of seeing the settlements (urban America) as somehow corrupt, especially as compared to those who live close to nature.

In *Six-Gun Planet* (1970), Jakes combines the conventions of the western with those of science fiction to produce a parable on the nature of man.

Set on the planet Missouri in the twenty-third century, the novella advances three rather bleak propositions: that, despite the veneer of civilization, there lurks within every man a capacity for violence; that, as power corrupts, so too absolute power corrupts absolutely; and that demagogues emerge when society demands them. The major towns on the planet Missouri bear names evocative of the American West: Shatterhand, Cooper, and Shane. These allusions to Karl May, the German author of over forty westerns, to the author of the Leatherstocking Tales, and to classic Hollywood westerns are indicative of influences on Jakes.

As Jakes juxtaposes Zak, the protagonist, and the people of Missouri, he draws sharp dichotomies of values: beauty versus violence, the law of the gun versus the law of reason, civilization versus a perverted individualism. One is reminded of Frederick Jackson Turner's observation in "The Significance of the Frontier in American History" that those traits of the American character elicited by the frontier may be for good or for ill. Frontier traits are not necessarily *virtues*.

In *Six-Gun Planet* Jakes suggests not only that all men have the seed of violence within, but that most men, facing such a force for evil, would prefer to live under the false security it grants than to challenge it and thus gain true freedom. Though written in 1970, the novella speaks powerfully to the political realities of 1996.

Not only has Jakes written western novels and short stories over the entire span of his career, but the western motif is prominent in his blockbuster family saga novels. In *The Seekers* young Abraham Kent wintered at Greenville with Lieutenants Meriwether Lewis and William Clark; at the Battle of Fallen Timbers he comes close to killing Tecumseh. In that book's epilogue, Amanda Kent is sold by a disreputable trader to the renowned Plenty Coups; in *The Furies* she survives the Alamo, and later, during the California gold rush, amasses the fortune which will undergird and undermine the Kent family unity for several generations. In *The Warriors* the West is posited as an opportunity for a fresh start; the construction of the transcontinental railroad is an important element, as is the conflict between nature and technology. *The Lawless* begins with a prologue, "The Dream and the Gun," which could be published as a stand-alone western short story. (Similarly, "A Duel of Magicians," published in *In the Big Country: The Best Western Short Stories of John Jakes*, is an excerpt from *Heaven and Hell*.) Later in *The Lawless* we have accounts of the postwar army on the Plains, the forces of Manifest Destiny, the Badlands gold rush, and the Custer massacre. In *The Americans* Theodore Roosevelt's cattle ranch in the Dakota Territory provides Will with an opportunity to grow up, to get his head on straight. The war with Mexico is a formative event in *North and South.* And in *Heaven and Hell* the West is both a catalyst for healing Civil War wounds and a means of inflicting still others, as, for example, at Washita, which demonstrated that perversion of national policy was not limited to the War Between the States.

One must also include *California Gold*, in which Mack Chance arrives searching for his fortune about thirty years after Amanda Kent has departed, having found hers; it draws a picture of much California history—railroad monopolies, land booms, the 1906 San Francisco earthquake, and the birth of the film industry. If California is America's America, as J. S. Holliday has suggested in *The World Rushed In*, the foundation for the analogy is laid in the social history portrayed in *The Bastard*, *The Rebels*, and *Homeland.* In each of these, America is portrayed as a land for the immigrant; a land of opportunity for the individual to redefine himself free from artificial social or economic barriers; a land of liberty which, it is true, could become a land of license. These values and verities are very western ones.

Thus, when Jakes writes about the western, it is with a very broad view of the genre. Rather than defining it narrowly, as some do, as including fiction of the American West between 1865 and 1900, Jakes takes a far more inclusive position. In part, Jakes' "West" is synonymous with Turner's "frontier." Unlike the European concept of frontier—a fixed boundary between sovereign states—the American frontier, the division between "civilization" and "savagery," was constantly moving, at least until the end of the nineteenth century. As Turner's line of settlement reached, was halted by, and then surged beyond natural barriers such as the Appalachians or the Missouri, so too Jakes' "West" moves. It may encompass traditional western locales and motifs such as the Sierra Nevada, Oklahoma oilfields, conflicts between ranchers and railroaders in frontier Kansas, or a riverboat gambler struggling against illness, age, and greed. But it can also include the British Carolina colony a half century before the American Revolution, as in "Carolina Warpath," as well as the twenty-third century outer space Missouri of *Six-Gun Planet.*

Introductions and afterwords to *In the Big Country* and *New Trails* reveal Jakes' conscious formulation of the theory of the western genre. "The word *west* is central to American reality and myth," writes Jakes in "The Western and How We Got It." It can be a geographic region: "where the buffalo roam. A vast space beyond the Mississippi"; a direction: "the way you go to reach the unpopulated country. The gold. Free land. Breathing room"; or a period of time in our national experience:

"roughly thirty-five to forty years duration—say, from the strike at Sutter's Mill to the massacre at Wounded Knee" (*In the Big Country*, 2).

But for Jakes, "west" is not simply a place on a map, a moment on a timeline; "west" is, ultimately, a place in the mind. "However it's used," he writes, "it brings with it a whole trove of secondary meanings. They speak an alluring language of hope; adventure; riches; escape; beginning again" (*Big Country*, 1).

Aside from these connotations associated with the West, Jakes feels it isn't hard to explain the popularity of literature about it. For the stay-at-home, "accounts of beauties and perils of remote, exotic lands have excited a strong appeal" (*Big Country*, 3). Thus the fascination with the travels of Marco Polo, the journals of Lewis and Clark, even the guidebooks to California goldfields, often written by people who hadn't been there for people who didn't plan to go.

The fictional western, practiced by others too, but invented by Americans, was, "in its first life, an Eastern" (*Big Sky*, 4), manifested in the works of James Fenimore Cooper and William Gilmore Simms. To both, Jakes is indebted. Moreover, Jakes argues, "three forces in nineteenth century popular culture propelled the Western to national, then global acclaim: the debut of the dime novel, the fiction of Ned Buntline, and the life of Buffalo Bill Cody" (5). Though Cody's Wild West Show "was not exactly the truth any more than the dime novels had been . . . no other entertainment, and no other man, did more to implant the myth and magic of the American West in the minds of his countrymen and millions of others besides. . . . Cody . . . has a just claim to immortality because he bequeathed the west to the whole world" (*Big Country*, 14-15).

Part of that world included Karl May, born in Saxony in 1842. He wrote only in German and visited America only once, four years before his death in 1912. By that time he had written forty novels set in "the American Wild West." By his death he had probably done more to promote the "splendor and excitement of the West to non-Americans than anyone except Buffalo Bill Cody," writes Jakes (*New Trails*, 297).

In his forty-plus novels, May's white hero went by various names—Old Surehand, Old Firehand, Old Shatterhand. Paired with him in exceedingly bloody adventures was a young Indian named Winnetou. It is, thus, intriguing to read Jakes' most recent story, "Manitow and Ironhand," the final selection in *New Trails*. Jakes means the story as an homage to, not an imitation of, Karl May. (The depth—or the length—of that influence is evident when one remembers the town of Shatterhand back in Jakes' 1970 *Six-Gun Planet*).

"Manitow and Ironhand" is set in the waning days of the fur frontier, when ecology (dwindling numbers of beaver necessitated seeking out secret streams) and fashion fads (the soiled block silk topper worn by a "disreputable German merchant of traps" at the summer rendezvous of '28) are twin harbingers of the end of an era. Old Ironhand, now an independent trapper providing competition to—and risking the ire of—the monopoly Four Flags outfit, is setting his traps in streams far into the wilderness. He is comfortable in nature, "far from the civilized per-fidy of other white men" (*New Trails*, 278). Traps set, he feels satisfied and at peace—until an assassin shoots him in the back.

He recovers consciousness at the campfire of a young Delaware, Man-itow, who had also been tracking him. (It is no accident that Jakes makes him a Delaware, a tribe who by 1833 have been driven two-thirds of the way across the continent by encroaching whites.) Manitow seeks Iron-hand out to revenge his brother Tammany's death. And there the two men's lives are inextricably intertwined, for both have suffered griev-ously at the hands of Little Joe Moonlight, henchman of Alexander Jag-gers, the factor at the Four Flags fort. Tammany, Ironhand's partner, had been beaten, drenched in whiskey, and set ablaze—presumably as a prank—by Little Joe and his buddies. When Ironhand, then going by his own name, Ewing, arrived at the fort and set upon Jaggers for Tam-many's charred, lingering death, Jaggers ordered him maimed. But, "looking pious as a deacon, Mr. Jaggers said that in the spirit of Christian forgiveness, Little Joe would only break the hand [Ewing] used least" (285). There follows an incredible passage in which Jakes alternates a description of their breaking every bone in Ewing's left hand, one by one, with the blunt end of a hatchet, while Jaggers pumps out, almost fanatically, Christian hymns on an organ he has transported from Phil-adelphia. Ewing's hand is mangled, "And Christ's great kingdom shall come on earth / The kingdom of Love and Light" (286).

In the two years since, Ironhand has gone his own way, setting his traps, believing Jaggers' insane farewell speech. "We part as competitors, but eternal friends. Christ counsels forgiveness above all" (287). But as Manitow observed, having heard the story, "Many traps are set in the wilderness. You were caught in the cruelest of all. Trust" (287).

There is, then, a blackness to the story, despite the satisfaction of dumping Little Joe's corpse on Jaggers' desk, of emptying five rounds from his revolver into the pump organ before continuing the demolition with his bare hands.

And there remains, even after Manitow and Ironhand have pledged trust in an exchange of knives, a haunting question. Just who is Manitow? For, in addition to his obvious name, Jakes provides details that make the reader wonder whether he's merely a young Delaware—or part of the creator spirit. He tracks Ironhand "to see what kind of a man" he is (283). Although Ironhand feels that Manitow accompanies him to "pass judgment," the young Indian, wise beyond his years, repeatedly saves him. And when, in the final shootout with Little Joe and his companions, when Ironhand, wounded yet again, must throw his rifle to the Indian but fears to do so ("He'll use it to kill me. . . . Don't dare. I can't trust"), Manitow yells, his voice almost muffled by the pounding of horses' hooves: "White man, if you don't, we'll die."

"There was a *halo* [emphasis added] of hoof-driven dust around Manitow's head. He looked like the ghost of one of his primitive ancestors. His outstretched brown hand opened, demanding. 'White man—*obey me!*'" Risking all, Ironhand threw him the rifle, "the supreme act of trust"—of faith?

There's a mysticism running through the story, one which encompasses, but transcends, the dichotomy between a pristine and an exploited nature. And this mysticism is powerfully juxtaposed to the terrifying hypocrisy of the hymn-singing trader, wreaking unmitigated horror while singing of love.

Jakes struggles once again in this story, as he has so frequently throughout his career, with the need to believe in good while facing the evidence of evil. It is in recognition of this, as well as for his lifelong work in mastering the western genre, for which he received the Western Heritage Award.

THE HISTORICAL FAMILY SAGA

John Jakes was not the first author to explore continuing family narratives. Perhaps the earliest was Sophocles with his fifth century B.C. Theban trilogy *Oedipus the King, Oedipus at Colonus*, and *Antigone*. Later the Scandinavian saga evolved—a prose narrative sometimes of legendary content but typically telling of prominent figures and events in the heroic age of tenth and eleventh century Norway and Iceland. Typical themes of such sagas included human tragedy, ideals of loyalty and heroism, and revenge (including the blood feud); action was more prevalent than reflection, but characterization was often surprisingly deep and subtle.

Although Jakes' blockbuster novels clearly share some of these elements, the Kent Family Chronicles "marked the virtual birth of a new and sustaining form of popular fiction—the paperback original, multivolumed, continuing-character, generation-spanning, romantic-historical family saga," as Dale L. Walker calls it (*In the Big Country*, xix-xx). Jakes shortens that nomenclature considerably to "historical family saga" and sketches factors which are essential to the form.

Of course, novels must cover more than one generation to be classified as family sagas. As a result, the historical element is strong. While not all historical novels are family sagas, the family saga is, almost inevitably, a historical novel. Jakes suggests that the historical family saga is popular today because it meets deep societal needs. Searching the past for "values and a sense of continuity" helps alleviate anxieties about the present. More specifically, because many modern families are disintegrating under social and economic pressures, family sagas about "idealized families that manage to survive ... harrowing test[s]" are reassuring (Jakes, "Historical Family Saga," 9).

Family sagas involve the characters in specific historical events. Thus "research is imperative: to set up story lines, to decorate the stage and clothe the characters, to give texture to the scene." Jakes argues that since one of the primary goals is to evoke a bygone era, the Ticonderoga cannon sequence in *The Rebels*, for example, could not exist without "descriptions of the sledge, the weather, the terrain"(10). Though research is arduous, it often simplifies plotting. Jakes comments that Gideon Kent's troubles during the Chicago fire were derived from facts found during research; once he introduced Gideon into the fire setting, "the complications and small turns of plot" came easily (10).

Most Jakes novels, like their Norse saga predecessors, have their fair share of violence. Violence is present, he says, because he enjoys action stories and enjoys writing them. Violence is, unfortunately, more interesting than day to day routine; but Jakes makes an effort not to trivialize such events. He also recognizes the streak of violence in our national personality, the frequency of violent events in American history (12).

Moreover, Jakes believes that violence can be a powerful catalyst for character change. He reminds us that the horrors of battle change Gideon's ideas of war in *The Titans* and the violence of the Union Pacific construction gangs changes Michael to a pacifist in *The Warriors* (12, 46).

Beyond these characteristics, contrasts with much of his earlier work help define Jakes' best-known genre, the family saga. Many of his books—such as the Brak the Barbarian books or the Johnny Havoc series—are told from the first person point of view. In others, such as *King's Crusader*, he may slip comfortably into a limited omniscient viewpoint, seeing through Blondel's eyes, for example, but with insight into his mind as well. In contrast, the family sagas—the Kent Family Chronicles, the North and South series, and the new one beginning with *Homeland*—make use of multiple points of view. In a chapter, or a section, or a book of the volume, he will use the point of view of one character; then, gaining narrative scope and freedom, he will shift to another character's point of view. It is important to note, however, that at any given point, he will include only what the character could legitimately have been expected to see or know. This means, sometimes, that research material may have to be scrapped.

Another trait of the family saga differentiating it from most of Jakes' other works is analogous to the multiple points of view: rather than a single plot line, he uses many intertwined plots. A corollary to this is that, instead of straight chronological development of plot, he may have events occurring simultaneously in different venues or he may flash back to earlier events to clarify the present.

However, like most of his other mature novels, Jakes' family sagas are character-driven. Plot emerges from character. And, in the saga, the characters through whose eyes we look and with whom we become most deeply involved are fictional, not historical characters. Thus Jakes is more free to interpret, to juxtapose, to shape his material rather than being bound by the rigors of known events, speeches, and behavior of actual people. These, however, appear repeatedly in the sagas, and the Jakes people interact with them.

These are among the central elements that define the historical family saga, the genre for which Jakes is best known. Not everyone, however, is enamored with the genre. Critics Nick Salvatore and Ann Sullivan see the genre as "a staple of mass-produced American culture," accessible in low-brow "drugstores, bus depots, and supermarkets." They believe the genre can be reduced to formula: "a facile style, obligatory soft core pornographic scenes, and a central romantic plot." Nonetheless, such novels carry the implicit message that our "collective past, [and] our present," are "personal, individualistic, and essentially asocial" (Salvatore and Sullivan, 141-42). Of Jakes, specifically, they write, "Predisposed merely to celebrate the success of the American people, Jakes never fulfills his promise of serious historical analysis within the form of fiction,'' instead writing ''celebratory pap.''

Jakes, I feel, would respond simply. He does not pretend to be anything more than a storyteller. He does not aspire to write the ''academic novel.'' But, equally strongly, he values America's past and how the country has transcended its tragedies. Like Walt Whitman, he hears America singing and shares in the song.

PART II

THE KENT FAMILY CHRONICLES

The Kent Family Chronicles was John Jakes' first true continuing family saga. Conceived by Lyle Kenyon Engel as an unabashedly commercial venture, timed to coincide with and capitalize on America's two hundreth birthday (indeed, the original name was the American Bicentennial Series), the series follows the Kent family from the Revolutionary War almost to the close of the nineteenth century. Although the plan was to bring the family and the nation up to 1976, thus covering the entirety of our national existence, the series stops some ninety years short of that goal. (Homeland, *the first of the newest Jakes series, picks up in 1890, almost exactly when* The Americans, *the last of the Kent Family Chronicles, leaves off.)*

Throughout the Kent Family Chronicles, Jakes uses the Kent family—individually and collectively—as a metaphor for the nation. They participate in America's major historical events—the Revolution, the War of 1812, the movement west, the Civil War, the urbanization and industrialization of the previously agrarian United States. They debate major social and political issues—when rebellion is right (the mid-eighteenth century) and when it is wrong (the mid-nineteenth); whether slavery can be tolerated; the ecological and cultural consequences of Manifest Destiny; women's rights and the union movement. They interact with major American figures—Ben

Franklin and Theodore Roosevelt, Andrew Carnegie and Lucy Stone, Robert E. Lee and Frederick Douglass. Permeating the entire series—whatever villains do, whatever cynicism or greed may appear—is Jakes' powerful belief in the United States and the principles for which it stands. The series is, thus, an anodyne to the national disillusionment resulting from political scandals and the war in Vietnam, an affirmation, conscious though not Pollyannaish, of America's goals, her strengths, and her ideals.

3

The Bastard
(1974)

The Bastard is the first of the eight volumes which comprise John Jakes'
Bicentennial Series, the Kent Family Chronicles. Thus, in addition to solv-
ing the problems of any historical novel—most especially how to integrate actual and invented characters in a plot which is part historical fact
and part interpretation and invention—the author also had to establish
a character about whom the audience cares enough to continue reading
for what was, at the outset, an indefinite, possibly infinite, number of
books. Jakes does this partly by creating a seventeen-year-old protagonist; we can watch him, in this novel and the two that follow, grow up,
live a productive life, found what will be an extraordinary family, and,
eventually, die. Perhaps more important, Jakes so intertwines the protagonist's life with that of the young nation that he may be thought to
be doubly a founding father—of the Kents ("I think the Kents will turn
out to be a very fine family indeed" [*Bastard*, 628]) and of the nation,
which Jakes unabashedly feels is "very fine indeed."

Because the novel concludes at Concord, with Americans streaming
off to fight the English, a discussion of neither plot, character, nor themes
in the Kent Family Chronicles can be complete here. However, by examining each of these in turn, we can begin to see how Jakes dramatizes
the birth of a nation, establishes values and conflicts central to the United
States, and makes what could be abstract come alive in characters the
reader will care about.

PLOT DEVELOPMENT

The Bastard begins in 1770 and follows Phillipe Charboneau, the illegitimate son of a French actress and an English nobleman, from his late
adolescence in the tiny inn near the hamlet of Chavaniac, which at the
outset was the only home he could imagine, to Concord, Massachusetts,
as he, with other American patriots, marches against the British to establish a new home, a new nation. The somnolent tedium of his early
life is disturbed by two forces. His tutor, Girard, introduces him to the
writers of the Age of Reason, the revolutionary thinkers Diderot, Voltaire, Montesquieu, and Rousseau. His mother, Marie, had hired Girard
to make Phillipe proficient in English, the language of commerce—and
his soldier-duke father; her monomania that he be recognized by Sir
James Amberly dominates the first two books of the novel and further
disturbs the tedium of Phillipe's life.

Inevitable conflict thus results when Lady Jane Amberly, James' wife
and the mother of Roger, Phillipe's half-brother, conspires with Roger to
remove Marie's challenge to their fortune; her efforts range from incredibly rude inhospitality, to faking James' death, to sending cutthroats out
to murder Marie and Phillipe.

Having fled from Kentland after James' "death," the Charboneaus arrive in London. There Phillipe learns the printer's trade, meets Benjamin
Franklin, and, against his mother's wishes, decides to start afresh in the
colonies. Symbolic of his change, he rechristens himself Philip Kent in
the final stages of the Atlantic passage.

Most of the second half of *The Bastard* intertwines Philip's fate with
that of the growing revolutionary sentiment in the colonies. Because of
his printer's skills, he gets a job with Benjamin Edes, and through him
meets many of the Sons of Liberty, among them Paul Revere, John Han-
cock, and Samuel Adams. We see, through Philip, the colonists' responses to the Boston Tea Party, the Boston Port Bill, the increased
number of English troops under General Gage, the virtual dismantling
of the Massachusetts provincial government, the Quartering Act.

The two halves of Philip's life—personal and political, European and
American—spark conflict when his half-brother Roger arrives in Boston
as colonel of a proprietary regiment. Subsequently, in saving Anne Ware,
the woman he loves, Philip has to kill Roger (he thinks) to rescue her
from Roger's assault during a search for a British army deserter. The
rising pattern of action and antipathy of the colonists to the British con-

tinues, leading to armed conflict and the outbreak of the Revolutionary War.

To lay the historical and philosophical groundwork for the novel, Jakes uses dialogue rather than long expository passages. Three examples will illustrate this technique: the tutor Girard's discussion with Phillipe of authors such as Rousseau establishes a political-philosophical rationale for the Revolution (20-21, 54-60). Mr. Fox, the innkeeper at Wolfe's Triumph, where Marie and Phillipe stay after their flight from Kentland, provides an explanation of the conflict between the colonies and the king, as well as pocket sketches of Ben Franklin, Samuel Adams, and Lord North; in addition, by noting that most colonists think of themselves as Englishmen, he underlines the ironic tragedy of the coming war (139-45). And Phillipe's conversations with Benjamin Franklin (249ff.) illustrate the American temper and growing dissatisfaction with English rule.

Another device Jakes uses to move Phillipe from adolescent Frenchman to rebellious American, to portray a character aware that one must stand up for what he believes, and to provide plenty of action for an audience that might become cloyed with discussions of political philosophy, is to introduce a series of killings. While Phillipe/Philip is the perpetrator in all instances, the reader views his actions as justified. This, of course, is crucial if the founder of the Kent family is to be viewed positively, as an almost elemental male force, to serve as a near-epic founder of a family and a nation. Jakes uses these killings as a means of advancing plot, building transitions between narrative segments, defining character, and stating major themes of the book.

The killings might suggest a masculinity bordering on the brutal were the motivation not usually self-defense coupled with a defense of others. Auguste and his cousin Bertram have already proven themselves louts and bullies by soundly beating up Phillipe after insulting his "whoring mother." Thus, when Phillipe comes upon them ganging up on the twelve-year-old Lafayette, he has to intervene, equalizing the fight somewhat, though it's still two boys against men. The young Lafayette's "trained grace" with his weapon is inadequate to the strength of the man Bertram, who wrenches it away, tossing it in Phillipe's direction. When Auguste advances upon him, dagger in hand, Phillipe instinctively grabs the lance and thrusts it forward; Jakes, however, does not here give Phillipe the desire to kill Auguste, who, "unable to check his forward momentum," impales himself on the lance Phillipe holds. The bully Bertram, Auguste's cousin, screams "murderer" at Phillipe. Lafayette, however, calmly notes that weapons are meant for killing, not for show;

the implication is that battle, once joined, should be won. One need not be sorry for the vanquished enemy who was the aggressor.

The friendship between Phillipe and Lafayette, established here, will be picked up in *The Rebels*. As an additional consequence of this encounter, Lafayette brings to Phillipe his Christmas gift—a sign of their soldierly, male comradeship—an exquisitely beautiful sword, an archetypally phallic symbol—which Phillipe from then on carries with him, treasures, and protects at great risk to himself. For most of the book, the sword shares a position of talismanic prominence with his father's letter; after he burns the letter, consciously affirming his personal independence, the sword remains, a central object of importance.

Beyond forging a friendship between Lafayette and Phillipe, the incident is important in a number of ways: it bloods Phillipe for the first time, forcing him to evaluate his actions; it also raises disturbing questions about the nobility, even his new friend. Do the nobility view others' lives as insignificant when their own are threatened? Do they believe themselves above the law, able to harm—even kill—their "inferiors" (70)? Such questions, based on experience rather than Girard's books, significantly undermine Phillipe's sense of destiny as James Amberly's son; moreover, they prepare the reader, if not Phillipe, for the demonstration of just how the Amberly family will treat Marie and Phillipe as claimants of Phillipe's rightful position as the Duke's son.

The two (or three) additional deaths Phillipe causes in England follow parallel patterns. Both are defensive; both protect others; both provide entree to people who will advance Phillipe's career; and both situations demonstrate some of the ugliness of eighteenth century England, to be contrasted later in the book with American idealism. When Phillipe kills the beggar, the General, on the steps of St. Paul's, he is protecting his mother and her precious letter acknowledging Phillipe as Amberly's son. This time, however, we see a tougher Phillipe; he feels nothing as he looks at the dead body, and he knows he has changed since killing Auguste. This, he believes, is "the price of survival," a phrase curiously echoed much later when Franklin introduces his fable about paying too much for the whistle. The incident, however, also introduces Phillipe and Marie to Hosea and Esau Sholto, whose role as rescuers is somewhat parallel to Phillipe's rescue of Lafayette in the earlier incident. More important, good people in the moral and social/economic quagmire of urban London, they take the Charboneaus into the Sholto home, eventually teaching Phillipe the printer's trade, so crucial to important connections for the rest of the book. When Phillipe, fleeing London from the murderous wrath of his half-brother Roger, kills the highwayman Captain Plumber, he not only dispenses with his own intended assassin, but he also becomes a hero to the other passengers in the coach. One of these, Hoskins, a rich iron manufacturer, has connections among sea captains, and secures passage for Phillipe and Marie aboard the ship *Eclipse* bound for Boston. However, the incident also isolates Charboneau, for, with his mother lapsing into terminal madness, there's no one with whom he can share his anxieties about the real reason for Captain Plumber's attacking *this* stagecoach; he is a hero, but a very vulnerable one. Jakes makes sure his reader does not view Phillipe as a cold-blooded killer: "It troubled him deeply that he had now been responsible for the deaths of three human beings. . . . True, none of the killings was deliberate. All had been done in self-defense. And his success in each case was, in fact, the source of an odd, guilty pride. Still, none of the deaths . . . rested easy on him" (287). The incident elicits from him his first defiant "I will survive." It also moves him further toward his eventual identity: "He reminded himself that he was no longer Phillipe of Auvergne. He had become someone different; harder, perhaps" (288).

He is no longer who he was, but he is not yet Philip Kent. His Atlantic crossing is significant, for it accomplishes the first stage of that transformation. The European Phillipe Charboneau is washed away in the storms of the Atlantic and the tears shed for his mother. For, in a real sense, Phillipe may cause her death as well. His pragmatic decision is that his (their) future lies not in London or in Auvergne and the pursuit of his legal claim upon the Amberly name and fortune; rather, it lies across the Atlantic in the American colonies, where a man may start afresh, may re-create himself, where what kind of person you are is more important than the position your father held. Phillipe's decision, however, is antithetical to all that Marie has striven for; it refutes her conviction that his rightful place is as an Amberly heir; it negates her sacrifices. And so Marie, even on the stagecoach ride to the port, is already partly dead; her lapse into French, her further lapse into a near catatonic state, underscores the death of her dreams. Their roles are reversed; Marie, sick in mind and body, is now helpless, childlike, dependent. It is as if, once the driving force that had for years sustained her was negated, she had nothing left. Her final legacy, in a brief, sudden moment of lucidity, is a curse, a demand that Phillipe once again promise, not merely the original promise never to be humbled into poverty or obscurity but now the oath to "repay them [the Amberlys] and damn their arrogant souls" (304). His oath, and her death, leave Phillipe shaken and alone, but even more determined to survive. And, in part because of the advice of Captain Cabot, master of the *Eclipse*, and in part to establish an identity that is American, not French, not English, he christens himself Philip Kent. The old man was dead—or so he would like to believe.

Philip still needs to kill, however. Once again, his killing of Captain Stark is self-defense. Once again, that death advances the plot, for this killing indirectly intensifies his relationship with Anne, who tends to his wounds after the lethal fight. Moreover, the incident elicits commitment, political and personal. Having killed not a bully, or a beggar, or a brigand, as before, but one of the king's officers, Philip muses, "I am a rebel now, I guess." But his decision also elicits Anne's "I want you for a lover." Thus the fusion between romantic love and love for country has been introduced.

Yet to come, of course, is Philip's mortal wounding of his half-brother Roger, now commanding a proprietary regiment in Boston for purposes not of patriotism but of self-aggrandizement. Once again, Jakes provides justification for Philip's actions: Roger is despicably attacking a woman, the woman Philip loves, as she attempts to shield a deserting British soldier who has become disillusioned with England's violations of the rights of its citizens. Philip's motives are multiple: revenge for Roger's attempts on his and Marie's lives, hatred of the aristocracy, so arrogantly personified by Roger and his mother Lady Jane, the fulfillment of his promise to his mother ("Repay them . . ."), defense of a woman being physically abused by a predatory male, and, not least, love for Anne and for his new country, both of whom Roger is assaulting. The apparent killing of Roger—only delayed, not foiled—leads both to Philip's exile near Concord and to his eventual final meeting with Alicia, Roger's wife and Philip's former lover.

After all these acts of violence, the final killing in the book is almost muted. As the Minutemen faced the British light infantry, drawn up across the bridge in street-fighting formation, they realized that the British were firing ball. Philip took aim; it seemed an eternity for his finger to tighten on the trigger; his musket fired; a British soldier spun and sprawled on his face. But, unlike all the other killings, when Philip used knife or lance or bare hands to effect his opponent's death, there is distance here, enough distance that he is unsure whether *his* musket—or someone else's—has killed the British infantryman. "But he knew that an era had ended and another had begun, both for himself and for all the shouting, cursing Americans who leveled their weapons and continued firing on the King's soldiers across the river" (621). The last death was, in terms of theme, the most significant, for through it Philip Kent had forged an unbreakable link to his new country, a country whose revolutionary ideals had been introduced to him long ago in those dangerous books of his tutor, Girard.

CHARACTER DEVELOPMENT

John Jakes has frequently observed that his plots are character-driven. Thus it should come as no surprise that the killings which punctuate *The Bastard* serve also to delineate stages of Phillipe's maturation from French teenager to American patriot. Four women also powerfully affect this transformation; the Alternative Reading section (below) discusses their impact on Philip's maturation. His coming of age will here be explored by examining the influence of male role models, by contrasting him with his half-brother Roger, and by probing the bastard motif, which is a paradigm of his search for identity.

Because Phillipe is illegitimate, there is no male role model for him within the family; indeed, he is seventeen before he learns that his father is alive in England and has been providing for him, albeit modestly. His mother hired Girard to prepare him for his future, as she envisioned it. He was to learn, not Latin, the language of the church, one of the professions accessible to a poor boy, but English, the language of commerce as England and its colonies came to dominate the world. Though English was a useful tool, Girard's far more useful legacy was to instill in Phillipe the ability to think for himself, a willingness to learn, and a rudimentary understanding of the revolutionary principles of Voltaire, Montesquieu, and Rousseau, which would shake the world's previous acceptance of absolute faith and absolute monarchs. That all men, not just aristocrats, have the right to life and liberty, that law must be applied equally to achieve justice, that a state may be overthrown if it violates its citizens' rights were to Phillipe and the world he inhabited revolutionary thoughts.

Phillipe has a whole series of less formal mentors. Young Lafayette taught him to stand up for himself and to accept the fact that it was sometimes necessary to kill to survive. The Sholto family not only taught him the printing trade, but demonstrated what a family could be, full of humor, support, and concern for each other. Fox the innkeeper had courage to protect Phillipe and Marie. Ben Franklin, estranged because of

politics from his oldest son, taught Philip that he must always be conscious of what he's willing to "pay" to achieve his goals but that those
who would sacrifice "essential liberty to purchase a little temporary
safety deserve neither liberty nor safety" (581).

Negative models also influenced Phillipe's character development: the
bullies who, functioning under a primitive philosophy of might makes
right, beat young Phillipe just for the fun of it, and the Duke, his father,
who, despite the letter claiming Phillipe as his son, has remained subordinate to his wife's wishes to ensure peace over the years.

The most important device Jakes uses to define Phillipe is the contrast
with his half-brother Roger. Once the brothers become aware of each
other, Roger becomes the crazed mirror image of Phillipe. Where Phillipe
is apparently a poor peasant boy, the illegitimate son of an actress, thus
doubly disreputable, Roger is a rich aristocrat, heir to an enormous estate, betrothed to a beautiful young woman, and virtually assured of a
financially rewarding career first in the military and then in politics. But
soon his glitter dims, and everything else we learn about Roger makes
Phillipe look better in comparison.

Phillipe is astonished when, at Kentland, he meets his half-brother.
Half a head taller, with broader shoulders, Roger is dressed in sharp
contrast to Phillipe's "plain garb," "in a long checkered coat much like
a dressing gown. His outfit was completed by loose Dutchman's breeches
and shoes of pink satin. He clutched a tall walking stick with a huge
silver head. The carry-cord was looped around one wrist. The young
man's wig was stuck through with pearl-headed pins. Phillipe had never
seen such a peculiar figure" (90-91). Roger was, in short, a fop, a "mac-
aroni," one of the superficial "young noblemen who adopted the latest
fads and aped the sputtering 'what, what?' of the King" (91).

Though his clothes may make Roger appear frivolous and shallow,
having little to do but to pretend boredom, his eyes are "ugly," totally
lacking "any softening humor." His face is marred by a small purple
birthmark shaped roughly like a U. On closer examination, Phillipe
noted a "cloven place" at the bottom of the U. He decided that the mark
didn't resemble a letter "so much as a broken hoof" (91). This image of
the cloven hoof—mark of the devil—dominates Roger's behavior. Jakes
plants in his reader's mind the likelihood that Roger will represent evil,
thus making him yet another of many antagonists Phillipe will face.

After being prodded by Roger's silver-headed cane, Phillipe flings the
cane away, arousing further ire and the likelihood of further physical

conflict with Roger. The incident, however, is not merely one of antagonism between brothers, the younger, richer one made vulnerable by what he perceives as a threat to his inheritance. In succinct dialogue Jakes connects it to thematic issues crucial to the novel, reflecting the new ideas Girard had introduced to his pupil.

"Under the law," Roger said with venom, "I could have you maimed for attacking me."

"If that's so, then your laws are as worthless as you" (95). Here we see Roger as a spoiled, arrogant, hotheaded, shallow young dandy, made vicious by a perceived threat to his fortune, oblivious to any sense of justice toward his brother, and certainly unable to comprehend the winds of change beginning to blow across Europe. Throughout the novel he does not change; he remains a two-dimensional character.

The reader's dim view of Roger is made even dimmer by Alicia's matter-of-fact assessment of her future with Roger. She responds to Phillipe's question about what career she expects her betrothed to take. He'll enter the army and purchase a commission, using the military as a "stepping-stone to a political career" which will, in turn, provide opportunities to increase his great wealth (113). Speaking as an aristocrat, she sees no irony, feels no shame, in so boldly stating Roger's venal motives. One cannot use the conventional term "serve in the army" for Roger. His time spent will not be service, but self-aggrandizement. There is no sense of service, of action in defense of a principle in which he believes, unless it is the acquisition of further wealth. Thus Roger is in sharp contrast to his half-brother Phillipe, already "infected" by revolutionary ideas, willing to make his own way, comfortable with questioning the status quo—even the law—when it contradicts principles of justice, and able and willing to fight for his beliefs. The first encounter between the brothers sets the stage for their later confrontation: colonel of a British regiment versus American patriot.

Jakes further integrates the destinies of Philip and his new country (his adopted *father*land) through his relations with Benjamin Franklin. Franklin, as one of Phillipe's chief role models, almost a surrogate father, has broken with his own son, incidentally a bastard, over politics. Franklin believes the colonies are taking the only road possible in the face of England's increasingly repressive actions. He believes that there's "no greater crime under heaven" than to let others put him or his country "in bondage" (581). As the breach with England approached, Franklin's son Billy, wanting an important position, had chosen to remain Royal

Governor of New Jersey rather than resign out of principle. Franklin explains his dilemma: despite his love for his son, "I love liberty more. . . . It's all choice" (582).

Franklin's renunciation of family bonds in the name of political principle helps Philip affirm his own identity. In a powerfully symbolic gesture of his coming of age, Philip burns his father's letter (612). The act, carried out at the very time he is committing himself to the future, not the past, to Anne and to America, states a very American concept: One must make one's own destiny, not inherit it.

THEMATIC ISSUES

As he does so frequently, Jakes makes use of the epigraph, or opening quotation, to suggest the theme of the novel. In this epigraph, from a 1766 speech by William Pitt the Elder before Parliament, in support of the repeal of the Stamp Act, Jakes links the bastard motif to central issues of the novel.

> This *gentleman* tells us America is obstinate; that America is almost in open rebellion. Sir, I rejoice that America has resisted.
>
> The gentleman asks when were the colonists emancipated. But I desire to know when they were made slaves. . . .
>
> They are subjects of this kingdom, equally entitled with yourselves to all the natural rights of mankind, and the peculiar privileges of Englishmen; equally bound by its laws, and equally participating in the constitution of this free country. The Americans are the sons, not the bastards, of England.

Pitt's words—his scorn of the aristocracy ("this *gentleman*"), his advocacy that all men be granted, equally, the natural rights of mankind, and his insistence on the rule of law to ensure justice—articulate the theme of *The Bastard*. Through word and action, Jakes' characters demonstrate these ideas, profound in themselves, and fundamental to American democracy.

European, particularly English, corruption, both social and political, demands change, and if not change, revolution. True justice must be based on fact and behavior rather than on social class. Roger asserts that Phillipe, a commoner, can be maimed for attacking him, an aristocrat.

Jakes' description of London is in sharp contrast to espoused English ideals. The opening sentence of Book 2 states the thesis of the obvious inequities which Jakes will develop: "The great city of London stank and chimed and glittered" (181). In the very shadows of Christopher Wren's greatest church, St. Paul's, the denizens of London are at work: rag pickers; toothless old women hawking ancient fruit; frightening prostitutes, their faces grotesquely painted, grabbing Phillipe's pants and aggressively manipulating his penis; and, on its very steps, a couple of drunks passing a gin bottle back and forth between the most "blasphemous, scatological" songs Phillipe had ever heard. It's a society of beggars only a step away from debtor's chains in the Fleet Street Prison, of children swilling gin to survive the brutalization of back-breaking labor suitable only for grown men, and who, if they run away, can be severely punished, their fingers or toes cut off (184-88). The chasm between the poor and aristocrats like the Amberlys shrieked for change.

Established religion, which might work to ameliorate these conditions, is portrayed as being in the pocket of the aristocracy. When Lady Jane comes to the Fox tavern to offer the Charboneaus a gift of fifty pounds to make them abandon what had been promised in the Duke's letter, Bishop Francis accompanies her. Jakes' description establishes his character—and the reader's response to him. Silhouetted against the fireplace (like Roger's birthmark, these flames suggest devilish intent), wearing purple (as befits his hierarchical position, in contrast to the simple black of a parish priest), is the Bishop. His round face is as severe as Lady Amberly's; his smile is fixed, insincere. His eyes are devoid of any emotion, any compassion. His lips are thick and moist; like the purple veins in his fleshy nose, they suggest his life of luxury. His entire demeanor radiates "affluence, importance, authority" (101). Jakes' description underlines the Bishop's allegiance (to Lady Jane rather than to church tenets) and his intent (to deny the Charboneaus what is rightfully theirs).

Jakes does not oppose religion, merely religion perverted and suborned by the aristocracy. The Bishop is of the Church of England. In contrast, we see the Sholto family, who saved the Charboneaus from the human predators who assaulted them on the steps of St. Paul's. They provide actual, not symbolic, sanctuary, nurse Marie and Phillipe back to health, teach Phillipe a trade, provide friendship to the sojourners, and, when Phillipe wishes he could repay them, reply that they expect no payment, wishing only to do their Christian duty (199). We also remember Mr. Fox, who dared to take the Charboneaus in when they were pursued from Kentland, risking personal danger rather than succumbing to hypocrisy (166). And the Ware family are Congregationalists, a denomination ruled not by a hierarchy but by the people themselves, an obvious denominational choice for those so deeply involved in the Sons of Liberty.

For, ultimately, the cause of liberty becomes, if not a religion for Philip and his American friends, a powerful, dominant article of faith. One remembers Girard's forbidden books and some of their messages: that there is a social contract among men which negates any king's divine right to hold a throne (54), that just laws come from the people (55), and that kings rule by the *people's* consent. That, although most government is eventually "evil and unnatural," neither oppression nor anarchy is acceptable; unlimited freedom, no matter how desirable, simply won't work (56). Liberty, as Paul Revere demonstrates when trying to save a political enemy from being tarred and feathered, must not be perverted by the mob (448-52). For the mob to pervert the cause of liberty is as evil as for Bishop Francis to pervert religion. Yet liberty for all, regardless of class, or religion, or gender, is, according to Jakes and many of his characters, important enough to defend with one's life. Part of the cause of freedom is the right to dissent *from* dissent. One must only do so out of conviction, granting the same right to others (581).

Thus, in the first volume of the Kent Family Chronicles, John Jakes has outlined some fundamental American political positions in addition to preparing us for the diversity of people and thought which will give impetus to all of his later novels.

ALTERNATIVE READING: FEMINIST CRITICISM

When the word "feminism" was first recorded in the English language, in 1895, it referred to the theory of political, social, and economic equality between the sexes and, by extension, the organized activity supporting women's rights. Feminist literary criticism as a self-aware or gender-aware conscious approach to literature emerged in the late 1960s and now ranges from the analytical to the doctrinaire.

Most feminist critics ascribe to three beliefs. The first basic belief is that Western civilization has traditionally been centered on and controlled by men and organized in such a way as to subordinate women to men in all spheres of activity. Many feminists believe that women have been socialized and taught to internalize this belief in male superiority. Accordingly, the masculine has come to be identified as active, dominating, adventurous, rational, creative; the feminine, by systematic opposition to such traits, has come to be identified as passive, acquiescent, timid, emotional, and conventional. Finally, most feminist critics believe that patriarchal assumptions pervade the writings that have been considered great literature, which, for most of history, has been written by men for men. Feminists point to the scarcity of female literary role models, female Hamlets or Huck Finns or Henry Flemings.

It is true that much in *The Bastard* demonstrates a patriarchal society. For example, even at a time when the institution of slavery was beginning to be questioned, women's roles were still defined as subordinate to and dependent on the men—father or husband—in their lives. (Anne's grandfather laughs at her mother's dream of managing the Sawyer shipyard; it simply isn't a woman's role. Moreover, when one compares Anne's and Phillipe's education, it is clear that Phillipe is being prepared to take his position as his father's son, to manage an inheritance, while Anne is provided with only the limited education of the Dame's School.) Those who challenged this order of things scandalized proper folk and were perceived as truly marginal, as were the prostitutes or, morally close, Marie, who chose to be an actress and was literally marginalized—excommunicated—by her church. But it must be argued that Jakes is writing historical fiction and, in doing so, *reflects* the society he describes, whatever his personal opinions. His portrayal of Alicia as the destructive temptress, "the gilded whore," no more implies advocacy of that role than his Hogarthian description of London, with its beggars, gin-riddled child apprentices, murder, and mayhem, suggests that these behaviors are, in his mind, utopian.

Though Jakes does not try to be "politically correct"—most of the Kent Family Chronicles were published before that term came into vogue—he admires strong women, and their recurring presence, in virtually all of his books, is one of his most apparent motifs.

Some doctrinaire feminists might argue that Jakes commits the sins of some other male authors who characterize women as either idealized projections of men's desires (the Madonna, the pale and innocent virgin, or Dante's Beatrice), or, in contrast, demonic projections of men's sexual resentments and terrors (the witch, Eve as source of evil, destructive temptresses like Delilah, or the castrating mother).

A radically different reading would be to suggest that Jakes, in his creation of powerful women, is actually a feminist author, *providing* female literary role models, especially in the character of Anne Ware. Jakes, however, would put it far more simply: "Strong women make strong characters" (letter, 6/22/95).

For, although Phillipe Charboneau/Philip Kent throughout the book illustrates very "male" traits—rationality and a propensity to violence—he is influenced by a succession of four exceedingly powerful women—Marie, Lady Jane, Alicia, and Anne. With the exception of the protagonist himself, these women are the strongest and most interesting fictional characters in *The Bastard*. (Even given the freedom fiction provides, it would be hard to top Benjamin Franklin.) For most of the novel, these four women have greater strength of character than does the protagonist, despite his obvious physical strength. For most of the novel, they are proactive, taking the initiative, defining the conflict, while Philip is merely reactive, responding to them and to other external stimuli. It is only when Philip, for himself, can choose among the women, reject false values, and purge himself of guilt that he becomes no longer the bastard, lonely and isolated, but the founder of a family of his own and one among the other Americans founding a nation.

Each woman influences him. Each defines values and traits among which he must choose to determine who he is. With each he wrestles, sometimes literally, sometimes for his very soul. Each dominates him physically: with Marie he's frozen into the perspective of the child looking up to the adult; Lady Jane consciously uses perspective, often railing down on Phillipe and Marie from the physical superiority of a flight of stairs; and Alicia attempts to ride him as she rides her horses—despite the pleasures of sex, she seems constantly to have the upper or whip hand. Only with Anne, who, as we learn in *The Rebels*, is actually taller than Philip, often described as "stocky," is there a sense of equality. Each also dominates him psychologically—his mother leaving him residual feelings of guilt each time he makes independent choices; Lady Jane from her exaggerated position of wealth and power; and Alicia, using her undeniable sexual favors as a means of control. Each dominates him—except Anne, advocate of liberty that she is, who offers him freedom—to accept as his own the cause of liberty or to retain his prior dreams of aristocracy.

Jakes portrays each woman as powerful. Marie is physically strong, with cascading black hair and, her genetic inheritance, good teeth, no rot, in an age of dental as well as social corruption. She, like Anne much later, is strong enough to choose her own lifestyle. She becomes an actress in an age when that profession—for women—was so ill-esteemed that those who chose the stage also chose excommunication from the church. Though there's a residual Catholicism (the Madonna and votive lights in Marie's bedroom at the inn in Aubergne), Phillipe never remembers seeing her pray at the niche. Rather, the object of devotion seems to be the casket of letters from James Amberly hidden behind it. Moreover, Marie takes on the church when she determines Phillipe's studies. In his nightmare she shrieks that he is to learn French and English, the languages of international commerce and politics, not Latin, the language of the church. He is to take his rightful place, claim what's his in England, "the greatest empire the world's known since Rome," and not learn Latin from that "bigot priest." Though one might suggest that Marie is embittered by her excommunication, she's also strong enough to take on the church, her family, and the aristocracy. Her goal, first for herself, is to seize the chance at something better; this becomes, by extension, her monomaniacal goal for Phillipe. For him she'll endure Lady Jane's haughty rage and cold disdain, battle Bishop Francis, endure London poverty. Only when Phillipe pragmatically recognizes that their very survival depends on a new goal in the colonies, when he gains a profession, a trade that will provide financial independence, when he abandons the oath she forced on him and begins to search for a goal other than to be recognized as James Amberly's heir, only then does her power wane. Indeed, on the stage they take to Bristol, the port of embarkation to America, their roles change. Phillipe increasingly fears for her sanity as, losing her dreams, she lapses into mutterings in French, the language of her happiest past. She becomes the child; he, the adult. Having announced that she *will not* sail to America, a land of tradesmen and farmers and hideous red Indians (237), she is rendered virtually catatonic once the ship sails. She cannot give up her dreams, her sacrifices, in favor of his. And although she rouses once long enough to absolve Phillipe before she dies, her legacy, in addition to the casket of letters from James Amberly, is guilt. For, in a waking nightmare, reminiscent of the one that opened the book, Marie, nearly hysterical, had screamed at him, "If you refuse to press your claim, then I've lived for nothing" (237). Her ultimate legacy is guilt, guilt heavy enough to destroy a man less strong than Phillipe, guilt which eats at him through most of the book, guilt which infuses his later relations with Alicia, complicates his political debates, and is finally purged by Anne's love and his love for America. But despite her sacrifices for Phillipe, and perhaps because of them, Marie is portrayed as the castrating mother.

No less powerful, though perhaps a lot less complex, is Lady Jane

Amberly, in some ways remarkably like Marie. Both women, of course, have sons by James Amberly. Neither has another child, though Marie seems to enjoy the pleasures of sex, while Lady Jane, after birthing Roger, seems curiously asexual. Both give all to their sons. The differences lie in the sons. Phillipe, the bastard, is nonetheless the elder, the stronger, the product of long-lived, albeit extramarital love. Roger, though legitimate, is weak, twisted, his birthmark the outward manifestation of a twisted psyche. He is the product, if we may extrapolate from Alicia's comments on her engagement to Roger, of an arranged marriage, the way the rich become richer in England. For Roger, and perhaps to maintain her own position, Lady Jane will go to any lengths—and her force is formidable. Though "only" a woman, she controls all the men around her, men of power as well as the servants. She spares no expense to engage Dr. Bleeker, one of the most respected physicians in London, to care for the Duke, but, equally important, to serve as a barrier against Marie's and Phillipe's claims; Lady Jane can, and does, buy allegiance. She obviously has Bishop Francis in her pocket as well. In his missions to confront the Charboneaus verbally, psychologically, financially, and eventually physically, and to convince them to abandon their claim, he is revealed not as a man of the cloth with religious principles and personal convictions, but rather as a vicious, hypocritical, cursing, brawling minion of Lady Jane. The Bishop's allegiance to Lady Jane personifies the unholy alliance between the church and the aristocracy that was still another cause of the revolutionary movements from the French Revolution to the Spanish Civil War. And when churchmen were willing to be corrupt, the secular forces—here Lady Jane—took control.

Besides dominating the doctor and the Bishop, Lady Jane was the only person who could control the sociopathic Roger, the monster whom, like Frankenstein, she has created. Despite Roger's murderous rage, Lady Jane's voice of steel can halt his aggression; though he must act out—smashing a vase with his walking stick—he obeys her command. Only her voice—and the force of personality behind it—brings him to heel. Finally, one wonders about her power over the Duke. Never in the book does he *speak* for himself: we read his letter to Marie; Marie tells Phillipe about him; and when Marie and Phillipe make their claim, based on James' letter, Lady Jane replies, "He cannot speak to your claim. *I am the Duke's voice now*" (132; emphasis added). Her extraordinary power is evidenced in her audacious faking of the Duke's death. The only thing she fears is the truth—as revealed in the Duke's letter—and she fights against it with every particle of her strength. One wonders whether, in the person of Lady Jane, John Jakes is asking whether all aristocratic despots must fear the truth, as revealed in writing. It is certain that in this specific case, truth threatens the status quo, and thus the *word* can be revolutionary.

Alicia, the third of the powerful women to affect Phillipe, is also a member of the aristocracy, the daughter of the Earl of Parkhurst. In many ways she's not the moral equal of Lady Jane. Indeed, Jakes describes her as a "fine lady—and a proper slut" (125). Phillipe, upon being introduced to Alicia at Kentland, is instantly reminded of Charlotte, the lusty French peasant girl who had initiated him, at seventeen, into the world of sexuality. Alicia, too, is a creature of the flesh, a gilded whore. She is capable of differentiating between marriages of convenience, such as that in her future to the strangely asexual Roger, and scenes of passion which she shares with Phillipe. Though defiant when she is reduced to the position of victim by Roger's brutality, she never questions the financial and social advantages of their forthcoming marriage. She knows she will have to seduce Roger, just as she's willing to seduce Phillipe. And in that first seduction, Alicia serves as a means for John Jakes to introduce exposition about the ugly underside of English aristocratic society. The scene also provides the basis for Roger's hatred of Phillipe, for not only has Roger been cuckolded before marriage, but the illicit affair elicits primal rage at the despoliation of his intended, for Alicia was physically, if not morally, a virgin. Indeed, she's a tease, a temptress who not only carries on her affair with Phillipe but demonstrates a suppressed streak of cruelty toward both men as she uses Phillipe to get back at Roger. To her, men are toys, tools to get what she wants, which is an even more assured position among the rich and powerful. Her loose morals may suggest the moral flaws of an aristocracy who believe, as does Lady Jane, that position can and should assure gratification of whims. Alicia drinks excessively; claret is her identifying mark. One may wonder whether this incipient alcoholism suggests an ambivalence toward her meaningless life, an ambivalence also expressed in her early, barely voiced fantasy of going to America to visit the Trumbulls. She's a bright young woman, providing Phillipe and the reader with an accurate reading of Phillipe's fundamental dilemma: whether he's a "proper nobleman's bastard" or a man who "spits on noblemen" (126, 128).

Though in many ways Alicia is weak, merely decorative, the product of her society, when she shows up in America after Roger's wounding, she still has sexual power over Philip. Moreover, by making him, for a time, feel like a kept man in the City Tavern in Philadelphia, she undermines his growth toward personal independence. She refuses to accept Philip Kent, the name he's christened himself with on the voyage to America, and insists on thinking of him as Phillipe Charboneau. She denies him *his* identity just as England has been denying the colonies theirs. Moreover, as Philip looks at her closely as she once again attempts to seduce him, her husband's corpse barely cold, she appears strained, worn, old, like the Old World and its value systems. And when, during his final argument with the gilded whore, he recognizes her desperate deception, he recalls the idealism of Girard, the dedication of Benjamin Edes to the power of the press to spread truth and achieve liberty, the personal courage and integrity of Benjamin Franklin. In contrast to their virtues, he sees her clearly, recognizes the danger as well as the futility of his mother's dream, and declares himself, once and for all, *Philip Kent* (593).

Philip's rebirth, however, would never have occurred had it not been for Anne Ware. She's every bit as willing as Marie to live unconventionally; she's every bit as strong as Lady Jane in fighting for what she believes in; and, like Alicia, she's capable of arousing Philip sexually. But she's a totally new woman. Not only has she read the political philosophers to whom Philip had been introduced by Girard, she applies them to herself. When the arrogant British officer Captain Stark seeks permission from her father to call on Anne, *she* refuses. Anne's response links the political freedom of the colonies to her personal freedom as a woman. Though she respects the broad rules set down by her government or her father, she demands freedom from arbitrary control (357). Anne has read—and taken to heart—those "filthy, blasphemous" writings Marie had forced Phillipe to read surreptitiously. Her rejection of an unacceptable suitor demonstrates a feminist interpretation of current political theory. She also rejects what James Amberly had called in his oft-cited letter "woman's natural role," bringing forth children. Anne feels sorry for Paul Revere's first wife, dead at thirty-six after far too many children. She wants a family of her own, but not at the expense of destroying herself. Anne strongly believes that, though her own mother died at thirty-five of smallpox, she was really dead in spirit years before. Marriage for her had been an admission of having given up her dreams, a response to her father's crushing rebuff of her ambition to inherit and run his shipyard. When Anne points out the formal education a colonial young woman was allowed—the dame school—we are reminded of Phillipe's private tutor. Both educations are to prepare the recipient for their "proper" place in society.

Anne is a passionate woman, but tempted as she was during the picnic in the meadow on Morton's Hill, she recognizes that sex alone is not enough. There must also be love. Otherwise "it's like the rutting of a slut and someone who's paid her" (397). One cannot ignore the ironic comparison to Alicia, the gilded whore. Moreover, Anne is passionate about politics and, as she talks to Philip about her views on marriage, she differentiates between surrender like her mother's and a voluntary bondage, mutually chosen by both partners (398). This philosophy infuses her relation with Philip and with the Revolution. From him she demands commitment—to a person and to a cause—if their relationship is to develop. But she also gives him freedom to choose. Unlike Alicia, manipulative to the end, she does not trap Philip by sex. On their reunion, just as the battles of Lexington and Concord announce a new world, he finds her, not like the perfectly primped, powdered, and coifed Alicia using her body and her beauty for personal gain, but a woman who's been heaving flour barrels out of the millpond. Her dress is torn and stained, her hair tangled, she's doing what she can for the Revolution; her integrity is whole. Though she'd decided she wanted no man but Philip, she would not use her pregnancy to hold him. Unlike all the other women, Anne has freed Philip to free himself—and to enter freely into commitment—to her, their new family, and their new country.

John Jakes has given us four powerful women as he develops the character of his protagonist. Marie, the castrating mother, Lady Jane, the witch, and Alicia, the gilded whore—these portrayals might outrage the most militant feminist. But he also presents Anne, lodestar for Philip in his search for self, catalyst to commitment; independent, unbridled, intellectual, passionate, idealistic, committed; a woman of integrity, courage, and strength—in short, a very modern woman, very much a feminist role model. Jakes transcends a narrow feminist interpretation, preferring instead to present women as varied, as powerfully good—or evil—as sacrificing, as conniving, as villainous, as manipulative, as true, as passionate, as honest, as any of his men. And in doing so, Jakes may have made a powerfully simple statement about human equality that transcends any topical ism and illustrates the ideals to which he is committed.

4

The Rebels
(1975)

The Rebels (1975) is the second volume of the Kent Family Chronicles. It picks up two months after the conclusion of *The Bastard*, but the tone is, for the most part, quite different. While *The Bastard* generally projected hope, however implausible, *The Rebels*, until almost the very end, is shot through with desperation. This reflects the military reality of the Revolutionary War, as a ragtag collection of colonies, reflecting differing economies, political philosophies, and social conventions, took on the world's finest military organization, the British army (22). The novel serves as a fine corrective to all those elementary and secondary school history lessons that make the Revolution seem, somehow, simultaneously heroic and strangely bloodless, victory inevitable. In contrast, *The Rebels* reveals what a very close call it was, making the victory—and the birth of a new nation—all the more precious.

PLOT DEVELOPMENT

The Rebels, continuing the adventures of Philip Kent in America, has obvious links to *The Bastard*; it also makes preparation for the six novels that will follow. In addition, *The Rebels* paints a broad panorama of American diversity—regional diversity, ethnic and religious diversity, and political diversity. Thus, Jakes must carefully provide a means to unify his plot if the novel is to have structural integrity. This he does by focusing exclusively on the Revolution. (The contrast on this point with the next two novels, *The Seekers* and *The Furies*, is marked.) *The Rebels* begins at the Battle of Breed's Hill, 17 June 1775, and concludes shortly after Cornwallis' surrender at Yorktown on 19 October 1781. This focus is essential because, unlike *The Bastard*, which was essentially Phillipe/ Philip's story, *The Rebels* truly introduces one of Jakes' signature techniques, the use of multiple points of view in the narration of multiple plots.

Aside from the war itself, there are two major plot lines. The Kent plot line finds Philip and Anne becoming the parents of a son, Abraham; the child is named for his grandfather, Abraham Ware, who will die only months later. His death, and Philip's commitment to Revolutionary principles, means that, except for brief leaves Philip can snatch away from the army, Anne is on her own. One of Jakes' strong women, Anne suggests to Philip during one leave that they take some of the money her father left them and invest it in two ships—privateers which will attempt to capture British ships, sell them and their cargoes, and thus return profits to the investors. Unwittingly, Anne thus sets in motion the events that culminate in her death.

A second plot line focuses on the Fletcher family of Virginia, slaveholders in fear of an uprising of their field hands—rightly so, it turns out. Thus Jakes introduces an ironic parallel: while the colonies are in rebellion against England for the "rights of man," some of those same colonies fear slave rebellions and institute increasingly harsh discipline to prevent them. Judson Fletcher, condemned by his father, Angus, for his atheism and for his soft treatment of slaves, is also condemned, or at least ostracized from polite society, for his drinking and womanizing. Judson, prevented by social conventions from marrying the one woman he truly loves, Peggy Ashford, now the wife of Seth McLean, fulfills his sexual desires with whores—Lottie Shaw in Virginia, and, when he goes to Philadelphia to participate in the writing of the Declaration of Independence, a ruined woman, "Alice," who when drunk asks him, "Why don't you love me enough, Philip?" (173).

The slave uprising occurs; amid violence and brutality on both sides, Peggy is raped by a slave, Judson arriving just too late to prevent it. Psychologically devastated, Peggy leaves the area to recuperate. Judson returns to Philadelphia. However, after he has once again disgraced himself in Philadelphia, he returns home, is disowned by his father, and visits Peggy, now returned to her plantation home. There, out of mutual desire, they make love but realize that it can never again occur. Judson sets off for Pittsburgh, the frontier, to rendezvous with a boyhood friend, George Rogers Clark. There he is mortally wounded saving Clark's life from the bullet fired by a Shawnee spy, who is working for the British.

The two plot lines are brought together in Book 3, "Death and Resurrection." After Philip is wounded at the Battle of Monmouth Court House, he returns to Boston to start his printing business; life, however, is not the same because of Anne's death. Eleven months after Judson's death in Pittsburgh, Lafayette visits Philip, and, trying to help him put his life back together again, demands that Philip accompany him to a dinner party. Going much against his will, Philip meets Peggy, in Boston on one of her frequent visits to Elizabeth, the child she bore out of wedlock, Judson's child. Late in 1781, Peggy and Philip marry, creating an instant family with two children, Abraham and Elizabeth. Almost simultaneous with the creation of a new nation in the surrender at Yorktown, Jakes has created the Kent family, with its rich, diverse, and contradictory influences, a family whose fortune he'll follow for six more books.

Jakes controls his materials carefully in *The Rebels*, almost like the driver of a six-horse coach, holding and controlling individual horses and thus allowing forward motion. First of all, the intricate plot lines of his invented people are carefully linked to actual chronology. More frequently than in other books of the Kent Family Chronicles, Jakes provides his readers with specific dates. A second technique, initially confusing, is to provide a different locale for each chapter, though chapters themselves are unified by place. Thus, in Book 1, for Chapters 1 through 7, the settings are Massachusetts, Virginia, Massachusetts, Virginia, Massachusetts, Philadelphia, and Philadelphia. This technique continues throughout the book. Once aware of it, the reader anticipates it. The result is another very important corrective to most people's understanding of the Revolution. While many school lessons seem to focus on New England, Jakes shows *all* the Eastern seaboard—New England, the Middle Atlantic, and the South—plus the West, the frontier. The effect, then, is that the reader truly sees the new nation as one forged from diversity.

Finally, Jakes has to work with plot to incorporate *The Rebels* into the ongoing Kent Family Chronicles. A number of times, he provides exposition of material covered in *The Bastard* (27, 33, 220, 513). At this point in his career (1975) he could not assume that his audience had read the preceding book; later, of course, the announcement of a new book in the series created an almost instant best-seller as readers rushed to catch up on the doings of the Kents. But in *The Rebels* he provides this explanatory material, interspersing it throughout the novel, usually through character musings or dialogue.

Other plot devices incorporate *The Rebels* into the entire saga. There are *continuing* plot lines or characters: Captain Caleb of the *Eclipse*—the ship on which Philip came to America—is now building a fleet of privateers; Lafayette and Franklin still give Philip advice; and, despite the fact that their nations are at war, Philip and his father, James Amberly, exchange letters. There are also *closing* plot lines. Both Anne and Alicia/ Alice die in this book. Although both, incidentally, die by water, their deaths otherwise are quite different. Alicia, though redeemed slightly from the "gilded whore" of *The Bastard* because she thinks she loved Philip, is now simply a worn-out, raddled prostitute who drowns herself because she has nothing to live for. Anne, with everything to live for— her husband, her son, potentially profitable business ventures, and a nation in which she believes—dies protecting the Kent investments; moreover, she dies strong, fighting off Captain Rackham's brutal and repeated rapes, resisting until they both plunge through a porthole into the Atlantic. Her last words, "a last strident cry of the soul: *Philip, I love—*" are, literally, drowned out by the element that destroys her. Finally, there are *opening* plot lines. Abraham is born, to continue the family name in *The Seekers*; the link with the Rothman family is forged on the battlefield, to continue in the banks and boardrooms of later novels; and, of course, Peggy unites two branches of the Kent family tree through her children Elizabeth (Judson's daughter) and Gilbert (Philip's son, born in *The Seekers*). Thus, both through the character of Peggy and by the technique of alternating locations, Jakes unites Virginia aristocracy and Massachusetts craftsman, the North and the South, the established Eastern seaboard and the frontier. The fusion of these disparate elements has created a nation and a family; it has also laid the foundation for other, regionally based plot lines in the novels that follow.

CHARACTER DEVELOPMENT

Through much of *The Bastard*, Phillipe/Philip is a relatively immature, unformed character, acted upon rather than initiating action. Not until he declares his interconnected love for Anne Ware and for the American colonies is he capable of independent action. He is still a very young man, and so John Jakes is able to continue his character development in *The Rebels*. Jakes does this in three major ways: he examines Philip's fear of death—and then of life; he juxtaposes him to Judson Fletcher, producing a contrast which defines both men; and he intensifies the connections to the American cause tentatively established in *The Bastard*.

Certainly the young Philip was no stranger to violence; he had been, many times, in mortal danger. But in *The Bastard* he seemed oblivious to danger, either unafraid to die or simply never considering the possibility. In *The Rebels*, mostly because he has the very pregnant Anne to consider, he worries about dying. As he sees others die on Breed's Hill, he wants to live. He mentally writes his own epitaph (17) but vows to survive for Anne. He knows fear, fear intensified by the disciplined British advance in perfect order, by the sound of the British drumbeat, the glitter of British bayonets, and, like Henry Fleming in *The Red Badge of Courage*, by having too much time to await action (23-24). Though he believes in the Revolution, "a cause was one thing, reality another. . . . He wanted to live. He wanted to see Anne again; see their child born whole and sound" (27).

Midway through the novel, during the disastrous retreat from Brandywine, he has seen so much death that fear has been replaced by pragmatism (297). Except for the emotional crisis when, concerned for Anne's welfare, he is talked out of returning home only by an appeal to his duty and a threat of court-martial, Philip maintains his equilibrium. Death holds no terror; it simply *is* as a possibility of life.

A more serious problem for him toward the end of the novel is his ambivalence about living. It is first demonstrated when he is wounded by a ball through his leg, and he comes close to whining about returning home a cripple. Moreover, once he learns from Captain Caleb about Anne's death, he seems to lack the will to live: he works at his press and he shares responsibility with Mrs. Brumple for raising Abraham, but, inside, he is a dead man. With Anne dead, he fears life more than death—until Lafayette snaps him out of it, first with the appeal to live so that Abraham can, and second with the introduction to Peggy.

Philip is also defined by contrast with Judson. Both love only one woman, but while Philip, inextricably bound to Anne, dies inwardly at her death, Judson, denied the possibility of marrying Peggy, seeks solace and release in prostitutes. Judson drinks far too much, far too frequently. (Jakes uses his drunkenness as a way to solve one problem for a historical novelist. His invented character Judson has helped write the Declaration of Independence. How, then, to explain the absence of his signature on the document? Jakes has the delegates request that Judson withdraw from the convention; drunk again when taking the floor, he had grievously insulted Dickinson, the delegate from Pennsylvania.) Where Philip is responsible, choosing duty to the army and the new nation over his desire to be with Anne, Judson succumbs to every desire. Only in his epic attempt to reach George Rogers Clark and prove himself does he almost overcome his weaknesses. But even his apparently heroic act of throwing himself in front of the bullet meant for Clark is, in part, acknowledgment that he is worthless and thus should be sacrificed to allow a good man to survive. As his father much earlier had shouted, he was "tainted"—and all his progeny after him. "Something in yourself has ruined you, Judson. Better to shoot any child you'd father than let him live his life with your devil's blood poisoning him and all his generations" (61-62). It is, thus, ironic that Judson's daughter with Peggy, Elizabeth, becomes, in effect, Philip's second child. The tainted blood which will appear in generation after generation of the Kents has been introduced to the saga.

The third technique Jakes uses to define Philip is to link him inextricably to the nation. This, of course, is yet another way Jakes connects books in the Kent Family Chronicles, for, in *The Bastard* it was only by internalizing the principles of the patriots so passionately held by Anne that Philip became, for the first time, his own man. In *The Rebels* the Anne-America-Philip chain is forged even more tightly. Several times he wishes to leave the army to be with Anne. (People *did* wander away from their units; poor discipline, a consequence, perhaps, of belief in personal liberty, was originally a real problem for the American army.) At first his desire to leave is simply that of a newly married man missing his wife, but "he and Anne agreed that he had to serve" (27). When, early in the marriage and the war, Philip grouses, "I wish the whole abominable mess were over, so we could go back to living like human beings," his father-in-law admonishes him: "Annie would scold you if she heard that, Philip" (81). She is his lodestone, reminding him that, just because the rebellion has minimal support—"less than a third of the people in the colonies are in favor of it" (91)—lack of support does not make revolutionary principles wrong. Thus, when his loyalty, his *duty,* is divided between Anne and the army on the receipt of the ominous letters about Rackham's behavior (377-81), his earlier conflicts are raised to a torturous dilemma.

A second major connection of Philip to his country is accomplished through Jakes' interweaving of passages from Thomas Paine's *The American Crisis* with scenes of camp life. Jakes quotes Paine's famous words:

> These are the times which try men's souls. The summer soldier and the sunshine patriot will, in this crisis, shrink from the service of their country, but he that stands it now deserves the love and respect of man and woman. Tyranny, like hell, is not easily conquered; yet we have this consolation with us that, the harder the conflict, the more glorious the triumph. (274)

Paine's words work wonders for the morale of the soldiers. Moreover, the discussion between Royal Rothman and Philip (273-76) points toward Kent and Son's first publication, except for handbills: a fine edition of Paine. Most important, Jakes allows the Paine passage to underscore Philip's dilemma between duty to family and duty to country. Henry Knox, feeling some guilt for having prevented Philip from leaving to check on Anne and perhaps save her, recalls Paine's words that "anything worthwhile—worth having, ultimately commands a high price. . . . if we win this war, we secure liberty." To which Philip, staunch patriot but also bereaved husband, can only reply: "Goddamn it, I know *very well* what we'll secure. But . . . you haven't lost the woman you love" (461-62).

THEMATIC ISSUES

The quotation from Thomas Paine's *The American Crisis*, so important to Philip, underscores a theme already introduced in *The Bastard* when Ben Franklin raised the question of what one is willing to pay to achieve one's goals. In *The Rebels* Philip has paid a great deal for his patriotic beliefs—separation from his wife and child, an emotional toughening necessary for his psychological survival, a wound from which he will limp the rest of his life, and, he believes, the loss of his wife because he wasn't there when she needed him. What he has purchased is suggested in Lafayette's toast: "To my comrade Philip. May he and his country live in liberty forever" (288). It is further emphasized by the epigraph Jakes chooses for the novel, always a clue to his major theme. He quotes John Adams, writing to his wife Abigail on 2 July 1776 about the Declaration of Independence: "I am well aware of the toil, and blood, and treasure, that it will cost us to maintain this declaration. . . . Yet . . . I can see that the end is more than worth all the means."

Aside from this major theme, Jakes presents three others. The book demonstrates Jakes' continuing interest in religion, especially his doubts about those whose Old Testament religion of law is not tempered by New Testament mercy. The scripture-citing, stiff-necked Angus Fletcher's condemnation of Judson is a case in point. But Jakes does not condemn religion. His portrayal of Peter Muhlenberg, an actual preacher/ general who sees George III as principal sinner, is one example (371ff.); Mrs. Bumple, Anne's neighbor, is another example of one who takes her religion sincerely, a practice even more admirable when combined with patriotism (391).

Another theme introduced in *The Rebels* which will be continued in many of the remaining Kent Family Chronicles is the frontier as a place of personal renewal, of hope and opportunity, a fresh start. George Rogers Clark lifts Judson's imagination with his narrative of immense western lands where a man could find himself and find freedom (40). Judson's near redemption dramatizes this idea. But Jakes does not ignore the consequences for the Native American. The Shawnee spy screams his outrage at the second wave of frontiersmen, not the hunters and trappers but the farmers who will inexorably change the land. "Steal our land, we throw down the red war belt"(482-83). And Judson, plantation born and raised, realizes a parallel—and the paradox of what will come to be called Manifest Destiny: the Tidewater planters had taken freedom from the blacks; frontiersmen were repeating that process with the Indians (483). Jakes, who has written westerns all his life, will return to the frontier as a tragically contradictory symbol in much of his later writing.

A final theme is the fusing of a united country from diverse people. Not only are there regional, economic, and cultural differences, but political factions cannot agree even on the issue of rebelling or not; the Tory majority early on cast doubt on the success of the venture. Nonetheless, a wide variety of people took up the cause: Tidewater Virginians like Thomas Jefferson and Blue Ridge mountaineers like Eph Tait; foreigners like the Polish engineer Kosciusko, the Prussian Von Steuben, and of course Lafayette; blacks like Salem Prince, who dies at Breed's Hill; and Jews like Royal Rothman. Rothman's case illustrates the process of Americanization. Early (226ff.) Rothman has to fend off a soldier who mocks his yarmulke, tries to snatch it away and, when Philip intervenes, explodes in an anti-Semitic outburst: "I didn't sign up to serve with no damn Israelites! . . . Robbers, usurers, every stinking one—" (270). Later, when the roles between Philip and Royal are reversed, Rothman now helping Philip survive after the battle of Monmouth Court House, Philip notices that his friend had lost his "little black wool cap" during the day (444). Royal Rothman is no less Jewish, but he is indistinguishable from all the other Americans.

Jakes borrows from Ben Franklin his symbol of this fusion of many diverse people into one. Franklin observed that trying to pull "thirteen colonies into concerted action was like trying to force thirteen clocks engineered by thirteen dissimilar clockmakers to chime all at once," an impossible goal. But, said Franklin, "We've done it, by God" (209).

ALTERNATIVE READING: A FOCUS ON FATHERS AND SONS

John Jakes uses the father-son motif to unify *The Rebels*. The term "motif" is very similar to, indeed often used interchangeably with "theme." However, a *theme* can usually be stated in a sentence; it is the thesis or central proposition of the book. In *The Rebels* one might identify as themes "A unified America was forged from a diversity of peoples" or "While the frontier offered vast opportunities to the pioneer, its settlement was a disaster to Native Americans." In contrast, a *motif* is usually expressed as a topic rather than a sentence: recurring dreams in *The Bastard* and *The Rebels*, the sound of drums in *The Rebels*, or, as we'll explore here, the relation between fathers and sons.

Jakes consciously connects the father-son struggle between independence and dominance with the struggle between the colonies and England. Although in some family struggles, especially in a Freudian interpretation, the sons literally wish the fathers out of the way, more frequently, as in this novel, there is a desire for acceptance, for more attention, for reconciliation. Nonetheless, almost always in this novel, the father-son motif is combined with yet another motif, that of separation. Here the separation between fathers and sons is used to underscore the novel's central historical event, America's war for independence from England.

Thus, the actual gulf between many father-son pairs is emphasized by repeated examples of other sorts of separation, many quite explicit. There's the separation between officers and men in the struggle to impose discipline while maintaining liberty. There's the stinking, rasping nightmare of the amputation of Cowper's arm, without anesthesia, as

Philip holds him down for the surgeon (308-11). Philip's own leg wound does not require amputation, but "there was permanent damage"; he was no longer able to soldier; "his separation orders were being prepared" (455). And, of course, there is the terrible, double separation from Anne. For most of the father-son relationships in *The Rebels*, separation is a central issue.

Philip, of course, in *The Bastard* had been kept apart from his father, James Amberly, by the conniving of his wife, Lady Jane. When, at the end of that volume, Philip learned his father was alive, he wrote to him. Now, in *The Rebels*, Philip receives a letter in reply, smuggled through the British blockade. Amberly is ecstatic to know that his older son is still alive. He is happy that Philip has maintained continuity by choosing Kent as his last name—for the family estate Kentland. He is happy at Philip's marriage, happy to be a grandfather. But he recognizes reality, too. An ocean, "a d——d debilitating war," and fundamental political differences separate father and son. They may never again hear from each other (228).

Ironically, although Philip has opened communication with his father, he cannot communicate with his son. Partly this is because, so long absent in the war, he is almost a stranger; partly it is because, mourning Anne, he is too dead inside to laugh, to play, to enjoy life with his son. Only Lafayette, his blood brother since their boyhoods in *The Bastard*, brings him to his senses. "You are driving that boy from you . . . you are counting as nothing all that's been spent to give him future—a country to grow up in that is unlike any other this world has ever seen" (501). Once again, while working on the father-son motif, John Jakes links Philip and his adopted country.

A second example of the father-son motif is the Fletcher family, also unsoftened by the presence of a wife and mother. Angus, the dour, religiously and politically conservative plantation owner, rejects both of his sons: Donald for his support of the Revolution, Judson for his drinking and womanizing. Angus' bitter denunciation of Judson as having tainted blood is one of the most shocking passages in the book (54-66). Only as Judson makes ready to go in search of George Rogers Clark (his personal attempt at redemption) is there any sense of reconciliation. But even then Donald carries the message of Angus' love (424). Father and son do not meet face to face.

This motif of separation between fathers and sons is, of course, used to intensify, personify, and dramatize the military/political plot—the separation of the colonies from England. Principle has come between them. Eph Tait puts it succinctly in his backwoods diction: "I'd rather have my kin remember me as a fella who died free an' sassy, instead of kissin' that old Dutchman's royal ass just to stay alive" (93). The ideas are put more elegantly in the quotations from the Declaration of Independence and from Thomas Paine which are woven through the novel. King George demands more of the colonies than, as maturing political entities, they are any longer willing to give; he is thus being replaced by George Washington, *father* of his country, who leads by personal example as he tries to instill discipline in his troops (a far cry from Angus' denunciations and rantings). Henry Knox observes to Philip: "The general's determined *to birth* an army out of this dismaying collection of ruffians" (76; emphasis added). Finally, it must be noted, by refusing to officially declare war on the colonies (338), England was refusing to acknowledge them as a nation, just as a parent may refuse to acknowledge his child's maturation. In both cases, a break occurs. In *The Rebels* John Jakes uses the father-son motif to emphasize, through casting them in familiar personal terms, the political issues of the Revolutionary War.

5

The Seekers
(1975)
and *The Furies*
(1976)

The Seekers and *The Furies* are volumes 3 and 4 of the Kent Family Chronicles. While they were published separately, they will be dealt with together in this discussion because their characters, themes, and historical considerations make them a cohesive unit.

The two volumes take the reader, the Kent family, and the United States from the first tests of the new nation along the borders of the Old Northwest to the prelude of the major test faced by this nation, the Civil War. *The Seekers* encompasses the years 1794 to 1814; *The Furies*, 1836 to 1852. In contrast to the tight focus on character in *The Bastard* or on events in *The Rebels*, both these novels are more diffuse. Perhaps as a corollary to the scope, major events are dealt with in an almost impressionistic fashion: daubs of color which, when one looks at them from some distance, take on the shape, the essence of that which is portrayed. Thus, instead of watching the Declaration of Independence being written, or seeing how independence plays out in regional arenas, or following the war through major battles from Breed's Hill through Brandywine and Monmouth Court House to the Yorktown surrender, as we did in *The Rebels*, we are now given representations of the historical whole. The battle between the *Guerriere* and the *Constitution*, for example, is a vivid rendering of the War of 1812, while the westering process is dealt with vividly in the fall of the Alamo and the excitement of the gold rush.

This skimming over almost six decades of American history may be accounted for, in part, by the fact that, as always, Jakes' characters drive his plots. In this case, two central characters dominate. When queried about whether these novels were meant to be one book, Jakes observed that the "characters ran away with me." That the two books probably began as one—or at least are closely connected—is clear from the central theme controlling both: the fall of the house of Kent, and its resurrection.

PLOT DEVELOPMENT

The Seekers and *The Furies* focus on two generations of Kents: Philip's sons Abraham (with Anne Ware) and Gilbert (with Peggy Ashford McLean) and *their* children, Jared and Amanda, respectively. Even *The Seekers*, the first of the two volumes, emphasizes the third generation, that of the cousins Jared and Amanda. *The Seekers* is mainly Jared's book; *The Furies*, Amanda's. A plot summary may be useful before discussing Jakes' techniques.

The Seekers opens with Abraham serving in the Legion of the United States under Gen. "Mad" Anthony Wayne. His immediate concerns are dealing with pre-battle jitters, fending off homosexual advances from Lieutenant Stovall, and acquitting himself well at the Battle of Fallen Timbers, where he almost kills Tecumseh. Returning home, he has the war veteran's difficulty of settling down, of adapting to peace. This is intensified by Philip's assuming that Abraham will take over Kent and Son, the publishing house Philip founded when he returned from the Revolutionary War. Abraham, however, wants to make his own way.

A hero to his younger brother, an ingrate to his father, he becomes the lover of Elizabeth, who is Peggy's daughter with Judson and Philip's stepdaughter. She, of course, carries the "tainted blood" from her father, the Fletcher blood, a wild streak which makes her resist the discipline and order of the Kent household. Despite grave parental misgivings, set aside for the sake of family peace, Abraham and Elizabeth marry, then head west to claim land near the frontier settlement of Cincinnati. Elizabeth, pregnant before the wedding, miscarries en route; Jared is later born on their homestead. Abraham, however, is no farmer; this frontier was no "gentle Eden" (183). He and Elizabeth were as much prisoners here as they would have been had Abraham worked at Kent and Son.

After Elizabeth is killed by Indians in full view of the toddler Jared, father and son return to Boston. Philip has just died. Unable to settle into the business, now run by his younger brother Gilbert, unaccepted by Gilbert's self-centered, snobbish wife Harriet, Abraham becomes increasingly erratic, fighting and drinking, till, amid an explosive family fight, the cerebral, physically weak Gilbert almost kills his brother. Abraham is banished from the house and disappears from sight.

Gilbert vows to raise Jared as his own; to Harriet, however, the boy is an interloper, a constant reminder of Abraham, whom she despises. Gilbert, a political liberal with important contacts, secures a place for Jared aboard the new ship *Constitution*, and the boy signs on for a year's service. There, he gains confidence away from Harriet's browbeating. He acquits himself well in battle, despite his blood phobia (legacy of having watched his mother's death, a phobia he'll have to fight all his life). Returning home on leave, he brings gifts—a bracelet made from tarred rope for Amanda, and a splinter from the battle-scarred *Constitution* for Gilbert—his contributions to the family's collection of talismans.

It is during this leave that Gilbert, aware of his own failing health and Harriet's fiscal irresponsibility, charges Jared to remember always that he is a Kent, a member of a family "not content to simply prosper without concern for [their] country" (*Seekers*, 432); to keep alive the family heritage and its symbols: "Don't let these objects vanish—or what they represent" (432); to live up to the words of the watch fob medal, a gift from Gilbert: *Cape locum et fac vestigium*: "Take a stand and make a mark" (300, 346); and, finally, "to take care of your cousin [Amanda]. I fear you are the only one who can do that adequately" (433). Gilbert dies Christmas Eve, 1812.

In addition to the symbolic presents, Jared also brings home the hatred of Lt. Hamilton Stovall, who, using the power of his office, made homosexual advances to Jared, repeating, almost exactly, his father's behavior with Abraham. Despite the advice of other ship's boys, Jared could not bring himself to murder Stovall, even though, during the heat of battle, it would have been easy. However, in their fight, a microcosm of the larger sea battle, Stovall, off balance, stumbled into a red-hot cannon, searing the right side of his face (406). Disfigured for life from the incident, Stovall becomes the major, truly evil antagonist to the Kents throughout the rest of these two novels.

Seven months after Gilbert's death, Harriet married Andrew Piggott, a man of many vices. Shocking to Harriet, who saw sex as an unpleasant duty, his sexual appetites were insatiable; rebuffed by his wife, he turned his eyes toward the ten-year-old Amanda, prematurely nubile. Moreover, he drank too much and was a pathological gambler. Stovall, looking for vengeance, capitalized on these flaws; Piggott gambled away the

Kent family assets—the printing firm and the house. A distraught Harriet, rushing to seek advice from her lawyer, was crushed by runaway horses. Meanwhile, when Stovall and his lawyer show up to claim Kent and Son. Jared, goaded beyond control, levels his revolver at Stovall, accidentally shooting Walpole, whom Stovall has seized as a human shield.

The fall is now complete. Philip, Anne, Peggy, Abraham, Elizabeth, Gilbert, and Harriet are all dead. All the family property has been seized. Kent and Son is in the hands of a man who cares neither for liberal political principles nor for good literature. And Jared, believing himself a murderer, flees with Amanda to the West as refuge—despite his horror toward it as a place which broke his father.

The two cousins plod through Pennsylvania, Ohio, and Kentucky, almost to Nashville. Jared is virtually incapacitated by fever when the ''Reverend'' William Blackthorn shows up at their camp. After beating Jared brutally in a free-for-all fight, he rapes the ten-year-old Amanda and abducts her to sell as a whore to fur traders. From Chapter 4, Book 4 of *The Seekers* until Book 2 of *The Furies*, Jared's and Amanda's plot lines separate.

Jared's goal is to find Amanda; unable to learn her whereabouts from Blackthorn before killing him, he eventually joins Elijah Weatherby as a partner in the fur trade. When beaver grew scarce, Jared went on to Oregon, where, with his wife Grass Singing, he raised a son, Jephtha. With his wife dead and his son grown, he responded to the siren call of gold in California.

Amanda, in those thirty-six years, had lived among the Mandan Sioux, having been sold by trappers to Plenty Coups; survived the Alamo, where she had stood up to Santa Anna after the massacre and had been protected by an honorable Mexican officer, Luis Cordoba, by whom she had a son, Louis. With Louis she had migrated to California and, in the sleepy village of Yerba Buena (San Francisco), established a hotel and enjoyed occasional visits from Bart McGill, captain of the clipper ship *Manifest Destiny*. Two things changed her relatively placid life: the discovery, in a bin of books, of one recently published by Kent and Son, establishing that the firm was still in existence, gave her the goal to regain it; and the discovery of gold gave her the means to pursue her goal. Jared shows up, but the family reunion is short-lived when he is shot and dies, leaving Amanda his share of a gold mine—in trust for Jephtha. Amanda turns east, vengeance on her mind.

Amanda, with income from the mine and from Gilbert's investment in New England mills, buys the Kents' Boston house just to get the family talismans. She establishes herself in New York City as Amanda de la Gura. There she tries to buy Kent and Son but is rebuffed by Stovall when her ambitions for the firm—better quality literature and a more liberal (i.e., anti-slavery) political position—become known. Despite flagrant anti-Irish prejudice abroad in the East, she hires Michael Boyle as her private secretary to join the coterie of wise and loyal helpers she has—Benbow the lawyer and the Rothmans, bankers—who know her true identity.

Louis, who hadn't really wanted to come east, who feels abandoned in Amanda's search for revenge, who has seen her single-minded pursuit of her goals and interpreted that as doing whatever she wants, who is a mass of teenage hormones, forces himself on an Irish maid in the Madison Square house. Amanda, one of the strongest of Jakes' strong women, continues to juggle business, family, and politics. She has become an abolitionist, a position put to the test when Jephtha, now working with the underground railroad, ships her a slave in a packing crate with the injunction that Amanda get her to Canada.

All elements of the plot converge, virtually simultaneously, on the Madison Square house. Captain Virgil Tunworthy appears with a U.S. marshal and a warrant to reclaim his slave. An Irish mob, further inflamed by Irish opposition to abolition because of the potential economic threat free Negroes will pose, comes to avenge Louis' rape of Kathleen the maid. And Stovall, furious at Amanda's stock purchases in an attempt to gain majority control of his enterprises, arrives to threaten revelation of her past and thus a ruination of Louis' future. The house is trashed. Amanda shoots Stovall, who has attacked Louis, and she herself is shot by one of the hoodlums. She dies seventeen days later, with her affairs in order, the foundation laid, she believes, for the continued prosperity of the Kents.

With such a convoluted plot, engaging so many characters in such diverse scenes over so long a time, John Jakes has violated every principle of Aristotelian unity of time, place, and action. However, especially in *The Furies*, Jakes is in firm control of his materials. *The Seekers*, relatively fragmented, almost picaresque in its characters' wanderings, is largely unified by the twin themes of guilt and redemption in Jared's character. There is also a quiet subtheme present: that Jared must find himself before he can find Amanda. *The Furies* is far more focused: all the subplots revolve around Amanda, with each having a different locus (the Alamo, California, the East) reflecting different stages of her life.

Her plot line is also unified by twin themes—survival and vengeance, both of which are intertwined with the larger unifying theme: to be a Kent.

This theme of living up to the Kent heritage is planted by Gilbert, quite consciously, in both Jared and Amanda (*Seekers*, 436). Family thus is a major motivating factor for both protagonists. Jakes further emphasizes this by using the family icons to unify and sometimes to advance the plot. The bracelet of ship's rope Jared brought to Amanda in 1812 is the recognition device between the middle-aged cousins when they meet again in San Francisco in 1849; Amanda buys the Boston house just to regain the family memorabilia; and, when she meets Stovall at the end, "struggling for control, for mastery of the inexplicable mixture of loathing and terror his presence generated," Amanda sits "beneath the portrait of Philip" (*Furies*, 513).

Jakes uses at least two other unifying devices. One is the repeated siege motif. The family, of course, is under siege by forces almost too numerous to withstand. In Book 1 of *The Furies* Amanda is among the Texans besieged at the Alamo; she survives through a mixture of luck, spunk, and Cordoba's intercession. In Book 3, the house on Madison Square is besieged by the Irish mob, Tunworthy and the law, and Stovall. This time Amanda is mortally wounded. But the repetition of the siege idea causes us—with Amanda—to reflect on all she's done in the intervening time to assure the family's survival.

Jakes employs one additional unifying device. The epilogue to *The Seekers*, "In the Teepee of the Dog Soldier," at first seems tacked on. However, it is crucial to Amanda's character development, especially her attitude toward sex and her determination to survive. It is also important to the narrative, for, through it, the audience learns what Jared cannot for another thirty-some years: Amanda is alive. (Jakes is punctilious in his treatment of point of view; he never slips and lets a character know what that character cannot know from his own experiences.)

Moreover, it is during Amanda's time with the Sioux that she learned that the "only honest verdict on a human life comes when it's over" (*Seekers*, 110), that "we see ourselves imperfectly. Untruthfully." She explains the Indian belief to Cordoba. When a person dies, a "great vine" sprouts from near the body. Invisible, it grows up toward paradise. The person's spirit begins to cling to the vine. "About halfway up is the critical point. Either you go all the way unmolested—or great hands reach down from paradise and break the vine, and your spirit falls back to earth, denied heaven because you lived an unworthy life" (*Furies*, 111).

This passage links Amanda's life with Plenty Coups to her life with Cordoba, father of Louis. It reemphasizes the strong woman motif, for the intercessor is a "very formidable [Indian] woman" (*Furies*, 111). And, as Amanda lay dying, trying to assess her life, "she remembered the Mandan legend of the vine; the great womanly hands left the vine alone or tore it, denying paradise. The meaning of the legend brought a certain comfort. Only a Divine intelligence could fully and accurately judge a human life, and find it worthy or wanting" (*Furies*, 536). She summarizes her life, balancing the ledger. Jakes links the Kent and the Mandan parts of her life:

> I am a Kent.
> I did what I had to.
> Let the verdict come down. . . .

"Suddenly, clear and sharp, she saw the vine to paradise. She spit on her hands and began to climb" (*Furies*, 537).

Jakes doesn't tell the reader the verdict; our emotions demand that the vine hold.

CHARACTER DEVELOPMENT

Although many characters populate *The Seekers* and *The Furies*, most appear only briefly, in cameo roles. They are at best two-dimensional, flat characters; one would not recognize them were they to walk into the room. They may be described by one or two words—Jephtha: "upright," "abolitionist"; Louis: "spoiled." Jakes uses them incisively—Gilbert establishes the family motto as a theme for the book; Blackthorn's rape and abduction of Amanda effectively separates the Jared and Amanda plot lines—and then lets them die. Though Hamilton Stovall and Blackthorn are appallingly villainous, they remain shallow. Instead, Jakes focuses on Jared and Amanda, especially Amanda. It is they, alone, who become truly rounded characters.

They share much: growing up as mischievous youngsters in Harriet's oppressive household; receiving Gilbert's charge to be true to the Kent principles; fleeing Boston after the apparent murder of Walpole; enduring the physical rigors of the flight west. Both have to recover from Blackthorn's rape of Amanda; both regain some of their strength through living with an Indian partner; and both become wealthy during the gold rush. However, by the time they meet in San Francisco, they have become quite different people, different both from each other and from who they were when they were last together over thirty years earlier.

The Jared we saw aboard the *Constitution* was a boy incapable of murder. He had, however, a violent temper which he was learning to control. Nonetheless, when the family and its enterprises were threatened, murderous rage erupted. Whether he shot the wrong man—or whether Walpole lived or not—was not the issue: he had *intended* to do grievous bodily harm. Ironically, the entire direction of his life—and of Amanda's—was changed by a murder he didn't commit. The guilt, however, and the fear of punishment by law, propelled them west.

After Amanda's rape and abduction by Blackthorn, revenge was added to Jared's psychological mix. Beaten into submission by the older man, he had witnessed the rape (as he'd earlier witnessed his mother's death), and that horror, plus the sense of personal impotence, intensified his guilt at not fulfilling his promise to Gilbert: "Take care of your cousin" (*Seekers*, 433). When finally he did catch up to Blackthorn in St. Louis, after Amanda had been sold, the two men aimed their weapons at each other. Jared fired first. Perhaps because wanton violence is so common, Gen. William Clark imprisons Jared for ninety days for shooting Blackthorn. Jared, in the depths of despair, feels responsible for the family's fall, for Amanda's fate. He accepts that, like his father, he has been defeated by the West, and that, like his mother's, his blood is tainted. He reaches his nadir, contemplating suicide. "But somehow he lacked the courage. Count that one more failure" (*Seekers*, 592).

Redemption comes in the person of Elijah Weatherby, a grizzled fur trapper who proposes that they become partners and, while trapping, pursue inquiries about Amanda. Most important, though, Weatherby teaches Jared that forgiveness for sins far worse than Jared's is possible. Weatherby is a windigo, accursed because he has committed cannibalism (610), a taboo he violated in order to survive (617). Weatherby encourages Jared: "What I'm sayin' to you is, the country west of here forgives just about anything a man wants or needs to have forgiven" (*Seekers*, 598).

So the two men set out—one an outcast, the other feeling like one; they go west together to the fur country. From Weatherby Jared learns the fur trade. More important, he learns to love the beauty of the land that he had feared and hated for breaking his father. Jared feels cleansed again; he has hope again; he feels part of a whole again—partner with Weatherby and with all the myriads of other Americans heading west.

And finally, with Weatherby's help, he is able to forgive himself and become free from guilt, and failure, and hate. "Even if you don't find [Amanda]," Weatherby says, "you got to remember it's the tryin' that counts most. It's the tryin' that makes a man worthy of the name" (*Seekers*, 620).

Weatherby saves him. With Grass Singing he enjoys love. Together they raise Jephtha, a wholly upright man for whom conscience and right will be ruling passions. And now, after Grass Singing's death, Jared has come to California.

This Jared, initially described as a loner, is not a hermit; he has partners on his mining claim. Though he chooses to separate himself from the drunken revelry at the bar, he is a man of courage, rescuing the black Israel first from the bigoted Know Nothings and then from the fire in the tented bar. Most important, Jared is a man living at peace with himself in the present.

As he and Amanda build a "bridge of words across the years since 1814" (*Furies*, 240), he sees their similarities: both have survived and prospered; both have had sons to carry on the Kent name; both are deeply moved at their unexpected reunion. But while he has no desire to return to the East (and if he does, it will be simply to visit Jephtha in Virginia), she is obsessed with returning to Boston to recover Kent and Son. He has mastered his anger except for the brief flareup when she tells him Walpole is alive—and he fights this back, along with the chance for revenge against Stovall, as part of a buried past. He remembers Gilbert's words about the Kents always taking the high road of cause, contribution, and commitment; though he may not have met Gilbert's expectations, at least he's lived "so I'm not ashamed of myself." She sees no "shame in taking what's ours" (*Furies*, 256). He pleads with her not to go back, to realize that vengeance is destructive, to recognize her son's fear of the driven woman his mother has become, to believe him when he says that hate only poisons the one who hates, to understand that to resurrect the Kents, to take vengeance on Stovall, will demand a price far too great to pay. It is at this impasse between cousins that Jared is shot. He dies, fearing that he had given her exactly what she shouldn't have—his share in the mine and the names of the Kent family attorneys.

Moments earlier, he had observed a woman as driven by monomania, as strong as Marie in *The Bastard*. He no longer knows her. This is no longer the mischievous imp of a cousin he'd sworn to protect; not even the suffering ten-year-old he'd failed to protect. For Amanda, with no mentor, no guide, no protector, has defined herself. In the course of the two novels, her roles and motivations have gone from survival to conviction to obsession to sacrifice. At virtually every stage her strengths have an opposite, reciprocal, capacity to destroy. After the excruciatingly brutal rape by Blackthorn, she has learned to use sex as a survival technique. More important, during her stay with Plenty Coups, she came to understand the Sioux attitude toward sex. "Sex was not a sin but a celebration" filled with "mystical reverence" (*Furies*, 36). Certainly this was a far healthier attitude than her mother's. It enabled her to run an honest brothel in Bexar after her husband Jaimie de la Gura's death; it brought her survival under Cordoba's protection and, through him, it brought her a son to carry on the Kent family line.

Not only a survivor, Amanda is a woman of conviction. Her loyalty is to her country and her family; the two are often interwoven in her thoughts. At the Alamo, when, with her late husband's surname, de la Gura, she could "pass" as Spanish, she insists on identifying herself as an American. She builds an analogy between the Texans' fight for liberty and that of the colonies two generations earlier. "Maybe it *is* time for another declaration of independence" (*Furies*, 39). When Buck Travis declaims on Washington's birthday that Americans in Texas had to stand up for liberty, Amanda remembers her grandfather, who did just that back in Boston sixty years earlier (*Furies*, 38). Amanda gains strength to face Santa Anna from the sight of the Mexican tricolor and eagle raised above the corpse-strewn plaza of the Alamo. To the dictator's order that she carry the message of the Alamo throughout Texas to demoralize the Americans, she retorts that it is better to die for the Texas republic than to surrender to Santa Anna's despotism (*Furies*, 75).

Even this early, her dream is somehow to recover the family icons— the tea, Lafayette's sword, the Virginia rifle. Her obsessive behavior is evident this early, too, for she refuses to return to Boston till she is worthy of the Kent name—which she interprets as being rich enough to "properly face anyone who might remember the family. Especially that son of a bitch Stovall or his heirs" (*Furies*, 110).

From the time she learns that Kent and Son is still in business, being ruined by Stovall, this determination becomes an obsession. Louis, once simply a child loved as the concrete manifestation of her love for an honorable man, Cordoba, as well as a means of perpetuating the Kent line, becomes subordinated to her desire to return east and wreak vengeance on Stovall. She fails to see that Louis doesn't want to leave California; that he misinterprets her killing the man blocking her way to the mines. She refuses the love of Bart McGill, who warns her that, although she's a good woman, a strong woman, she's tempting fate by her obsession. "You've somehow got in your head that you're one of those avenging goddesses of the Greeks or the Romans. . . . But the difference between you and one of the furies, sweet, is just this. They lived forever. You can't. You can be injured" (*Furies*, 295). Later, after she once again rejected his marriage proposal in favor of duty to her family, Bart observed that her feeling for family is a curse, not a blessing. "You're wrong," she said. "It's both" (*Furies*, 303). She had become a zealot, a fanatic.

Bart knew such fanaticism could be self-destructive, as did Michael Boyle, totally loyal though never an obsequious yes man. So close that he was almost a member of the family, Michael observes her increasing obsession with destroying Stovall and regaining ownership of Kent and Son. He supports her efforts to buy the firm; he goes along with her stock manipulation schemes; but he draws the line at blackmailing Stovall about his sexual perversions. If she acts on those plans, she will have sunk to Stovall's level.

Fortunately, Amanda realizes what has happened. Vengeance has taken on a life of its own, consuming the higher Kent ideals. Having recognized this, Amanda is ready for her final role—sacrifice. For at the end she dies for others—for the slave Mary and for her son Louis.

On that final evening when the Madison Square house is besieged, as was the Alamo so many years earlier, Amanda can pause briefly in satisfaction that she has helped Mary to escape. In the tradition of her revolutionary grandfather, she has broken the law, the Fugitive Slave Law, in the name of a higher law, freedom.

However, the incident drew newspaper attention, and with it, Stovall's awareness of her link to the Kent family he has sworn to destroy. The story, having alerted him, scuttled her hopes of secretly buying up a controlling interest in his company. And that meant she had no leverage to negotiate a purchase of Kent and Son. She sees the irony of her situation: her choice to help rescue the slave girl has undercut years of hope, hard work, and struggle to restore her family (*Furies*, 511). Was the slave's freedom worth the sacrifice of all that she'd dreamed of? Amanda had been caught in a classic dilemma: could she sacrifice Kent principles to gain Kent property? That her choice, freedom for the slave, had a direct chain of consequences, chief of which was the loss of all she had striven for, was appallingly clear. Her obsession had died as she reaffirmed her principles.

At that very moment, Stovall arrived at the house to confront and

threaten Amanda, morally stronger than she'd been in months, but emotionally shaken. Jakes uses descriptive words and phrases to indicate her
fragility, words surprising when applied to the woman who had faced
Santa Anna. Now she is shaken; she "struggl[ed] for control" (*Furies*,
513); "she churned with overpowering hate." At the same time, she "felt
unclean" (516), "she shivered" (517) in the face of the man, a physical
grotesque whose "very soul—if he had one—was malignant" (516). The
strong woman is as vulnerable as we've seen her in either novel. Nonetheless, she absorbs his assertion that he will instruct his attorneys that,
even were he to die, neither she nor her heirs could purchase Kent and
Son. She shrugs off threats to expose her checkered past. But when Louis'
future success is threatened by her past, she becomes desperate. She does
the hardest thing she had ever done—she begs Stovall for a truce (520).
But one cannot negotiate with absolute evil.

The moment is interrupted by the Irish mob attacking the house. Louis,
panicked, brings the rather redundant news to the door of the parlor. In
his rush to escape, Stovall slashed his gold-headed cane against the boy's
temple. Unthinking, Amanda acted, a mother protecting her son: she
pulled out her revolver and shot Stovall. Though the boy had already
been knocked unconscious into a coma from which he took days to
emerge, and thus Amanda didn't literally save his life, she *did* save his
future; Stovall, dead, could not implement his threats. Like Jared, decades earlier, Amanda was not able to murder Stovall in cold blood, but
could respond to a real threat from him.

As she had shot Stovall to protect her son, so too she shot two hoodlums as they threatened the family talismans. Her back to the mantle
(the portrait of Philip thus, literally, backing her up, she shot them as
they threatened to "tear the fuckin' place apar[t]," and as they reached
for the mantel and the family icons (*Furies*, 556).

Whatever sins she'd committed, whatever obsessions she'd let rule her,
however low she'd almost sunk in pursuit of her goals, Amanda died a
Kent, living Kent values, sacrificing herself for Mary's freedom, Louis'
life and future, and the family icons.

THEMATIC ISSUES

Because the Kent Family Chronicles is a continuing family saga, themes
introduced in earlier books resurface in later ones, as do the characters
who espouse them. Sometimes even when characters are dead, the prin-

ciples for which they had stood, the themes they illustrated, are perpet-
uated. This occurs in this brace of books every time Jared feels guilt for
having failed to carry out his promise to Gilbert or whenever Amanda
wonders what her grandfather Philip would have done. The Kent family,
in many ways, personifies American values. This will be especially important as we follow Louis from *The Furies* into *The Titans*; the character
flaws he manifests as a young man—feeling, for example, that it is his
right to do whatever he wants in his rape of Kathleen—become more
pronounced, and his lack of values produces a dramatic tension all its
own. However, in these two books, characters so frequently dramatize
ideas that thematic issues inevitably creep into discussions of plot or
character. Such themes include the necessity for personal choice, especially when it is difficult; the sacrifice of—or willingness to sacrifice—
self for principle; the strong woman motif; the necessity of making peace
with oneself in the face of failure, so long as one has done all one can.
(A corollary, from Jared, is that guilt can destroy; and, from Bart, that
while hate can destroy, love endures.) In the following discussion, three
themes will be explored: the meaning of the West, the nature of family,
and redemption.

   Although the West was a factor in earlier books and will continue to
be so in the Kent Family Chronicles at least until 1890, in *The Seekers* and
The Furies, the significance of "the West" is as varied as the region itself.
For the frontier is moving. In *The Seekers*, Pittsburgh, Cincinnati, and
Louisville are at the limits of civilization; by *The Furies* the frontier is St.
Louis and the upper Missouri, Texas, Oregon, and California. Jakes' use
of this moving frontier alludes to the thesis of Frederick Jackson Turner's
"The Significance of the Frontier in American History": that the existence
of the frontier and its continuous movement westward is the central
factor defining and shaping American character. Jakes, too, in these bicentennial novels, is defining American character.

   For some, the frontier offers economic opportunity. Characters in these
books seek fur, gold, and land in an effort to better their positions. For
some, like Daniel Clapper, Abraham's nearest neighbor on the farm, it's
the satisfaction of an "itch" to move (*Seekers*, 161). Others move west to
flee crowded cities or simply because they're not happy. Clapper says,
"It really ain't a matter of goin' *toward*, it's a matter of runnin' *from*"
(*Seekers*, 168). Certainly for two of the villains of these books this is the
case. Rumors surround the elder Stovall before the Battle of Fallen Timbers; not only is he a sodomite, but word of a scandal follows him: an
apparently incestuous relationship with his sister, whose miniature he

wears in a locket on a chain (*Seekers*, 33-34). Blackthorn, masquerading as an evangelist, is a perverted parody of the frontier circuit-riding minister—but he stays a jump ahead of the law. The frontier, for renegades like Stovall and Blackthorn, was a haven, a sanctuary from punishment for those unable or unwilling to live according to society's conventions.

For Abraham, the frontier army was a chance to escape differences with his father. When later he returned as a settler, he came west because he knew what he didn't want. To Mr. Clay of Kentucky, "the west is the rising star" (*Seekers*, 340); to Abraham, it is "this accursed place" (*Seekers*, 222). The West is a test for some, like Jared, with the real possibility of defeat. For Elijah Weatherby, it provides a cleansing of his soul from sin. Thomas Jefferson defines the West in terms of what will be called Manifest Destiny: contiguous lands must one day belong to the United States for their natural resources, for political security, for a new chance for the yeoman farmer. "I believe our country's true future lies not in the east but in the west," he says (*Seekers*, 109). Amanda uses the resources of the West to attain her goals in the East.

Despite—or perhaps because of—the diversity of responses to the West, the frontier, Jakes, like Turner, feels that it is fundamental to the definition of American character.

A second important theme is family. On the one hand, this is obvious: much of the discussion of plot and character dealt with what it means to be a Kent. Beyond this, it is intriguing to compare the first books of the Kent Family Chronicles. The dominant motif running through *The Bastard* was the strong woman; in *The Rebels*, it was the father-son motif. Both, of course, continue here, but the scene in *The Rebels* of George Rogers Clark setting off from Pittsburgh with families on flatboats foreshadows the Clappers and Abraham and Elizabeth on their ark in *The Seekers*. While single men, for the most part, trapped and hunted and prospected, families *settled* the West.

The family motif is also played out in the continuity of generations. Both Abraham and Jared, father and son, face the Stovalls, father and son, as sinister threats. If anything, the evil intensifies, for Hamilton, who is also Amanda's nemesis, is almost certainly the offspring of the incestuous relationship between the elder Stovall and his sister Lucy. Another point worth mentioning is that, even for the Kents, by the third generation the family seems to be dying out. One may support this by noting the weaknesses in Abraham and Gilbert, or by remembering Abraham and Elizabeth's stillborn child. An infusion of fresh blood seems necessary. Amanda marries de la Gura; Cordoba fathers Louis. Jared marries Grass Singing; his son Jephtha is referred to as the "Indian preacher." As Philip identified himself with the emerging nation, this generation of Kents reflects an America expanding its gene pool. Michael Boyle's virtual adoption into the Kent family as guardian for Louis further exemplifies this process.

The "new blood" of the previous paragraph is an example of Jakes adding multiple layers to a single word, almost like a complex pun or the richness of a poem. "Blood" in these two books has multiple connotations and denotations. There is, of course, the blood of battle: Fallen Timbers; the battle between the *Guerriere* and the *Constitution*; the Alamo. There is the blood of free-for-all fighting; the blood of the deflowered Amanda; the blood of Israel congealed into the scars that affirm his hatred of slavery, his insistence on equality. There is plenty of blood in Amanda's drawing room; she probably kills more people than any Kent since Philip. But there is also the blood that Jephtha, the defrocked minister, warns of when assessing the nation's coming dissolution over slavery. In his letter to Amanda, which results, eventually, in her complicity in helping the slave Mary to escape, he writes, "We have sinned as a nation." The nation's sins must be punished. Jephtha quotes the Apostle Paul's Letter to the Hebrews: "almost all things are by the law purged with blood. And without shedding of blood is no remission" (*Furies*, 431).

With this quotation, Jakes introduces the concept of redemption through Jephtha, probably the most moral character in the novels, the polar opposite to the other "preacher," Blackthorn. Jakes seems to suggest that redemption must be attained consciously, of one's own volition. (One remembers Judson's unconscious "redemption" in *The Rebels* through saving George Rogers Clark.) Some cannot achieve redemption at all. Abraham, his opportunity for redemption—participation in the Lewis and Clark expedition—arranged, does not go; he is too weak physically and morally. Many must have others' intervention and help to achieve it; one wonders whether Jared, without Weatherby and Grass Singing, could have gained redemption and peace. And Amanda, despite all her efforts at being true to Kent—and American—principles, has sinned. As she tots up the balance sheet in the seventeen days between being shot and her death, she seems unsure of the verdict on her life. Her final sacrificial role, however, her shedding of blood for others, suggests that she *will* climb the vine to paradise.

ALTERNATIVE READING: ARCHETYPAL CRITICISM

An archetype is a "primordial image, character or pattern of circumstances that recurs throughout literature and thought consistently
enough to be considered universal" (*Merriam Webster's Encyclopedia of
Literature*). Among archetypal symbols are the laurel and olive leaves,
the snake, and the eagle. A common archetypal theme in literature is
initiation, the passage from innocence to experience. Archetypal characters include the blood brother, the rebel, and the prostitute with the
heart of gold. Jakes' titles *The Seekers* and *The Furies* are clear allusions
to literary archetypes.

The Seekers suggests a quest for something, an odyssey in that search.
Clearly these are concepts that appear frequently in literature from Ho-
mer to Steinbeck. *The Furies* is a direct allusion to the Greco-Roman goddesses of vengeance. (Amanda clearly plays that role here.) The Furies
may have originated as personified curses or perhaps as ghosts of the
murdered. This motif of vengeance extends from the Biblical " 'Vengeance is mine' saith the Lord" to modern police procedurals where
crime is punished by the state *in loco deum*. Many archetypes may be
found in *The Seekers* and *The Furies*. For the sake of brevity, however,
this discussion will focus on the Garden of Eden, the Fall, and Death
and Resurrection.

The archetype of the Garden obviously has its origins in the Bible. The
Garden of Eden is a place of innocence, as close to heaven as is possible
on earth. Not only *is* there no evil, but there is no conception of evil,
until the ultimate outsider, the snake, brings awareness, knowledge previously untapped. As a consequence of their fall from innocence, Adam
and Eve are thrust out from the Garden, condemned to wander. The
Kent family is a tightly knit enclave, all the more so because both
branches of the family tree are united by Philip's (the first father?) marriages to Anne and to Peggy. There are virtually no outsiders. But in *The
Seekers* Gilbert marries Harriet LeBow, clearly outside the Kent philosophy of duty, and, when widowed, she marries yet another outsider, Andrew Piggott, a thoroughly unprincipled man whose vices bring
destruction on the Kents. Figuratively speaking, with these marriages,
the snake has entered the garden. After Piggott, the children are forced
to wander, cast out not *because of* evil, but *by* evil. Amanda settles in
California, described in early accounts as the "Terrestrial Paradise."
There she lives happily with the love of Bart and her son Louis; she

owns a business that provides adequately. She has a good life, *until* the "snake" enters—the knowledge that Kent and Son is still in business, which knowledge begins the obsession and hatred (sin) which nearly destroy her. It might also be noted that the Indians called Anthony Wayne "Blacksnake." Admittedly, this is for the pattern he used in moving his troops back and forth, but for the Indians, the defeat at Fallen Timbers effectively casts them from their Eden onto a century-long wandering west to exile on reservations. Finally, there are the snake images connected to Hamilton Stovall, epitome of evil. At the Frederick Douglass lecture, he "hisses" repeatedly to express his opposition; and, when Amanda prepared to meet him, "fear crawled in her like some venomous intruder" (*Furies*, 512).

Adam and Eve's expulsion from the Garden was as a result of their fall from innocence, fall from grace. (It might be noted that Jared's middle name is Adam.) One can discern the decline, the fall, of the Kent men in these books. Gilbert, physically weak—presumably a flaw introduced by the bad Fletcher blood—is, nonetheless, morally strong. In contrast, Abraham, son of the strong Anne, is weak in character. While Philip was strong physically and morally, neither son is *both*. Moreover, the wives of Abraham (Elizabeth) and Gilbert (Harriet) are far weaker than either of Philip's wives. It may be significant that the last child born in the Boston house is Amanda, a girl—not therefore weaker, but, under normal circumstances, a hint of the end of the Kent name.

Yet another indication of the Fall, the expulsion from the Garden, is that Abraham is beaten by the West, generally a land of opportunity. Admittedly, having Elizabeth killed by the Indians is traumatic, but even before that, Abraham is not a good farmer and wants to leave the land. Unlike Jared, who eventually controls his blood phobia, Abraham can't recover. Jared grows stronger, first physically, then, in *The Furies*, morally; he is redeemed. In contrast, Abraham, the last time we see him, is a syphilitic wreck.

Absolutely essential to an examination of this motif of a fall from innocence is the rape of the ten-year-old Amanda, especially heinous as it is perpetrated by a self-proclaimed man of God who alternates his thrusts with Biblical quotations. The cacophony (literally, "bad sound") reaches a crescendo as Amanda's shrieks provide contrapuntal commentary on desecrated scripture. The "preacher" is crazed; the world has gone mad.

Indeed, this may be a final evidence of the Fall. Even sin seems more heinous in these two books. Roger, of *The Bastard*, despite his birthmark shaped like the devil's cloven hoof, is, as a villain, a rank amateur compared to Hamilton Stovall or Blackthorn. And although the self-styled preacher can be variously interpreted, whether he is a psychopath or the personification of absolute evil is surely irrelevant to Amanda as he is raping her. There may be a suggestion—corroborated by all the forces moving the country toward the Civil War—that society as a whole has suffered moral decline since the time of the Revolution.

The ultimate "fall" is perhaps death. In these two volumes Jakes has killed off not only the patriarch Philip but both his sons as well as their wives. The scythe has swept so broad a path that when Jared and Amanda are out of touch with each other for over thirty years, each would seem to be the last of the line. Both, however, are so conscious of that possibility that having children is, for them, more than the result of the act of love with a cared-for person; it is a kind of resurrection of the Kents. Before he'd even met Grass Singing—but after his own personal resurrection from despair initiated by Weatherby, Jared realizes that "he had it in his power to begin the family anew. He must do it as best he could" (*Seekers*, 619). Amanda, too, is "resurrected." Having experienced a fate worse than death at the hands—or penis—of Blackthorn, she emerges, eventually, a strong woman. Her final words in *The Seekers*, after she has gentled Plenty Coups, are "I will live. I have found a way. I will live" (*Seekers*, 634).

Both Amanda and Jared survive, bringing to life the fourth generation of the Kent family. It is, however, Amanda's behavior at the very end of *The Furies* that assures its survival. She takes seventeen days to die, for she has much yet to do. In almost excruciating tension between death and duty, Amanda's painful day-to-day actions ensure that her goals— and the family—will endure. She has demonstrated the ultimate archetypal pattern—sacrifice. Because of her suffering and death, the family will live.

6

The Titans
(1976)

The Titans, Volume 5 of the Kent Family Chronicles, along with the following volume, *The Warriors*, has as its focus the cataclysmic events of the American Civil War and the westward expansion that follows. (John Jakes returns to these topics in the North and South trilogy.) One of the surprising characteristics of *The Titans* is that, despite the epic dimensions implicit in the title, the novel encompasses a relatively brief time span. Though the prologue begins on election night 1860 and the epilogue carries the conflict to 31 May 1862, the date of the birth of Gideon's daughter and his disappearance while fighting with the Army of Northern Virginia to repulse McClellan's vast army, the bulk of the book covers only three months. Those ninety days are bracketed by the Confederate attack on Fort Sumter on 12 April 1861 and the Battle of Manassas in July 1861. The events at Manassas emphasize the irony of expectations, North and South, at the beginning of the war, that it would all be over in ninety days. The reader, of course, knows better.

PLOT DEVELOPMENT

The Titans emphasizes the tragic error of belief that the war would end quickly. Because Jakes' plots are character-driven, *The Titans* focuses on Jephtha Kent and his son Gideon from April to July 1861. Though time is fairly limited, place is relatively more expansive. The novel is set in Washington City, Richmond, and Baltimore (representing Federal, Confederate, and Border mentalities) and on the battlefield at Manassas, where armies and spectators from Washington—who brought picnic lunches to eat while watching—were disabused of their ideas of the war's brevity and bloodlessness.

Two kinds of plot lines run through the book: those dominated by physical action and those focusing on emotional relationships. The war, of course, and Gideon's participation in it, serving in the cavalry under J.E.B. Stuart, is full of tumult, confusion, blood, and carnage. No less threatening and violent is the plot to kill Gideon's father, Jephtha. Since leaving the church because of his abolitionist activities, he is now a Washington-based reporter for the family newspaper, the New York *Union*. The murder plot was instigated by Edward Lamont, actor acquaintance of Wilkes Booth, husband of Fan Kent Lamont, Jephtha's ex-wife, but, most important, a southern zealot who is willing to do anything, however scurrilous, for the cause. The goal is to kill Jephtha and thus gain control—for the Confederacy—of the money from the Ophir mines, which Amanda, in *The Furies*, had earmarked for Jephtha and his sons. (One wonders whether Lamont's marriage to Fan is at all based on love rather than political machinations. One also sees a method Jakes uses to unify the book: both its chief villains—Louis and Lamont—are dominated by material concerns, specifically acquisition of the California gold; of the two, perhaps Lamont's murderous schemes are more virtuous, for they are subordinated to a political cause rather than being the manifestations of totally amoral greed.)

Emotional relationships also provide substance to the plot. Jephtha, divorced from Fan and, through much of the book, feeling little but hatred toward her for the schism she has created between him and his sons, has found refuge in Molly Emerson, proprietor of a Washington boarding house. Her unconditional love helps to heal him, not only from his loss of family but also his loss of faith in God. His proposal of marriage near the conclusion is not the sappy happy ending of a romance novel but an affirmation of the power of good in a world gone mad, of order in a world controlled by chaos. Gideon too finds—and loses—and regains—love. Margaret Marble, however, provides more than a love interest. Because her father was horribly maimed in the war with Mexico, returning literally "half a man" to live in an alcoholic haze where the horrors of war can be hidden by its glories, Margaret has no illusions about war. While Gideon is idealistic, she is realistic, and that difference, as well as her adamant refusal to grow attached to a man she fears she'll lose, very nearly destroys their relationship. Only when she becomes as brave in love as Gideon is in war—both now totally aware of the potential for disaster—do they marry.

In the midst of gathering war clouds, where division and disintegration seem the dominant motifs, some reconciliation occurs: Jephtha with Fan, Gideon with his father, whom he saves from Lamont's murderous assault.

In addition to reconciliation between characters previously in conflict, Jakes uses a number of other unifying techniques. For one, he is very careful to work within the points of view of his two protagonists. Jephtha's job as a reporter, of course, gives Jakes the opportunity to include any historical figures—Lincoln, Lee, Davis—Jephtha can interview and any battles he can observe. Similarly, by utilizing Gideon's point of view, that of the soldier trying to find his unit, Jakes can select from among the materials he has researched and thus provide focus to a book, which otherwise could be unmanageable and out of control.

In *The Titans* Jakes seems more conscious of crafting the novel's structure than in previous works. The two books, "Black April" and "Red July," use color symbolism to provide an incisive indication of substance. "Black" suggests the desperation and despair of Americans on both sides and the seemingly inevitable dissolution of the Union, achieved at such cost almost 100 years earlier. "Red" quite obviously elicits an awareness of battlefield carnage. Moreover, the colors may be an allusion to Stendhal's novel *The Red and the Black*, whose central character, though less admirable than either Gideon or Jephtha, seeks advancement first in the military and then in the church. In this novel, of course, Gideon chooses the military; Jephtha, although disillusioned with God, regains his faith and, at the end of the novel, is again a minister.

Although most of the action occurs in Books 1 and 2, Jakes also experiments with structure by adding a prologue, interlude, and epilogue. These establish central conflicts within the novel and prepare for future ones in the Kent Family Chronicles. The prologue, by capturing Michael Boyle's mixed responses to Lincoln's election victory—elation at the victory of American principles but awareness of the inevitable consequences—establishes a mood for the novel through his "sense of failure and foreboding" (15). It establishes a rift within the Kent family which parallels the emerging national schism. Jakes makes these points very explicit in the concluding sentences of the prologue: "In all [Michael's] life he'd never been more pessimistic. God alone knew what would be left of the Kents—or the country—a year from this night" (53).

The epilogue, "Captain Kent, C.S.A.," continues this mood. At first it seems almost tacked on. The book seemed to reach a satisfying and structurally viable conclusion with Jephtha's last comment, "I must buy another Testament." But that is far too upbeat for historical reality and the Kent family futures. For the war has barely begun; it will, people now know, continue for far longer than earlier optimistic projections. And Gideon, despite having saved his father's life and married Margaret, despite collecting his own talismans (a lock of hair from his baby daughter, his horse, and the new Stars and Bars flag), which remind us of the Kent family propensity for symbols, despite his change from a naive young soldier dominated by idealism to a battle-weary man committed to duty—Gideon must ride once again into harm's way. This book cannot end happily; historical honesty will not allow it.

Most fully developed of these segments outside the major plot lines is "Interlude: The Girl I Left Behind Me." It demonstrates some of Jakes' narrative techniques, techniques often influenced by his love of theater. Indeed, in a master class on fiction writing, he railed against excessive modifiers: "She replied *tearfully*." "He asserted, *strongly defending his argument*." Instead, Jakes suggested, try to eliminate modifiers. Let the dialogue itself carry the meaning, for all else is merely stage directions. In others words, show, don't tell.

It is instructive to examine "Interlude: The Girl I Left Behind Me" in light of these principles. Set primarily at Kentland, Louis Kent's Westchester County Gothic Revival attempt to demonstrate his position among people of power and money, neither of whom quite accept him, the interlude portrays a microcosm of motivations for events played out in Books 1 and 2 of the novel; it prepares for *The Warriors* by introducing Louis' shocking plans for the family, and maintains suspense—"What will happen?"—about the future. It is one further demonstration of a house divided against itself.

We are introduced to Michael Boyle's personal dilemma: he feels guilt because he has not gone off to war with the Seventh New York Militia; however, as a loyal defender of Amanda's legacy, he believes he must *not* go to war, for Louis Kent needs to be watched (318-19). Even before Louis' announcement of his plans, Michael has been aware of his surreptitious communication with Confederate businessmen.

Some of the complexities and contradictions the nation faced are evident in the dinner table conversation. There is racial prejudice, even in the North, evident in Julia's "Clotilde is a lovely woman—for a nigra" (321). Israel Hope, the escaped mulatto who had helped Amanda build her boarding house in San Francisco and who now manages the family's gold mine, is clearly aware of this. Responding to Miriam Rothman's (wife of the Kent family banker, Joshua) idealistic liberal criticism of the President for not having freed the slaves, Israel realistically replies that an emancipation proclamation might make the blacks' lot even more difficult. Though he favors emancipation, he's aware of latent prejudice even in the North and believes that such a proclamation "would only end one struggle and begin another" (327). Like Lee and Lincoln, these adversaries, Miriam and Israel, may differ, but they respect each other, for they are people of principle.

Louis, however, interrupts the discussion with his astounding manifesto. The family need not rue the war. Indeed, "the war will help us do even better" (328). Like so many civilian vultures who profit from war while others lose everything, Louis sees the Civil War as an opportunity, not a tragedy. He announces, quite pragmatically, that the Kent businesses will trade with the slave states and profit from their lack of industry. He's willing to practice duplicity, maintaining a public stance of support for the Lincoln administration while trading with the enemy; even the name of the company, Federal Suppliers, is carefully chosen to mask its practices. He's willing to violate his mother's deathbed wishes, planning to tap the resources of the Ophir gold mine to support his venture, despite her desire that those funds remain segregated for Jephtha and his sons. This parody of personal freedom and independence is, instead, a manifestation of greed and disrespect, a clear demonstration of hubris, excessive pride. In the face of such callous disregard of Kent family principles, those unrelated by blood but bound by integrity to Amanda and everything her ancestors stood for, can only disavow Louis. When Louis can no longer be watched, controlled, and corrected, his aberrations modified, Israel Hope, the Rothmans, the Benbows, and Michael have no option but to separate from him, despite his threats of severe financial loss. Their secession is at once revolutionary and conservative, schismatic and loyal.

While one of the functions of the Interlude is to allow for exposition of material that cannot readily fit into the rest of the book's narration, it follows dramatic principles and demonstrates dramatic techniques. Jakes applies the conventional dramatic plot structure: rising action, climax, and falling action. The interlude follows this pattern: sections i, ii, and iii, a mix of narration, exposition, and dialogue, are the rising action; sections iv and v, almost totally dialogue, present the inevitable schism within the Kent family (family by blood—Louis—vs. family by loyalty— Michael, the Rothmans, and Israel). These sections, in which the dialogue could easily be transferred to the stage, increase the reader's tension till it is almost unbearable; they are clearly the climax. The rest of the interlude, sections vi, vii, and viii, comprises the falling action, including Michael's near rape of Julia and his search for absolution, first from a priest and then by enlisting in the army. This clearly is the denouement of the interlude; however, because the novel will continue into Book 2 and the Kent Family Chronicles into subsequent novels, one cannot use the near-synonymous term for denouement, resolution. Much remains to be resolved.

CHARACTER DEVELOPMENT

As usual, Jakes' characters are people we care about—love or hate, but find it impossible to treat with indifference. As Jakes interweaves the lives of his characters with those of historical figures, he presents an entire spectrum of important events: the election of Abraham Lincoln as President after a divisive campaign; a young businessman (Louis) rejecting family principles in an attempt to amass even greater wealth, no matter the means; young people falling into a seemingly hopeless love affair; a minister abandoning God because he feels God has abandoned him; riots, attempted murder, and, ultimately, the Civil War itself. Many of these events include at least an element of disaster for participants. There may, however, be some question as to who is the protagonist, the central character. Because in this book, as in so many others, Jakes uses the technique of multiple points of view, a number of characters are thrust to the fore, their disastrous destinies often intertwined. Is the protagonist Jephtha Kent? his son Gideon? the Kent family in general? or, ultimately, the United States, that miraculous and fragile political union? The fabric of this novel is woven of many threads. Ultimately it is America's story, revealed through the Kents. Since *The Bastard* Jakes has linked the Kent family to the nation. Now both are divided against themselves.

In developing characters in *The Titans*, Jakes again utilizes a motif introduced in *The Bastard*, the strong woman. Each has a powerful impact on the men whose actions dominate the plot lines.

Julia, Louis' wife, shares his love for material things. She is also a sexual tease, a trait used by Michael to strike back at Louis for all his arrogant threats.

In contrast to Julia, Fan Kent Lamont is sexually repressed; she merely endures the conjugal bed, though she loves her three sons and fears for their safety as the nation rushes on to war. In this, she quietly underscores Margaret's more strident antiwar sentiments. Fan, though she was introduced as a zealot like her current husband, Lamont, a supporter of slavery like her father Virgil Tunworthy, and a bitter ex-wife of Jephtha, is strong enough to change and to admit prior errors. Though she doesn't abandon the South, her philosophical motivation becomes states' rights rather than slavery. She recognizes her previous personal vitriol toward Jephtha; they effect a kind of reconciliation because of their sons, the link that makes them family. When Jephtha hesitates a bit, almost asking permission to look in on their youngest, Jeremiah, Fan quietly notes that the boy is Jephtha's son too. Fan is strong enough to give him this—and to recognize the truth about Lamont, that his warped zeal might very well hasten Jephtha's death.

Molly Emerson provides a haven for Jephtha at his most despairing. She heals his wounds, physical and psychological. A strong woman who since her husband's death has made her own way running a boarding house, she reminds one of Amanda before she became almost monomaniacal in her goals. Molly risks violating social convention: she sleeps with Jephtha, never pressing him toward marriage; the physical connection is neither teasing nor repressed; it is a healthy, comforting fusion of one human being to another, body and mind and spirit. She is Jephtha's equal—or stronger. Their relationship, especially when Jephtha is finally strong enough to suggest marriage, provides hope that the forces of dissolution and division, so prevalent in the novel, will not triumph.

Margaret Marble, Gideon's love, also fulfills a number of functions. For one, she links the book to the past and to a time (during the war with Mexico) when a younger nation seemed destined for expansion, victory, and ebullience. However, this is tempered, for because her father came home grotesquely mutilated from that war, she provides an opposition to Gideon's early naive enthusiasm for combat. Finally, she demonstrates that love demands courage; that, especially in time of war, love may result in the pain of loss; but that true commitment transcends such fear. Thus, in addition to providing a love interest, Margaret echoes old Kent family values, especially the willingness to sacrifice self for something larger.

It is also necessary to look at two minor characters, the villains Josiah

Cheever and Samuel Dorn. It is, perhaps, indicative of the power of historical forces as antagonists in this novel that villains here can be described as minor characters. Neither has the horrifying omnipresence of a Hamilton Stovall from *The Furies*: morally unclean, physically repulsive, driven by the combined goals of revenge and destruction. But each is, in his own way, insidiously worse. Cheever, that ferret-faced, conniving turncoat with a name worthy of a Dickensian villain, pops up repeatedly as an actor playing his bit part in the plot to kill Jephtha. He thus functions against one protagonist, although he is hardly significant enough to be called the novel's antagonist. His reappearance, however, once we are aware of him, is yet another way Jakes unifies plot; whatever else is going on simultaneously, Cheever does not let us forget the danger to Jephtha.

Dorn, not only because he is more powerful physically, is far more dangerous, for he represents not simple treason, as does Cheever, but excess—ostensibly in defense of the state. One of Pinkerton's operatives, Dorn first appears observing travelers crossing the bridge to Virginia. A "disreputable bully" (85), he is constitutionally unable to speak the truth; he cannot accept Jephtha's term for what he is doing—"spying"—but prefers the ethically effete euphemism "watching." That such unofficial spying was going on demonstrated how deep the mood of distrust and fear had become in the nation.

Dorn, a man with "no humor in his eyes," is one of those few human beings who are "wholly and inexplicably cruel" (174). He is capable of shooting an innocent man so that he can get his hands on Edward Lamont and beat him to a pulp because of his performance of "Dixie's Land." Freedom of speech has no meaning to him. Nor does any other constitutional right. He is one of those men drawn to a profession, which allows him to bully and brutalize anyone who challenges his authority (90).

Dorn, like all criminal investigators who will suborn truth for victory, like all prosecutors who, in order to "protect society," will compromise the very rights granted by that society, is an evil more insidious to the nation than was the firing on Fort Sumter. Such men's perversions are greater than Stovall's because they are less honest. The danger they pose to the state is all the greater because of their lying profession of its defense. Thus, while Dorn is a minor character, he represents one of the major threats to American democracy.

THEMATIC ISSUES

One of the reasons Dorn appears so evil is his absolute inability to comprehend fundamental principles of American democracy. Central among them are the principles of liberty crucial to the Kent family heritage, principles for which Philip Kent fought during the Revolution, principles Amanda Kent wanted to be extended to all Americans, black or white. Established in earlier novels, especially *The Bastard* and *The Rebels*, these principles of liberty permeate this book; they are, however, multiple and complicated.

Early in the novel we learn that the principles of political liberty are not easily come by. Michael Boyle, the young Irishman who had worked for Amanda Kent as a confidential clerk, had initially felt a strong prejudice against free blacks. As one of thousands of Irish immigrant laborers in New York and New England city slums, Michael recognized the economic threat and increased competition for jobs that would result from freeing the slaves. Even as *The Titans* opens, he asks himself why God had allowed the black man to be brought to America. He believes that the conflict generated by slavery—and its end—was about to "cause a disruption greater than anything seen since the Revolution" (21). Yet Michael had eventually concluded that Amanda was right: the principles of liberty had to apply to all Americans. Now he "thought as she had. He thought as a Kent" (18), even to having voted for Abraham Lincoln.

For Louis, Amanda's son, freedom means economic freedom, free enterprise. Discreetly ostentatious, Louis single-mindedly seeks out greater and greater capital, willing to plunge into moral debt. One recalls the fears Amanda had for his character. One wonders at what point his plans for perpetuating family wealth and power became a perversion of family values. Louis certainly seems to lack any hint of his mother's principles: He doesn't "give a damn about a lot of unwashed niggers." He doesn't care whether they're "free men or property so long as they keep supplying the Blackstone mill with cotton" (48). He sees the incipient war as economic opportunity: "Alert men should be able to find ways to profit from the wants and misfortunes of both sides." Michael's moral explosion—"It's a somewhat broader question than supply and demand! It's a question of whether this country can be torn apart at will" (49)— is, to Louis, incomprehensible. Liberty, to Louis, is the freedom to profit; for him, freedom brings no corollary responsibility.

Abolition of slavery, freedom for black Americans, is yet another manifestation of this motif. As a rallying cry for both sides, the issue is a prime example of inflamed passions ignoring the facts in the name of a cause. Ironies abound: Jephtha, a good man, suffers for acting on his beliefs; for his belief that all men should be free, he loses his ministry, his family, and almost his life. Yet John Brown, viewed by men like Jephtha as little more than a murderous fanatic, is extolled as a martyr by abolitionists like Ralph Waldo Emerson and Louisa May Alcott. In the name of an idea and in response to that idea, people on both sides became irrational, lapsing into dangerous emotionalism. And, though by 1861 relatively few Southerners held slaves, the right to maintain that peculiar institution became a rallying cry for others. Even the potential effect of freedom for the blacks contained ironies and contradictions. As Isom, the body-servant who had come with his master Rodney Arbuckle to the Confederate Army preparing for battle at Manassas, said: "Folks up north—old Linkum—they gonna set us all free if they win. Then it's gonna be worse. . . . Deep down, I don't b'lieve most of the Yanks really want us free. They just want to punish the South. . . . It's a bad war, sir, a bad war. It's goin' places nobody ever dreamed" (465-66). Besides fulfilling the role of prophet in Greek tragedy, Isom here introduces another momentous issue, regionalism versus states' rights.

Many characters make the analogy between the incipient schism between North and South in 1860 and that between England and the colonies in 1776. How can the principles of freedom espoused by Jefferson then be denied now? Aunt Eliza comments to Margaret that John Quincy Adams had once said that if the sections of the country no longer felt "a magnetism of common interests" then it was better for the sections to separate: "Let the disunited states part in friendship" (375).

Despite such direct statements of certainty by some, for others, leaders on both sides, personal dilemmas dominate. Jakes has Lincoln explain to Jephtha the newspaperman: "The very idea of Americans quarreling is grievous to me. . . . I bear no ill will toward the Southern states. . . . [But] I have [taken] a solemn oath . . . to prevent . . . the destruction of the Union. . . . We must settle the question *now*. In a free country, does the minority have the right to sunder the whole whenever they choose? I say no" (70-73). Ironically, Jefferson Davis also answers this question. "Any people, anywhere, so inclined and having the power, have the right to rise up and shake off the existing government and form a new one that suits them better. That's a . . . sacred right—a right I hope and believe can liberate the world." The major irony came when Davis identified the original speaker: a "certain gentleman" who, during his first term in Congress, spoke on behalf of the Texas rebellion against Mexico. "His name was Lincoln" (604).

The tautness of historical irony is further evident in Lee's interview with Jephtha. Lee, whom Lincoln had called "the best soldier in the United States army," commented, "I see no greater calamity than a dissolution of the Union." Though he would free all his slaves if it would save the Union, and though he believes secession is anarchy, he is adamant: "I could never draw my sword against my native state" (107). Good men of conscience struggle once again with the principles of political freedom and political stability. Thoughtful individuals on both sides, as opposed to the rabid and incendiary propagandists, are torn within themselves, thus becoming small metaphors of the impending cataclysm.

Such adherence to principle is evident also in Jephtha Kent, an advocate, even in time of war, of the rights of free speech and the freedom of the press. He recognizes in the Pinkertons, especially the loose cannon Dorn, the threat of covert police surveillance of citizens to freedom of speech. "The national interest" does not justify the suppression of fundamental rights granted by that nation. "Nobody's yet revoked the right of free speech," he reminds Pinkerton. And, to his ex-wife, Fan Lamont, astonished that her husband had sung "Dixie's Land" at the Canterbury Hall demonstration: "Singing has yet to be declared an act of treason" (210). When examining the behavior of the Pinkertons, one is reminded of tyrants'—from Sophocles' Creon to the China of Tiananmen Square—fear of public opposition. The novel reaffirms that freedom of speech and, by extension, freedom of the press are essential to a free society. Yet Jephtha twice imposes, in effect, self-censorship. He keeps his word, values his promises to Lee and to Pinkerton, and refuses to write the stories that could make his career. He withstands the pressures of his editor because he recognizes the responsibilities, as well as the freedoms, of the press. Jephtha, who has already suffered for his beliefs, maintains personal integrity. He differentiates between personal probity and state suppression of the news. His behavior here is perhaps a model of ethical professionalism which could provide lessons to all the dubious denizens of the editorial offices of the *National Inquirer* and *Hard Copy*.

While reiterating the primacy of liberty in the American system, John Jakes raises the puzzling and often contradictory considerations of personal responsibility and public order. It is an equation that must be solved in every generation if the values fought for when establishing the nation are to be maintained.

ALTERNATIVE READING: AN ARISTOTELIAN PERSPECTIVE

In many ways, *The Titans* resembles Greek tragedy. Like *The Furies*, this title suggests Jakes' familiarity with the Greek classics. Indeed, examining *The Titans*, one may see astonishing thematic links to Sophocles' *Antigone*. How does one reconcile life's dilemmas requiring choice between conflicting virtues—civic duty and divine law? Must virtuous men be destroyed by unintentional sin? How does one choose between loyalty to the State and loyalty to family when these are in conflict? When does adherence to principle become fanaticism and subject one to the sin of hubris or excessive pride? Is division of family, of nation, of self an inevitable component of the human condition? Is death with honor or pusillanimous life preferable? What constitutes honor?

These questions, and others like them, led Aristotle to examine the plays of Aeschylus, Sophocles, and Euripedes and to formulate a critical theory of drama, especially of tragedy. Thus it may be instructive to apply Aristotelian criticism to this novel. The discussion that follows incorporates only some relevant Aristotelian principles. The reader might find it fruitful to explore the critical approach further.

In *The Poetics* Aristotle defined tragedy as "the imitation of an action which is serious and also, as having magnitude, complete in itself." One can readily grant that *The Titans*, like most of Jakes' novels, has magnitude. There is a sweep that is almost epic: dozens of characters, from presidents and generals to porters and seamstresses, populate its pages, creating a cross-section of mid-nineteenth century American society. Though freedom is only one of the motifs that gives *The Titans* "magnitude" and "seriousness," it is a central one, in part because of the Kent (and the American) heritage. Jakes in this novel also provides other parallels to and illustrations of Aristotelian theory.

Tragic action, according to Aristotle, will incorporate "incidents arousing pity and fear, wherewith to accomplish the catharsis of such emotions." Because of Jakes' multiple point of view, a discussion of these concepts must be multifaceted; they may apply to more than a single character. Margaret Marble's father, the Sergeant, veteran of the Mexican War, elicits these responses. Overcoming our shock, we can't help pitying this physical and psychological wreck of a man. Nor can we ignore his fanatical faith in military glory, in the meaning of his sacrifice.

Though we may pity him for his mutilations and the overcompensation that results, we cannot totally deny his belief that serving his country is the most honorable vocation a man can have. It is, moreover, a test of whether he can endure the unendurable. "That's why war can be a glorious thing" (438). We can understand the Sergeant, and perhaps pity him, for, in truth, he *needs* to believe that his sacrifice, his unimaginable mutilation, has meaning; it must not be for nothing that he is now half a man. He can't, given his own destruction, minimize the importance of The Cause. There is pity, too, for Margaret, whose childhood was amputated as surely as were her father's legs, who has known hardship and suffering and anger—and, yes, probably guilt for those other feelings. And through Margaret we feel fear—that such a thing could happen to Gideon. War has already destroyed the first man she loved. An even more cataclysmic event could destroy the second. In a much less graphic way, we may pity Michael, Israel, and the Rothmans in their conflict with the unbending and powerful Louis; certainly we can fear for their financial survival.

Pity and fear, however, are not gratuitous emotions; they must lead to catharsis. Thus Aristotle explained the fact that many tragedies, portraying suffering and defeat, left the audience feeling relieved, even exalted, rather than depressed. In Greek, *catharsis* literally means "purgation" or "purification." This product of pity and fear is evident in Jephtha's story. We may well pity him. He has suffered separation from the family he loves, become an outcast for his advocacy of abolition and his demonstration of that faith in his work with the underground railroad; he is befriended only by the seemingly eccentric professor of military science Tom (later Stonewall) Jackson; he is reduced from minister to a menial laborer; he so doubts God that he burns his Testament. We can feel fear for him. As he crafts a new life through excellence as a writer and his reciprocated love for Molly, his integrity (plus the power of the press: the word vs. the Word) puts him in mortal danger from Lamont and Cheever and all those others who would silence the truth. Yet Jakes provides us with the basis for catharsis too. Jephtha's salvation by his son Gideon in the Almshouse when Lamont attempts murder leads to reunion with Gideon and Fan, reaffirmation of his faith in God, and a proposal of marriage to Molly.

But Jakes doesn't end the book there. The epilogue thrusts *Gideon* onto center stage as object of pity and fear; the audience is plunged once again from happiness to uncertainty and foreboding. Though some *family* reunification has been achieved, the war goes on—in the Kent family as well. One is reminded of Sophocles' continuing the tragedy of Oedipus through several plays, creating perhaps the first ongoing family saga.

Aristotle further argues that the audience will most effectively be moved to pity and fear if the tragic hero is neither totally good nor totally evil, neither a saint nor a villain. Jephtha, if he is considered the protagonist, demonstrates just such an integration of contradictory traits. He is a man of principle, willing to suffer the negative consequences of his beliefs; he has the fortitude to endure, re-creating himself as a competent, honorable journalist rather than wallowing in self-pity. Nonetheless, he may also be seen as too unbending, too stiff-necked, even arrogant when it comes to his stand against slavery; and when we meet up with him in this book, he has renounced God, by whom he feels abandoned, and he is living with Molly without benefit of marriage. Gideon, too, is neither all good nor all bad. While he is brave, patriotic, loyal to his mother, and capable of great love, he is also bombastic, resentful of his father, and brutal toward him, beating him with his cane in an uneven display of youthful strength against middle-aged exhaustion; he seems almost arrogant as he prefers losing Margaret's love to accepting her opinion; he is blind to his personal vulnerability. Finally, if the North and the South are seen as twin protagonists of the novel, the pattern is once again evident. Neither has the monopoly on political virtue; on both sides good men are plunged toward catastrophe with the best of intentions; on both sides scoundrels rapaciously plunder or overtly demean the causes they ostensibly support.

The tragic impact, according to Aristotle, is intensified when the hero is greater—of higher moral values—than the audience. Using Jephtha's point of view, Jakes writes: "Neither Lincoln nor Lee was a hothead. Both were men of principle; conviction—titanic figures who seemed to loom larger than life because of their prominence on the national scene. . . . It seemed a wicked irony that men of such character had been helpless to prevent the storm—and an unspeakable cruelty that they now had to suffer its fury" (110).

Such observations might suggest yet another element often present in Greek drama: the intervention of the Fates or other superhuman forces, often foreshadowed long before they act. Lincoln was fatalistic about his own death, and his wife interpreted one of his dreams as meaning that he would be elected for a second term but not survive it (76). From the very first page, Michael is troubled by a "sense of failure and foreboding" (15). "In all his life he'd never been more pessimistic. *God alone* knew what would be left of the Kents—or the country—a year from this night" (53; emphasis added).

Change in the novel, however, is not exclusively catastrophic. Much that occurs, of course, demonstrates the end of the world as America knew it: political and moral disintegration, a rushing forward from an agrarian society to a technological one, impelled by a fascination with advances as varied as the transcontinental railroad, Mathew Brady's photography, Bessemer's steel-making process, and Minie's new rifle ball; previously unthinkable personal freedoms and unimaginable battlefield horrors. And although the Aristotelian formula requires change in fortune from happiness to misery, of which there is plenty, not least the carnage of war, the suspicion where previously there had been trust, the fracturing of one into several, there is also change which is positive. Jephtha learns that he must change—or suffer as a "prisoner of the past" (99). Gideon recognizes that love and duty need not be mutually exclusive. And, as Jephtha tells Molly, in the midst of catastrophe, there are forces—the better angels of our nature—which can bring America through this war and heal the wounds afterward—if we only let them (627).

Often, however, man's very nature makes this difficult. We see example after example of hubris, "that 'pride' or overweening self-confidence which leads a protagonist to disregard a divine warning or to violate an important moral law" (Abrams, 212). There's Gideon's sense of invincibility, his failure to pay attention to Margaret's warning, his belief that what happened to the Sergeant was a fate only for "old" men over thirty. There's Louis' failure to listen to advisors advocating ethical business practices. There's the belief, on both sides of the Mason-Dixon Line, that the war would be over in ninety days; the faith, despite—or perhaps because of—contrary evidence, in the glory of war demonstrated by the Sergeant; and the zealotry, the passion for The Cause demonstrated by patriots both North and South. The new Jephtha might observe that "pride goeth before a fall." There is a universality in this principle that links the Bible to Aristotelian criticism.

The pity that tragedy evokes is all the stronger because, as the protagonist is not an evil person, his suffering is more than he deserves. One may extrapolate from Jephtha, who suffers too much, to all those good men slaughtered and mutilated in the carnage of this war. Moreover, all of us, wherever in the United States we live, live the heritage of the Civil War. We *have* been affected by those events over a century ago.

This introduces a final element to this discussion: dramatic irony. We, the audience, know what the characters do not. We are aware of what fate has in store for the Americans of 1860. Unlike the picnickers who went out to watch the Battle of Manassas, we know how brutal the war will be. We flinch at the small-minded voices of hate calling the President Abe the Ape. We cringe at references to the young tragedian, John Wilkes Booth. We know what is yet to come. We, like the ancient Greeks, who also were familiar with the plot lines of their tragedies, know how the story ends. Consequently, part of the catharsis, the relief, the exaltation that we experience from this novel, which in so many ways resembles a Greek tragedy, is the recognition of the rightness of Lincoln's words, used by Jakes as an epigraph to *The Titans*: "We are not enemies, but friends. We must not be enemies. . . . The mystic chords of memory, stretching from every battle-field and patriot grave, to every living heart . . . will yet swell the chorus of the Union, when again touched, as surely as they will be, by the better angels of our nature."

7

The Warriors
(1977)

The Warriors, Volume 6 of the Kent Family Chronicles, carries members of the Kent family from 2 May 1863 and the Battle of Chancellorsville to the spring of 1868, a period encompassing half of the Civil War, the beginning of Reconstruction, and the postwar movement west, including the construction of the transcontinental railroad. To give the historical events faces, John Jakes here focuses primarily on Jeremiah and Gideon Kent and Michael Boyle; Louis and Jephtha Kent are treated more briefly.

PLOT DEVELOPMENT

Jeremiah, the youngest son of Jephtha and Fan, enlisted in the Confederate army to his mother's concern and with her advice to "fight well and . . . *honorably*"(53). Carrying news of his commanding officer's death to his family, Jeremiah witnessed the worst excesses of Sherman's march through Georgia. Completely disillusioned with war, he declared the old Jeremiah dead and headed west. Rootless, wandering with his Sioux friend Kola between Texas and the towns growing up along the railroad, Jeremiah remains a killer—of buffalo for railroad construction crews, and of men who cheat at cards, mistreat whores, or attempt to steal from him. To his father, Jephtha, who has searched army records, he is dead; and, in a very real sense, he is, living under one of a series of aliases.

But he has a remnant of honor left, a belief in fair play; acting from these fundamental though vestigial beliefs, he saves Michael Boyle's life.

Along with the Rothmans and the Benbows, Michael, once Amanda Kent's private secretary, had broken with Louis over his unsavory business practices. Having served with the Union army in an Irish brigade, having grown disillusioned with death and destruction, he wanted instead to *build* something; consequently, he headed west to work constructing the Union Pacific. But violence followed him in the guise of a crew chief who couldn't forget the Civil War, Indians agitated at the coming of the railroad shortly after the Sand Creek Massacre, and small-minded men fighting others for racial or ethnic slights. Becoming increasingly interested in the forthright, outspoken, honestly religious Hannah Dorn, Michael vows never again to engage in violence. When the Union Pacific reaches the 100th Meridian, Michael chooses a new future—with Hannah, establishing stores along the railroad right of way.

Gideon, too, served in the war, witnessed Stonewall Jackson's death, and was captured, to spend the rest of the war in a prison camp. There he is blinded by a sadistic sergeant who burns one eye with a stick heated to glowing. After the war ends, Gideon works first in the press room of the *New York Herald* and then in the switchyards of the Erie Railroad. He becomes increasingly conscious of the exploitation of workers and the owners' disregard for those injured, maimed, or killed struggling to earn little more than subsistence wages. As the novel ends, Gideon, though he had promised not to get involved in any more lost causes, takes up the cause of labor unionism.

Unlike Jeremiah, Gideon, and Michael, who all did their military duty, though on opposite sides, Louis paid a trifling $300 for exemption from the draft and spent the rest of the war multiplying his millions. Under his ownership, Kent and Son has declined even further, now publishing almost nothing but half-dime novels. Louis, willing to do almost anything to gain money, power, and personal recognition, has gotten involved with the robber barons Jim Fisk and Jay Gould. He fails to fully recognize their ruthlessness, however, and, when he inadvertently causes Gould embarrassment, the monopolist sends thugs to attack him, leaving him partially paralyzed.

Jephtha and Molly now live in New York, where he is minister of a small Methodist church. Almost fifty, aware he can't live forever, Jephtha commits two highly symbolic acts: he rewrites his will, giving Michael Jeremiah's portion of the inheritance from the California gold mine, and, after Louis is paralyzed, he purchases Kentland, recovers the Kent family heirlooms, and orders the mansion torn down.

With so broad a canvas, covering the eastern two-thirds of the continent over five years of major historical events, John Jakes has to impose control on his materials to keep the novel manageable. He does this, first of all, by his choice and treatment of historical events. Clearly he cannot be encyclopedic in his narrative; therefore, *what* he includes is as important as *how* he deals with it.

In "Prologue at Chancellorsville: The Fallen Sword," Jakes chooses Saturday, 2 May 1863, on which to focus. Gideon, carrying a message for Stonewall Jackson, isn't able at first to find him. This allows Jakes time to show—through Gideon's eyes—the condition of the Confederate army and—through his reflections—the army's morale. Though not quite twenty, Gideon is a major, worn out and edgy (15). The Confederates are outnumbered two to one. The previous winter had been brutal: he remembered fifteen-year-olds in tattered uniforms, grubbing in the forests for wild onions to cure their scurvy (19-20). Having already experienced many brushes with death since his first at Manassas in '61, he felt "his luck was playing out" (22).

Coupled to that personal premonition was an omen spreading among the soldiers: that Jackson had stood his scabbarded sword against a tree; then, with no one touching it—or even near it—the sword had suddenly fallen to the ground (18). The reader will, of course, remember the dream-premonition of Lincoln's death in *The Titans*. The omen here is clear. The consummate irony of Jackson being shot by North Carolinians amid chaos, rumor, and confusion increased the tragedy, for Jackson was more than a superb tactician. He personified the South's one advantage—"raw courage in the face of superior numbers and industrial strength" (31). The South couldn't afford to lose Stonewall Jackson. Eight days later, Jackson died. Though the Confederacy won a victory at Chancellorsville, it was a Pyrrhic victory, with morale irrevocably weakened, the South's hope no longer to win the war but mainly to achieve a truce. Jakes has carefully chosen a battle that defined the war's eventual outcome; he has filled his narration of that battle with foreshadowing of doom.

The prologue is told from Gideon's—thus the Southern—point of view. But Michael Boyle had also been at the Wilderness, fighting in Union blue under an emerald Irish flag. Three years later, at the railhead, Michael is still having the nightmare of "gray-faced men cleverly hiding"

among "gargoyle trees"; of walking bloodless corpses pleading for
mercy, of walls of burning underbrush replicating images of hell from
his Catholic boyhood, of being shot once, twice, six times, of a bell tolling
his death (283-84). He has survived, but in many ways he is suffering
from post traumatic stress syndrome, not even defined till a century
later. Jakes not only uses the Wilderness to unify the prologue and Book
3 but to universalize the impact combat had on soldiers on both sides.
Neither Gideon nor Michael is any longer fighting for abstract ideals;
both are changed. Gideon fights "unmanly thoughts," but fears what
will happen to his little family if the South loses. How will he make a
life for them? War is the only trade he knows (37). Michael fights back
a desire "to scream" and flee from this "impossible battle taking place
below the Rapidan" (282). Only by gripping his rifle tightly can he remember duty and avoid flight. And interwoven with the description of
the battle is the lure of Julia Kent, the woman with whom he is infatu-
ated.

One might object to this parallel between Michael and Gideon. Michael's experience of the battle, after all, is revealed by Jakes in nightmare, not reality. But is Gideon's experience any less nightmarish? By
letting Gideon and Michael share similar emotional responses to the
same battle, Jakes reemphasizes the oneness of the nation and the awful
tragedy which had torn it asunder.

Sherman's March to the Sea consumes most of Books 1 and 2. There
Jakes paints a frightening picture of total war—of pigs slaughtered, sil-
verware stolen, food requisitioned, wells polluted, houses and barns and
cotton gins torched; of women raped and ex-slaves incited to violence.
This is not the war anyone expected. It is not idealistic. Reason has been
replaced by rampage. This is the war called by some "the first great
modern war." Concepts of chivalry, sanctuary, and honor seem outmoded. Sherman's "War is hell" sums it up.

It is this attitude, as well as that of the carpetbaggers and scalawags
Jakes briefly discusses in the epilogue, which marks an end of an era
and creates new hatreds which endure long after the war. We see this
most vividly in the character of Leonidas Worthing. In the prison camp
with Gideon, he labeled General Lee's order disbanding the army "cowardice"; he would prefer that the Confederate army continue to fight
guerrilla actions. And, when he shows up as crew chief on the Union
Pacific construction project, his hatreds have not cooled. Any Union veterans, as well as the few blacks on the crew, become his targets. For
Worthing, the war is not over and probably never will be. Worthing and

men like him were created by defeat, their attitudes hardened by retribution, rampage, and Reconstruction. Thus, although Jakes stresses Lincoln's desire for humane and forgiving policies, he also suggests, through the historical events he chooses to include, that real reconciliation will be difficult if not impossible to achieve.

Once again, with so broad a canvas, Jakes must be especially careful to achieve unity. To accomplish this he experiments with a pattern of manipulating point of view. Each book is dominated by the point of view of a major character (Jeremiah in 1 and 2, Michael in 3 and 4, and Louis in 5). But, usually toward the end of each book, a chapter is presented from a different character's point of view. Not only does Jakes thus continue to juggle narrative balls, but he maintains suspense in the main plot line and, by suggesting simultaneous but different actions, he universalizes the trauma of the war. It becomes far more than the possibly atypical experience of one individual. Thus, at the end of Book 1, as smoke begins to rise from neighboring plantations, and Jeremiah, "just as terrified as . . . when he'd first climbed toward Union marksmen at Chickamauga" (148), is alone with the women and loyal slaves to protect the plantation from Sherman's forces—at that moment Jakes shifts to Gideon in prison camp. One additional effect achieved by thus uniting the two characters is to emphasize the actuality of terror, rarely discussed as an emotion of a combat veteran, but one which Jeremiah admits and the entire audience shares with Gideon as the red hot stick comes closer and closer to his eye. In both chapters, Jakes breaks off the narration. For the Jeremiah plot line, the effect is to create a cliffhanger (148); the audience wants to know what's going to happen as Union soldiers arrive. In the Gideon chapter, however, Jakes utilizes a technique from Greek tragedy—letting the most horrible things occur offstage, unseen. Thus Jakes avoids telling all the graphic details of Gideon's blinding (175). This, however, is not to save the readers' sensibilities, for he has told us enough to allow our imaginations to fill in the details, creating a horror perhaps more intense than if he had shown us everything.

Quite a different purpose is served at the end of Michael's Book 3 in the chapter titled "Kola." This chapter provides connections to Books 1 and 2—for here we find out what's become of Jeremiah, now Joseph Kingston, since he left the war. We see that he can be a cold-blooded killer but that he can also be a loyal and tender friend. In addition, through Kola, an Oglala Sioux, the audience gains insight into Plains Indian culture and religion (404). This cross-cultural perspective is more than intrinsically significant, for it also provides a link to the antagonism we see developing between Indians and whites in Book 4 as the railroad becomes a more and more obvious threat to the Indian way of life.

Jakes integrates his multistranded plot a number of other ways as well. A bit of exposition, such as that about the Sand Creek Massacre (335), will show up later as the basis for distrust when Guns Taken captures Tom Ruffin (428-29). Many times Jakes breaks into one conflict (Worthing's hatred toward Michael) with another, as when Michael interrupts Casement's discipline of Worthing with news of the Indians (435). Or, later, Gideon applies a principle learned from his cavalry days with J.E.B. Stuart to his strategy in union organizing: to stick together to ensure their safety and make success more likely (586-87). The Erie Railroad links the Gideon and Louis plots: Louis as a Vanderbilt/Gould/Fisk wannabe monopolist-exploiter; Gideon fighting for the rights of the workers. And twice Jakes uses juxtaposition of Biblical passages (475-77) or hymns (107-9) to link exterior action and interior reflection and thus to provide ironic commentary on events. To Michael, the passage from Ecclesiastes—"a time of peace"—is a lie. Earlier the arrival of the Yanks, come to "forage liberally," had cast doubts on the hymn's "Under the shadow of Thy throne / still may we dwell secure."

Several additional comments need to be made about Jakes' narrative techniques. First, he seamlessly integrates his research into the narrative, so that the reader picks up interesting pieces of trivia: transcontinental telegraph poles tilted at a 45 degree angle because buffalo had pushed against them, scratching off some of their shedding hump manes; or the passage Michael reads (397) from an eastern journalist describing the "anvil chorus" of railroad construction. Jakes shares the fruits of his research but does so inconspicuously, reinforcing rather than interrupting his plot lines.

Finally, Jakes has to solve a problem created by intermingling actual and created characters in the plot lines. Louis conspires with Jim Fisk and Jay Gould to combat Cornelius Vanderbilt for control of the Erie Railroad. How, then, to account for the fact that no "Louis Kent" appears in railroad histories? After Gould is threatened by Louis, the financiers vote to remove him from the board of directors (660). Jakes' attention to detail here reminds us of a similar ploy in *The Furies*: Amanda did not show up on a roster of Anglo survivors of the Alamo because she was using her husband's name, de la Gura.

That *The Warriors*, wide in its scope, multiple in its points of view, and sometimes convoluted in its plot, hangs together so well is, thus, a product of Jakes' attention to details and his conscious attempts to draw connections.

CHARACTER DEVELOPMENT

Just as John Jakes carefully controls elements of plot, so too he is conscious of how he develops character. When Jeremiah reflects on the tension and barely restrained violence between Catherine and Serena Rose, he doesn't particularly want to probe the cause of the antipathy, but he can't ignore it. "The women were revealing more and more of themselves as each day passed. Perhaps the stress of living with the threat of Sherman's army made such a situation inevitable" (124). The passage reveals a good deal about how Jakes works with character. Rather than giving long introductions, he reveals a few salient details when we meet the characters; then, bit by bit, in small increments, we learn more, by their speech and actions and by others' reactions to or comments on them. In addition, the importance to character development of psychological stress, whether or not it escalates into physical conflict, is explicit: "the threat of Sherman's army." Later, when Michael laughs that Hannah Dorn frequently takes him by surprise, her speech constantly demanding new assessments of her character, she replies, "That . . . is because people are not books containing just a single page to be understood in one quick reading" (493). Hannah's comment suggests Jakes' methods of developing characters in increments and his goal of creating multidimensional people.

Sometimes he begins—or intensifies—the process by using stage props, objects with which the characters surround themselves, thereby revealing something of themselves. The books at Rosewood are an illustration of this technique. They suggest culture, gentility, civilization. Once this is established, their destruction by the Union scavengers underscores the barbarity and excesses of the march to the sea. Throughout the Kent Family Chronicles the family talismans achieve a similar effect: they recall, as symbols, the values held by the Kents and thus go far to define their characters. In *The Warriors* Gideon carries a lock of Eleanor's baby hair; Worthing's hacking Jephtha's letter to Michael (the letter itself a talisman) into shreds demonstrates his insane hatred; and Michael scoops up a handful of mud and crushed rock from between the ties as a relic of participating in the construction of the transcontinental railroad, "the greatest marvel of the age" (549). In contrast is Louis' treatment of the Kent mementos: Jared's fob medallion has become "tarnished," and Louis views the motto, *Cape locum et fac vestigium*, "Take a stand and make a difference," as "pretentious" (557). Jim Fisk calls the icons "trinkets"; he asks who's the "mean-looking fellow" in the portrait on the mantel. His query whether these objects have some significance to the family received this response from Louis: "They did at one time. . . . I should have gotten rid of them long ago" (558). One may recall that it was to defend these "trinkets"—and the family they stand for—that his mother Amanda died. Jephtha, in the letter giving Michael full membership in the family, writes that Louis has "no regard for the tradition or the ideals they symbolize," and it is to restore them to "clean hands. Honorable hands" (350), that he ultimately buys Kentland (680-82). And on a national, rather than a family scope, the transcontinental railroad itself is such a symbol. Aside from all its practical economic and military purposes, its "binding together of the oceans with iron cords" (474) is a metaphor for the Union now again being forged after the war.

Jakes also makes use of foils to help define character. The technique is to juxtapose in the reader's mind—if not literally side by side on a page—two characters who serve mutually to define each other. Examples of this are numerous. Price and Maum Isabella on the Rose plantation demonstrate the diverse responses among slaves to emancipation and to their former owners. Oliver Tillotson's gratuitous brutality in blinding Gideon may be juxtaposed to Dr. Cincinnatus Lemon, the humanitarian who viewed war as "the filthy, immoral waste of God's gift" (166). Hannah and Gustav Dorn, daughter and father, illustrate the sharply differing influences of the East on the West; while Gustav brings the saloon and its accompanying violence, Hannah lives a pragmatic Christianity, helping whomever she can. Early in Michael's relationship with Hannah her image—and Julia's—swim in his mind as mutually exclusive love interests; this reminds the reader of Philip's having to choose between Alicia and Anne in *The Bastard*. Finally, when separated from the army, neither Gideon nor Jeremiah has any skill but killing. But while Gideon spends his time in prison camp reading, gaining necessary skills to support his wife and baby, Jeremiah, having discovered that he enjoys killing (257), sets out to practice skills learned through "excellent training, directed by Mr. Jefferson Davis. After you kill one or two, the others come easy" (420).

A final way Jakes differentiates and defines character is by calling the reader's attention to the personal vows each man takes. Each man's personal oath reveals his values and provides contrast to the other characters.

Michael, recognizing that the violence he had hoped to leave behind with the war has followed him west, realizes that it wasn't enough to condemn violence; he must act on his convictions. And so, invoking the spirit of Amanda, turning his face to the sky as if she were an intercessor angel, he vows: *"If you're there, listen to me. . . . Never again while I breathe will I lift my hand against another human being, no matter what the provocation. Never"* (503; emphasis in original). His new pacifism makes him vulnerable; Jeremiah must save his life. But it also prepares him for a new life with Hannah.

Although Jeremiah can admire Michael's determination and, like him, recall the war as anything but uplifting or pleasant, his conclusions are different. When he came out of the war, whole in body but wounded in mind, he decided never again to let anyone defeat him. Nor would he "suffer the behavior of dishonorable men" (540). Though he recognizes that Michael's decision calls for more courage, Jeremiah will abide by his vow and wander the Plains, a kind of twisted knight, loyal to his own standards of virtue.

Unlike any of the other major characters, Louis is not willing to sacrifice anything of himself. After Julia had become active in women's rights and, eventually, divorced him, Louis took a "silent pledge" never to get involved with another woman. Women were "bad investments" requiring too many "unpredictable and therefore unacceptable risks" (583). Louis is capable only of acquisition, unwilling to give. He is, thus, the mere husk of the man Jeremiah is, however much a renegade the latter may be from law and society's conventions.

Finally, Gideon has to rethink his vows. After the war he had sworn never again to fight for any "lofty principle." To survive was "struggle enough" (592). Like Jeremiah, he had experienced the plunge from high ideals to abject disillusionment. But unlike Jeremiah, Gideon defines himself within society. The antagonist is now monopoly capitalism; feeling guilt for failing to prevent the accident which killed the switchman Daphnis Miller, he vows to provide for his widow and children. By extension, this means that he must take on the railroad, fight for workers' compensation, enlist in a new, perhaps hopeless cause. Gideon knows his decision is quixotic. But the alternatives are to do nothing or to take a stand. Unless he acts on his beliefs, he will be unable to live with himself (625).

As Jakes differentiates among these men, using their vows as touchstones of character, he also places them on a continuum of Kent-ness. Of the four, only Louis is unwilling to live the family motto: "to take a stand."

THEMATIC ISSUES

Because a Jakes novel is neither a sermon nor a diatribe, it usually does not have a single, all-encompassing theme. However, in *The Warriors* the theme of honor is central.

We first become acutely aware of the theme of honor in the prologue. Stonewall Jackson is the personification of the trait. He is stoic, suffering great pain in silence. He is selfless, putting others' safety above his own needs: "Never mind about me," he says to his stretcher bearers (33). He is a courageous military leader, instilling hope where there should logically be none. Gideon reminds us of what we recall from *The Titans* and *The Furies*, that, when everyone turned against Jephtha for his abolitionist beliefs, Jackson gave him sanctuary. When this man of high moral purpose died, something very honorable, almost chivalric, faded from the war. This is yet another reason for Jakes to center on his death in the prologue, for it prepares for the dichotomy between honorable and dishonorable behavior which will dominate much of the book.

Jeremiah's dilemma about whether to obey Rose's order and thus appear to desert is, at heart, a conflict between two mutually exclusive demonstrations of honor. He cannot break his solemn word of honor to his commanding officer; yet no honorable soldier can desert his comrades in arms. He is torn between courage (an honorable quality) and cowardice; the difficulty is that the criteria defining them have blurred. Like Michael later, for whom it was more courageous to refuse to fight, it took courage for Jeremiah to keep his word and thus *seem* to abandon his post. Lee's order demanding the disbanding of the Confederate army was an honorable declaration, though some, like Worthing, called it cowardice. So was Lincoln's desire for an "easy peace." Both men recognized that after honorable battle between men who differed out of principle they were willing to defend, there must be a victor. But humanity—and honor—decreed respect between former antagonists. None of the villains of this novel—Worthing, Tillotson, Grace—is capable of comprehending this truth.

While Jeremiah struggles to act honorably, he comes face to face with mass behavior of the most dishonorable nature. The total war practiced against civilians was not an honorable way to prosecute war. Most believed that war should be waged against combatants, not civilians, and especially not against women. Jeremiah naively vowed to himself that, when Sherman's men came, he would stand up to them and "demand they deal honorably with the residents of Rosewood" (132). The height of his idealism was a major cause of his disillusionment. "He'd tried to be honorable, and this was how it had ended. There was no place for honor in war. Or in the world" (259). Yet, despite his bitterness here, he continues to behave according to a tightly defined personal code of honor. He shoots a crooked monte dealer (413), is disappointed in a former Confederate officer caught stealing his buffalo (416), and explains to Kola why he killed Cutright: "Dishonorable men deserve to be treated in kind. . . . A man should know better than to do a dishonorable thing" (419, 421). Verities, presumably, remain.

Villains, ipso facto, are men lacking honor. One can see this by contrasting Captains Poppel and Grace at Rosewood, Dr. Lemon and Tillotson at the Fort Delaware prison camp, and Casement and Worthing at the Union Pacific railhead. Additionally, Jephtha wants to get Kent and Son away from Louis and back into "honorable hands" (349-50). Men of honor do what's right, even when it would be more advantageous not to. Michael's telling Jeremiah about the California gold and offering to surrender the share Jephtha granted him is an honorable act, even though it could cost him millions. Jeremiah recognizes it as such: "You could have kept the information to yourself. You're a proper Kent, all right" (543).

Honorable behavior, then, rather than blood alone, defines a Kent. To be honorable is to stand for what's right, regardless of personal cost; to remain honest and maintain personal integrity; and to recognize humanity in all people and to treat them accordingly. Thus Michael, not related at all, can be a Kent, as can Jeremiah, outlaw though he is. Louis, however, though Amanda's son, casts himself out of the family. He stands for nothing save the acquisition of wealth; he will engage in corrupt business practices; he demonstrates no desire to treat others fairly. He will die as he lived, alone and dishonored, victim of his own moral vacuum.

ALTERNATIVE READING: DECONSTRUCTIONIST CRITICISM

Deconstruction is a method of literary criticism initiated by the French critic Jacques Derrida in the late 1960s. In some ways, it may be seen as an extension of New Criticism (see Chapter 8), for it requires a close reading of the text. However, the deconstructionist reading attempts to subvert or undermine the assumption that the system of language can establish coherence, unity, or meaning in a text. Rather, a deconstructionist reading starts with the intention of demonstrating that, within the text, there are conflicting forces which destroy the apparent clarity of structure and meaning and create instead multiple and incompatible possibilities of interpretation. Deconstructionist critics believe in the "arbitrariness of the verbal sign"; they undermine "logocentrism"—literally the focus on the word—as a basis upon which other concepts such as truth, identity, or certainty can be validated. They take apart the logic of language. They believe that every text undermines itself with unconscious "traces" of other positions exactly opposite to those it sets out to uphold. It is, thus, not surprising that deconstructionists believe that the meaning of a text bears only accidental relationship to the author's conscious intentions. Indeed, Derrida would argue that "there is nothing outside the text," *including* the author's intentions. He would assert that any close reading of the text requires a "double reading," resulting first in the "standard reading" based on the logic of language but then progressing to the second reading, which reveals incompatible or contradictory meanings. Barbara Johnson, another deconstructionist critic, describes this process as a "careful teasing out of warring forces of [meaning] within the text itself" (Abrams, 229).

Deconstructionist criticism is thus "subversive," questioning, among other things, many "hierarchical oppositions"—pairs of polarized terms in which one is usually considered superior. Examples include male-female, cause-effect, reason-emotion, and truth-error. Not only do the deconstructionists invert the hierarchy—suggesting, for example, that "female" may be superior to "male," but they often destabilize the hierarchies completely, leaving them in a "condition of indecidability." Which is superior? Even which is which? Deconstructionists may thus expose societal bias. One may apply this questioning of hierarchical opposites to *The Warriors*. An entire array of such polarities can be found by a careful reader: courage-cowardice, victory-defeat, chivalric war–modern war, civilization-savagery, success-failure, white-Indian, ethical behavior–corrupt behavior.

We all know—or think we do—the meaning of "civilization" and "savagery." And we might grant that "civilization" is the preferable, "superior" state of being. Yet, examined critically, these terms may become indecipherable, their edges blurred. Which, ultimately, is which?

Kola, Jeremiah's Sioux friend, ostensibly a "savage," believes in and practices his religion. He knows that Jeremiah's saving his life had been an intervention of the gods—"*Wakan.* Holy" (402). He does not hate white men. He is disturbed by Jeremiah's love of killing, preferring instead the Sioux practice of counting coup (403). He is a "savage"? To protect "civilization" and assure the safety of Denver, an ordained Methodist minister, Col. John M. Chivington of the Third Colorado Cavalry, led a raid in 1864 on Sand Creek and there massacred and mutilated Cheyenne women and children. Denver citizens enthusiastically celebrated the triumphant return to "civilization" of these troops, who proudly displayed their trophies—children's scalps and women's pubic hair (428-29). "Savagery." "Civilization." Inherent in each word is its diametrical opposite. Similarly, the construction of the transcontinental railroad is called, in a newspaper article, a second "grand march to the sea." This allusion to General Sherman's rape of Georgia, described by the correspondent as "glorious" (319), requires a contradictory interpretation of both events. Implicit in the reporter's praise of both events is their condemnation. A similar deconstructionist reading might be applied to all the hierarchical oppositions found in *The Warriors.*

Repeatedly, Jeremiah's character offers opportunities for deconstructionist criticism. His personal philosophy, indeed, has deconstructed the usual meanings and standards of "virtue." He ignores the legal and Biblical injunction "Thou shalt not kill"; instead he enjoys killing those who "deserve" it (414-21). Readers, most of them not murderers, find little fault with him, accepting, at least momentarily, his rejection of a fundamental verity of Western civilization. Moreover, Jeremiah deconstructs himself, appearing to surrender to the cattle thieves led by Cutright (410) before attacking them viciously. His companion Kola is initially confused by these incompatible manifestations of Jeremiah's character. Like many deconstructionists, Kola "realized he would *never understand* [his friend's] *unfathomable* behavior" (421; emphasis added).

Finally, the deconstructionist critic could completely undermine the interpretation presented in "Thematic Issues," above, and in a "second reading" deny even the existence of honor. Jeremiah's disillusioned reflections—"He'd tried to be honorable, and this was how it had ended. There was no place for honor in the war. Or in the world" (259)—provide the basis for such a second reading. Jeremiah's double-bind demands that he choose between mutually exclusive definitions of courage and honor. Jakes would have us believe that Jeremiah chose the difficult, honorable option. The opposite is equally possible. And Jeremiah's inability to choose between conflicting interpretations of his behavior haunts him throughout his life.

A second illustration of this critical process involves Louis Kent, whom Jakes has presented as devoid of honor. Though he gets his comeuppance from his erstwhile partners, Jim Fisk and Jay Gould, we realize that those robber barons, far from being punished for their unscrupulous, dishonorable business practices, live to profit yet another day. Gideon only ameliorates the loss of family honor by retrieving family talismans; the Kent name has been publicly tarnished. Moreover, Gideon's symbolic gesture of tearing down Louis' mansion, Kentland, to regain family honor, is totally inexplicable to the general public, represented by Patrick Willett (680-82).

Finally, in the epilogue, "The Lifted Sword," the meaning of peace is subverted and undermined. The Civil War is over; peace has been declared. Yet war—economic, political, social, and ethnic (Jakes provides an entire catalogue)—goes on. The cessation of battle is not peace, but merely the opportunity for other sorts of violent conflict. And while war fought for a Cause could be honorable in a conventional sense, the participants in peacetime conflicts make little pretense of honor.

Thus, while Jakes consciously affirms the existence of honor and decency, the novel, especially the epilogue, undermines that very affirmation. Despite Jakes' arguments to the contrary, *The Warriors* seems to cast doubt on the validity—even the viability—of honorable behavior. It thus reinforces the bleak interpretations of American history—and of human nature—which Jakes has fought much of his life.

8

The Lawless
(1978)

The Lawless, Volume VII of the Kent Family Chronicles, explores American history and its major themes as personified by the fifth and sixth generations of the Kents during the years 1869-1877. Jeremiah, thought dead in the Civil War, resurfaces in the West of Kansas and Dakota, the West of cattle drives and cattle towns, of Sioux Indians (like his friend Kola) who anguish over sacred grounds invaded by gold-seekers, of law being maintained precariously by the U.S. Army and by marshals like Wild Bill Hickok. Now a killer and a card sharp, Jeremiah, under various aliases beginning with the initials J. K., has, by the end of the novel, sold himself as a security guard to the unprincipled railroad tycoon Thomas Courtleigh. Matthew, who had discovered his talent for drawing during his Civil War naval service, has become disillusioned with an America he condemns as greedy and corrupt and has chosen the expatriate life, first among the Paris Impressionists and then in London; he is now a dedicated artist living the bohemian lifestyle. Gideon, fiercely dedicated to the cause of the American worker, has, with his wife Margaret's help, become a writer; conflict with her emerges, however, when his dedication to social justice seems to require time away from her narrowly conceived concept of family. Along the way, Gideon makes an ally, then lover, in the crusading Julia Sedgwick, widow of his cousin Louis and forceful advocate of women's suffrage. In his commitment to the cause of labor in particular and fairness in general, Gideon also makes an enemy of Thomas Courtleigh, epitome of the oppression, corruption, and lawlessness of the postwar era; the vendetta between the two men is intense and personal as well as philosophical, and provides much of the impetus for action in the novel.

PLOT DEVELOPMENT

The plot of *The Lawless*, like all other novels in the Kent Family Chronicles, has internal unity as well as connection to the other novels in the series. At first glance, the interior structure seems complicated and potentially fragmentary, with a prologue and three interludes which alternate with four books. Each book is unified in plot line, concentrating, though not exclusively, on one of four central characters: Matt, Gideon, Margaret, and Eleanor. Though the point of view is usually that of the central character, others provide insights and commentary. For example, Gideon's and Eleanor's insights are crucial to "Margaret's Wrath," perhaps because we're never sure whether Margaret is sane—and thus capable of rational thought—or not. The prologue and the interludes tend to initiate action, provide motivation, or intensify conflict; they are not, however, primarily expository but, rather, dramatic. "The Dream and the Gun" introduces the plot driver and a thematic motif for the novel as a whole, that, despite his good intentions to abandon violence, Jeremiah will once again take up his guns and eventually be killed by a member of his own family. "And Thou Shalt Smite the Midianites as One Man" passes the torch from Jephtha to Gideon, providing the son more ambitious means for fulfilling his goals of serving society. "A Shooting on Texas Street" shows Jeremiah falling toward his personal nadir, his expulsion from Abilene seemingly casting him irrevocably as one of the lawless. And "Summer Lightning" intensifies the Gideon-Courtleigh vendetta and foreshadows the denouement in Book 4. Despite multiple plot lines, the central conflict throughout is that between Courtleigh and his corrupt materialism and Gideon's idealistic drive for social reform. The denouement at least partially resolves the theme of class conflict; provides a satisfying conclusion of the mutual motives of Courtleigh and Gideon to achieve vengeance; reveals Jeremiah (Jason) as the agent for saving his brother from violence—either as victim or perpetrator; and allows the prophesy of Kola's vision to be played out.

The novel is unified in part by the frame of Jeremiah's fate—prophesied in the prologue and fulfilled in the final chapter. Jakes also utilizes other methods to achieve unity. Simultaneity—having things happen at the same time—provides linkages; at virtually the same moment Jakes has Thomas Courtleigh in Chicago plotting to destroy Gideon ("Summer Lightning"), Matt in Boston proofing an etching ("100 Years"), and Eleanor in New York City realizing that a career in the theater might provide an escape from her dysfunctional home life ("Imprisoned"). A similar technique is the use of accident or coincidence, as when Jeremiah, aboard the train after having been run out of Abilene, picks up the brakeman's copy of Gideon's paper, *Labor's Beacon*; or when Courtleigh, too penny-pinching to pay the Pinkertons, hires "a man who once had a pretty big reputation out west ... Jason Kane" (615). Sometimes Jakes uses devices like letters to unify: Gideon's to Matt, hoping to convince him to work on *100 Years*, thus integrating the expatriate of Book 1 with Gideon's ongoing story. Similarly, the gun Gideon chooses prior to going to Courtleigh's office to kill him is a LeMat, the same model he had carried for protection at the labor rally at the time of the Chicago fire, the model with which he was familiar from his Confederate military service. Themes and characters are sometimes linked by small details and incidents. Margaret's adamant refusal to entertain Eleanor's ambition to become an actress and her insistence that she prepare for the traditional role of wife and mother is yet another way force lines are drawn between Margaret and Julia. And the bohemian artist Matt's advice to Eleanor underlines the novel's subthemes of the necessity of choice and the need for personal integrity. Finally, although there are many other such examples of unifying techniques, the national nightmare of Custer's defeat at Little Big Horn is linked to Margaret's phantasmagoric, then real, men in the park through her deranged observation about the Watchers: "They've come to punish me, just the way the Indians punished poor General Custer" (584).

As carefully as Jakes unifies the novel, he also links it to others in the series. Often this is done by reminding readers of past events—of Jeremiah killing his first nine people during the Civil War (15), of Matt's escaping from the painful reality of the war through sketching (54), of Gideon's self-improvement with the help of Margaret during their courtship and early years of marriage (199). And when Jakes realizes that in *The Lawless* he has essentially repeated a scene from *The Furies* in which the Kent family home has been pillaged and desecrated, its women and children vilely assaulted, he meets the potential criticism head on. The banker Joshua Rothman (another link to prior works) reflects on the "sad and interesting" parallel: twenty-five years earlier Amanda had been killed because of her advocacy of a poor black woman's freedom; now Margaret is killed because of Gideon's stand for workers' rights. The Kent idealism has, once again, led to Kent sacrifice and suffering (697).

There are links not only to the past, but to the future as well. *The Lawless* virtually writes *finis* to a generation of Kents, already adults in the previous volume. Now they're characterized by disillusionment (Matt), disintegration (Jeremiah), aging (Gideon and Julia), and death (Jephtha and Jeremiah). This book's children—Tom, Eleanor, Will, and Carter—will be *The Americans'* adults.

CHARACTER DEVELOPMENT

Because, as always in a Jakes novel, plot is character-generated, it's important to examine some of his techniques of characterization. Because, as always, the protagonist is the entire Kent *family*, Jakes uses multiple points of view, and thus many characters are integral to the plot.

Even with very minor figures, Jakes pays attention to detail, providing people with quirky traits, or human foibles, that make them beg to walk off the page. One such person is the man who, hoping to survive the Chicago fire with as many of his possessions as possible, runs into the street with five hats stacked atop his head. Other characters have more than a walk-on part. Some of these tend to personify concepts, provide unity, or catalyze major characters. Strelnick is one of these, representing late nineteenth century revolutionary movements in Europe or in America. Courtleigh's lawyer, Lorenzo Hubble, personifies bloated, corrupt materialism. Other figures, such as the Princes, Dan and Martha, provide support, almost like surrogate parents, to Eleanor as she enters her theatrical profession. They're among the kind, decent people of the book, despite the brevity of their appearance; they demonstrate the uniqueness of the theater as one of the few remaining democratic institutions where one may succeed with talent and desire; moreover, in Dan Prince, Jakes presents a positive portrayal of a homosexual, counterbalancing the sinister Lepp.

While minor characters are relatively quickly drawn, Jakes lets us know major ones more fully. His first means, of course, is to have us follow them through the plot; however, we become aware of at least four corollary methods of characterization. Some are revealed through personal growth. Gideon, a virtual illiterate in *The Warriors*, becomes the publisher of the pro-union paper *Labor's Beacon*; ultimately he achieves a wider audience as publisher of Kent and Son. Eleanor, similarly, broadens her horizons as her character grows. Initially simply one of two siblings, she becomes a child with too much responsibility, a preadolescent dreamer, a victim of a merciless attack, a young woman defining herself and leaving security (going *to* her art, not merely running away from home), and, finally, achieving a tentative maturity in her reconciliation with her father.

Sometimes we learn about people through others' commentary. It is through Eleanor's eyes that we see much of what is wrong in the house dominated by Margaret. It is from Carter—his actions as well as his words—that we see Julia as a good mother. But two major methods of defining characters are enmeshing them in conflict and juxtaposing them to others for contrast.

The use of conflict clearly demonstrates Jakes' belief in the linkage between plot and character. A major theme of the novel, that no responsible adult can avoid difficult choices, is bound up with this principle. Often choice is raised almost to the degree of dilemma. Jeremiah seems to be fighting the "Fletcher blood"; he is dissipated, often violent, and, once Kola is murdered, he seems incapable of love. Yet he tries repeatedly to put aside violence, adhering to his personal code of killing only those who deserve to die, feels guilt when he violates the code of the West, and ultimately kills—and dies—to save his brother. Matt must choose between his art and his mistress, Dolly, who, after, in effect, forcing him to marry her in order to give their unborn son legitimacy, abandons him, knowing conventional family life would stultify his artistic talent. Gideon is forced to choose between family and social responsibilities. While Dolly frees Matt out of love, Margaret, increasingly domineering, tries—unsuccessfully—to bind Gideon to her. Such monomaniacal behavior inevitably requires that Gideon make yet another choice, that between Margaret and Julia, who is not only a sensuous and forceful woman, but shares with Gideon the intellectual drive to reform society. Eleanor, too, must choose between a dysfunctional family and a beckoning career, and, before her eventual reconciliation with Gideon, between her father and mother, who systematically poisoned Gideon's relationship with his children.

Obviously, Jakes uses comparison and contrast as a method of portraying his characters. Matt the bohemian and Gideon the reformer disagree about nearly everything except brotherly love. Jeremiah and Gideon are both prone to violence; close co-workers and friends—Kola and Strelnick and Theo Payne—are aware that this tendency can destroy them. Their difference appears most pronounced in the final chapter when Gideon abandons his intent to murder Courtleigh, recognizing that he can no longer kill, and thus makes himself vulnerable, saved only by his brother's honesty—and gun. Both Margaret and Courtleigh's wife are mad, a possible coincidence that, by making the two men more alike, heightens their fundamental difference. Courtleigh's Gwendolyn, already psychologically fragile (perhaps a commentary on the fundamental weakness of the ruling class), is apparently driven over the edge when, during the engagement party, Gideon throws at Courtleigh's feet the blood-soaked shirt of the child Courtleigh had murdered. Margaret, once strong (indeed, in *The Titans* and *The Warriors*, she'd been able to care for her father and to initiate Gideon into the world of letters), now is either insane or pathologically manipulative or both. She who earlier endured much in near poverty seems unable to function in the luxury environment she'd demanded. Of all the major characters, she is the least plausible. How did such a likable woman of earlier volumes become such a whining, devious bitch here? Her alcoholism doesn't explain enough. But she's a wonderful foil for Julia, who is everything Margaret no longer is: a sensuous woman who has demonstrated her capacity for growth and independence, a woman who shares Gideon's desires for social reform and is willing to sacrifice money, reputation—even her life—for the cause in which she believes. It is, thus, appropriate that Jakes concludes the novel with the telegram from Theo Payne to Gideon: *She will live.* Julia, representative of much that is right with America, *must* survive, despite all the corruption, evil, and violence that exists. Not only does this conclusion provide Jakes with a transition to another book, but it also suggests his fundamental optimism about America, despite the dark tones in *The Lawless.*

ALTERNATIVE READING: THEME AS A FUNCTION OF HISTORICAL CONTEXT

Like all of the previous volumes in this series, *The Lawless* examines the meaning of America. But, in contrast to earlier novels, the America Jakes describes in *The Lawless* is a society disillusioned by the Civil War and fractured along the fault lines of gender, race, and class.

For the first time, this book is retrospective. Indeed, one of the events it covers is the Philadelphia Centennial Exposition, intended to celebrate the accomplishments of our nation's first 100 years. In that, it was remarkably similar to one of the early publishing goals for the Kent Family Chronicles: to examine 200 years of American history through a single American family. But while the intended tone of the Philadelphia Exposition was celebratory (marred, in fact, by the telegraphed news of Custer's defeat at Little Big Horn, an event John Jakes, curiously, plays down), the tone of the book—as well as its retrospection—is generally much darker.

The destructive effects of the Civil War, long after the last shot has been fired, are seen in Jeremiah. He is representative of a generation of young men who went to war, as yet untrained in any civilian occupation. Survival, for many, was not kind. Taught killer's skills, desensitized to the value of human life by the carnage he'd witnessed, disillusioned by a society and its leaders who had sanctioned such carnage in the name of political abstractions, Jeremiah is representative of many such men who drifted to the West of the plains, as had renegade frontiersmen of previous generations—but who are now far more bitter. His own conscience haunts him, along with ghosts of those he has killed, however much they deserved that fate. His conscience is evident in his dissipation: the need to submerge his actions in alcohol diminishes his skills as a gunman and gambler; at the conclusion, he is a wreck of the man he once was—a consumptive alcoholic with rotten teeth. Yet the essence of the man is not rotten, for when, at the conclusion, Gideon is being framed for killing the evil Courtleigh, only Jeremiah speaks the truth, refuses a bribe, and dies in defense of his brother. Through Jeremiah, Jakes demonstrates that despite all of the evil legacy of the Civil War, some good remains.

For Matt, too, the Civil War and its consequences have exiled him from his home. Though it may be argued that he is running toward something (his art) and not just away from his country, his rejection of America remains unchanged even after working with Gideon on the commemorative *100 Years*. He has traveled America anew, and painted America—but as an artist, not a patriot. While Gideon sees *100 Years* hopefully—as a celebration of America's first century, the achievements of the common man as well as of national heroes; as an opportunity to resurrect the excellence of the family publishing house; and as a means of attaining personal satisfaction through creative collaboration with a brother too long absent—it is family loyalty that moves Matt, always wary of anything jingoistic about the project.

While Gideon sees the wrongs and tries to right them, Matt simply wants no part of modern America. He tells his friend Paul Cézanne that if America were to be swallowed up, the only real loss would be its baseball teams (49). And when Cezanne questions why he hates America so much, Matt replies that it's because social position and money, not idealism, have become people's prime motivations. Nor can he forget the Civil War. The politicians and profiteers had grown rich from the war while "virtuous young men" they sent into battle had perished (55).

Thus Matt analyzes the catalyst for his expatriate life. He can no longer accept those people in power who, through war, destroyed a generation of young men like his brother Jeremiah. That, as the robber barons of industry, they continue to exploit the common man in their mines and factories and railroads, growing rich from others' labor, is a belief he shares with Gideon. Yet Matt, despite occasional spasms of homesickness for his brother, cannot do what Gideon chooses to do—fight corruption and injustice. Though he helps Strelnick and his family immigrate to America, he sees all too clearly, albeit cynically, how Strelnick will be treated in America if he dares to express his revolutionary economic ideas openly. Thus Matt's disillusionment with America also functions to underscore one of the novel's central themes, that of class conflict in post–Civil War America.

For the wars of this book are no longer regional and military; now they are wars of economics and ideology, of class, race, and gender. And, like the Civil War, many of these conflicts are fought with new rules—or with no rules at all.

The first battle was often one of personal decision; indeed, for most of the positive characters, the necessity of choice is a salient feature of the plot structure. For some, such as the immigrants of the book, the personal decision to tear up roots and move to America was a step toward freedom and opportunity. Once in America some, like young Leo Goldman, spout near clichés of America, the promised land, and dream of making their fortunes in a land where every man is his "own king" (401-3). Other immigrants, like the Irish waiter, are more conservative in granting others seemingly outlandish opportunity. In response to Jakes' and Lucy Stone's discussion about women voting, he insists that his wife will know and keep her proper place. "Females don't have the head to understand a subject such as politics" (444).

Thus Jakes links one struggle—the economic struggle of the immigrant—to another, that of women for equality. And just as the right to vote will prove difficult to achieve (Lucy Stone notes that when it comes to votes for women, "you'd think it had been proposed by Satan himself" [445]), so too will economic parity be difficult for the immigrants;

for, in an increasingly urbanized industrial America, there is a large and growing class of the poor, evident in Jakes' descriptions of the Chicago fire, the Pittsburgh railroad strike, and even the "cowpoke," bottom man in the hierarchy of the cattle industry. For there was, increasingly, a hierarchy in America, a dichotomy between the haves and the have-nots, a tarnish on the Gilded Age.

The tarnish extends to the national capital. Though neither John Jakes nor the character Theo Payne questions the personal integrity of President Grant, Payne's description of the national capital tends to reinforce Matt's low opinion of the United States. Washington is the "auction room" where everyone is for sale. Votes, influence, honor, and physical favors all may be bought for the right price (194).

While the rich and powerful schemed for greater wealth and power, American workers suffered exploitation. To feed their families, laborers had to submit to the men who controlled the factory system (244). Labor reformers proposed an eight-hour day, the formation of a federal labor department, elimination of abuses in the child labor system, and workers' and survivors' compensation. To achieve such goals, a union of workers was necessary.

Such unity of workers was a solution, but not one easily achieved. On the one hand, Jay Gould observed, "I can hire one half of the working class to kill the other half"; on the other, radicals like Strelnick asserted that the only way to deal with the bosses was ruthlessly (214). Violence seemed inevitable, especially with people like Thomas Courtleigh among the haves.

For Thomas Courtleigh is almost a caricature of the evils of capitalism. He has built his wealth through exploiting both his employees and his customers. At a time when railroads came to represent capitalism run rampant, Courtleigh bragged about owning one of the most repressively managed lines in the entire country (254). He thought nothing of arbitrarily reducing the pay of his employees, to $1.15 for a twelve-hour day, 34 percent below the national average. And when Wisconsin dairymen protested his exorbitant rates for shipping their milk, he retorted that everyone is entitled to the maximum profit he can earn. "The farmers milk the cows and we milk the farmers" (255).

Courtleigh's success is clear in the descriptions of his home and office. His home and its landscaping claim an entire block on State Street, a three-story edifice of marble and stained glass whose very air "smelled of costly perfume, expensive cigars—and wealth" (338). His office, "joyless and dark," was hung with "idealized paintings of W and P rolling stock and with trophies of hunting expeditions" (782). The paintings, idealized rather than realistic, suggest his refusal to look at the oppression and exploitation upon which his wealth is based. The glassy eyes in the stuffed heads of a bison and a big-horned buck deer stare with "sinister life" (782), suggesting that Courtleigh is, in all ways, a predator, and contrasting him sharply with the Indians of the West, whose land and cultures have been transgressed by railroads like his. Courtleigh has no respect for the truth; manipulation of public opinion—whether to set up a straw man by associating the union movement with communism or to discredit Gideon as a Marxist—is simply another management technique. The truth is irrelevant, he tells Gideon. If an allegation is repeated often enough, the public will believe it (784). His arrogance and his power make him almost untouchable. When Gideon proposes exposing him in the press, Julia cautions that everyone already knows what Courtleigh is, but his vast wealth, and the influence it buys, make him unassailable (334). Thus Courtleigh seems free to exact revenge on any, like Gideon, who cross him. And he accepts no conventional rules—unlike even Jeremiah, who respects the gunman's code—and wages war on women and children, his minions causing Margaret's death and raping Eleanor. Truly, Courtleigh (his name is well chosen for its symbolic value) is a personification of the nadir of American capitalism.

But Jakes does not overgeneralize, for Julia, too, is very rich before losing her wealth in the Panic of 1873. Indeed, she was Thomas Courtleigh's next-block neighbor. But she can also be compassionate. She invites those made homeless by the Chicago fire to camp on her property; Courtleigh, in contrast, posts guards to keep them off his property and complains about the riffraff at Julia's destroying property values. Thus, although class conflict is the major battle in the book, Jakes' portrayal of Julia argues against a Marxian interpretation of the novel.

Through Julia, Jakes introduces yet another struggle, that of women for equal rights. In expository passages, as well as in Julia's speeches, he sketches the careers of Margaret Fuller, Fanny Wright, Lucy Stone, Susan B. Anthony, Julia Ward Howe, and Elizabeth Stanton; he discusses the 1848 Seneca Falls Convention and the struggle for suffrage, first granted by Wyoming; he examines the planks in the women's platform dealing with equal property rights and the right to have equal access to the guardianship of their children. Julia, initially stigmatized by her divorce from Louis Kent, knows social ostracism (Thomas Courtleigh and his mother consider her "no better than a whore" [275]) and real danger (from the Bible-spouting, shotgun-toting miner in Deadwood) in her advocacy of women's suffrage. Yet she firmly believes that what the abolitionists had done for the slaves, someone must do for women (271). In her zeal, however, she does not abandon her son Carter, whom, as a single mother, she raises with affection, common sense, and loving discipline. In this she may be contrasted to Margaret, who, despite her strident advocacy of family, virtually ignores her children, leaving them to fend for themselves as she wanders in an alcoholic haze.

Yet another conflict in post–Civil War America was that between the Native American and the forces of Manifest Destiny. The transcontinental railroad has already bisected the grasslands of the buffalo and the Indians dependent on them; gold-seekers, having already plundered California, are now probing new finds in the Sioux's sacred Black Hills. There are some, like Jeremiah (perhaps *because* he was a fugitive from white society?), who were sworn lifelong friends of the Indians; he is literally blood brother to Kola, whose death he avenges and whose body he buries, respectfully, according to Sioux tribal custom. Julia, too, has an affinity for the West and its Indians. Unlike Courtleigh, who relished trophy hunting, she had from the first fallen in love with the "grandeur of the west" (454). On the stagecoach to Deadwood she dares to observe that the land being invaded by the gold miners is sacred, and thus Custer's 1874 exploration was illegal, that treaty commission proposals of money for this land were "robbery," and that the United States government policy toward the Indians is "muddled and despicable" (460).

Jeremiah and Julia, however, are in the minority. Sergeant Graves, responsible for killing Kola, justifies his actions because an Indian should know better than to walk into the dancehall like a white man (23); moreover, townsmen believed Indians killed off the cattle business in Ellsworth, Kansas, even before it began, and believe "Custer did right" (24) in punishing the Cheyenne at the Washita. Julia is told that gold is "a lot more sacred" to the white man than land is to the Indian, an observation ironically echoing Matt's disillusionment and broadening the arena of capitalists like Courtleigh. In addition, Hickok observes that the "hostiles" had better not defend their sacred territory. If they do, they'll get "scorched earth" because people are sick of Indians "standing in the way of progress" (459-60). The tactics of Sherman marching through Georgia are seen as viable methods in the name of Manifest Destiny. Progress—and profit—define policy.

Thus, in these postwar years, America remains mired in struggle—struggle to resolve conflicts of class, gender, and ethnicity. The ultimate struggle is that over law. Each of the previous struggles—for economic equality, for women's rights, for the march of the nation west—is in some way revolutionary and thus disruptive of the status quo. In the name of law and order, society enlists the police force to put down the Tompkins Square riot, the Philadelphia militia and the Pinkerton Agency to control the strikers in Pittsburgh, and the United States Cavalry on the plains. The irony is that each of these forces is not only repressive (which could simply be the point of view of their opponents) but, as Jakes portrays them, also corrupt. At Tompkins Square, Gideon notes that it was a police riot, not a labor riot (440); the Pinkertons with their logo/symbol of a wide-open eye (the origin of "private eye"?) are an unregulated, almost renegade force of hired spies and thugs; and Sgt. Amos Graves, who kills Kola, is not only a bigot and a usurer, but also representative of "the Plains Army . . . a haven for men who couldn't control their craving for alcohol" (28). Compared to such officers of the law, Jeremiah, despite his disintegration, despite his career as gunman and gambler, despite his having violated the loose code of the West when he shot the miner abusing Julia—but hit him in the back—Jeremiah, on balance, appears virtuous. Certainly he does in the ultimate chapter when his morals are juxtaposed to those of Courtleigh, who maintained a facade of respectability while considering himself above the law. For Jeremiah has personal integrity: he will not lie, he will not be bought, and he kills only those who deserve it.

Such a portrayal, however, causes the reader to reflect on the meaning of law. We applaud Jeremiah while we are appalled at him. We see further ironies in that descendants of American revolutionaries are afraid of modern revolutionary ideas. And, as we see an America now as part of a larger world, we realize that might (the Prussian militarism of the Franco-Prussian War) does not always make right. In *The Lawless* Jakes asks his reader to reexamine the meaning of America in the postwar years. A nation which plunged into the cataclysm of the Civil War out of idealism and conviction, misplaced or not, must reexamine its values and decide its goals: to squeeze the nation dry, like Courtleigh, to abdicate one's responsibilities, like Matt, or to fight for change, like Gideon and Julia. Writing at the time of the second centenary, Jakes suggests that such reexamination is as important today as it was a century ago.

ALTERNATIVE PERSPECTIVE: NEW CRITICISM

Since its introduction in 1941, New Criticism has been followed by many newer forms of criticism; yet it retains the name. Defined by John Crowe

Ransom, it dominated American literary criticism until the 1960s. New Critics believed that a work existed for its own sake, independent of external factors. Thus a close reading, or explication, of the text was more important than social history, literary history, or the author's biography. New Criticism is word-oriented; central to its methodology is careful examination of how words work in the context of the literary piece. Thus New Critics pay close attention to the meanings and interactions of words, to figures of speech, and to symbols.

Although it may seem improbable to separate a John Jakes novel from historical context, a close textual, New Critical, reading is not only possible but perhaps profitable. This discussion will focus on simile, metaphor, personification, and symbol.

A simile compares two distinctly different things by the use of "like" or "as." The simile is often used to make description more precise and vivid. Jakes does this in describing the glowing ash and sparks blown about during the Chicago fire: "Gideon had never seen an effect as strange and lovely as that produced by the sparks. It was as if he were caught in a snowstorm in which every flake was lighted from within" (309). Sometimes such description suggests character. Courtleigh's mansion was "shuttered and curtained like a fortress" (308). He thus is made to seem unassailable. Julia is portrayed as a powerful woman: She was "like some natural force. . . . like a hurricane that blew away whatever resistance it encountered" (276-77). Courtleigh's white-haired mother moves into the ballroom "like a warship under sail" (340). A simile may also indicate a character's response to a situation. Matt, when Dolly insisted that they talk about their future, "felt . . . as if she'd announced an execution" (73). In addition, Jakes sometimes uses simile to provide unity with previous books. Matt depends on his painting teacher's help explaining his aversion to marriage: he clung to Fochet and his advice "as tenaciously as he'd clung to the spar that had kept him from drowning in the Gulf" (105). Finally, Jakes recognizes others' use of the simile as effective—and quotes them for his own purposes, as when he cites Goethe: daring ideas—for Gideon, labor reform—are "like chessmen moved forward." Although they may be beaten, they may open a "winning game" (219).

Closely connected to the simile is the metaphor, which also makes a comparison between unlike things, but without using "like" or "as." Twice Jakes uses this technique to describe Gideon's newly discovered feelings for Julia. After they've made love while fire is consuming the city (fire itself is often a metaphor for passion), someone far off detonated an explosion, a "fitting capstone to the incredible experience" (320). Making love with Julia was, literally, explosive. And earlier, when Gideon first kissed Julia prior to leaving in search of a doctor for the wounded Ericsson child, he went out into a "night grown brighter than day" (307). The brightness, of course, is both from the fire and from a newly kindled love.

Frequently Jakes makes use of weather metaphors to underscore emotion or to achieve foreshadowing. "We've been having unsettled weather, Dolly" (65) literally describes the climate but also introduces potential discord to the Matt and Dolly relationship. "[S]torm clouds moved in" (59) precedes one of Matt's first encounters with the ominous Colonel Lepp. And, when Gideon returns to New York City after the threats from Courtleigh and the beginning of his affair with Julia, a "cold autumn rain poured down," whipped by the wind, which drove "silver needles" through the beam of the locomotive's headlight. The locomotive's smoke added to the "murk" of an afternoon already "dark and dreary"; "fast-flying black clouds" filled the sky (355). Danger and depression fill Gideon's world.

An extended metaphor emerges in the descriptions of Chicago before the fire. Along the river was a "jumble" of wooden office buildings, grain elevators, masts—"wood everywhere." In addition, nearly everywhere near the workers' small frame houses are piles of shavings and wood scraps—winter fuel (250-51). Gideon recalls the word a fellow pedestrian had used:

> Tinderbox.
> Chicago was that . . .
> In more ways than one. (257)

Thus Jakes foreshadows the labor unrest, the passions of love, hate, and vengeance which will soon ignite. The metaphor also indirectly comments on the book's theme of the haves versus the have-nots, for clearly it is the wooden houses of the workers, not the granite and marble mansions of the rich, which will be consumed in the Chicago fire.

Yet another extended metaphor, that of the snake, unifies the pages of Gideon's confrontation with Courtleigh after one of the latter's minions has murdered the Ericsson child. Courtleigh's eyes "flicked" over Gideon; his threats to "crucify" his servants for admitting Gideon are "sibilant." Gideon had never heard "such venom" in a voice. And, when Courtleigh's mother orders Thomas to silence Gideon, the invited guests add their "hisses": "Socialist!" "Communard!" (343). Courtleigh later continued his threat at Julia's house: to crush Gideon, his family, and his beloved Julia. Afterwards "the venomous hazel eyes lingered in Gideon's mind" (354). Courtleigh is the Snake in America's Garden of Eden, the seemingly omniscient destroyer amid the Terrestrial Paradise.

Indeed, Courtleigh has become a personification of all the evils of the rich. Even his name, Courtleigh (courtly), suggests class conflict. Similarly, Colonel Lepp (leprosy?) comes to personify the corruption of Prussian militarism. Jakes takes Lepp, and Courtleigh, to yet another level. Both become symbols, one of materialism, one of militarism. Matt rejects both of these evils of modern society, as does Jakes.

Matt remembers his mentor Fochet's observations on the role of the artist in society: art is a "high calling," the artist a priest privileged to emphasize the shared traits of humanity rather than their differences, privileged to show them beauty rather than ugliness and, thus, to help people endure (100). Thus it is eminently appropriate that Jakes unifies this novel with the motif of art. Recurring throughout are references to art: Courtleigh's idealized paintings of the W and P rolling stock (782); descriptions—of the Sunflower Cafe, where Jeremiah confronts the corrupt Sergeant Graves (here too the name is significant): smoke and amber chimneys on the ceiling lamps softened the figures as if they were "images in an old, soiled painting" (26), or of the "grand mural of New York" (211); or, simply, "a blue sky worthy of a Constable" (64). These constantly remind the reader of Matt, the painter, the expatriate, the man of "high calling," the member of a "priesthood," the critic of America. As Jakes sharpens our sight by reminders of the artistic world, he asks us to sharpen our insights as we reexamine post–Civil War America.

9

The Americans
(1980)

The Americans is the eighth and last volume of the Kent Family Chronicles. Although he had originally intended to bring the exploits of the Kents up to 1976, Jakes felt that after "eight long books in a little over five years," it was "time to step back, take a breath, reflect on the past and consider some alternatives for the future" (795).

Thus Jakes, for the first time in the Kent Family Chronicles, does not anticipate future volumes at the same time as he creates an aesthetically satisfying conclusion to the one in hand. This is in sharp contrast to *The Bastard*, which brings Philip to the opening salvos of the Revolution, demanding that *The Rebels* follows; to *The Furies*, which does more than complement *The Seekers*—it completes it; or to *The Lawless*, which ties up most of the loose ends of the Civil War generation of the Kents introduced in *The Warriors*. With *The Americans* Jakes wants to end the series. His solutions are apparent in his treatment of plot, character, and theme.

PLOT DEVELOPMENT

The Americans opens on New Year's Day 1883 and concludes during the 1890 Christmas holidays. The initiating premise for the novel is Gideon Kent's awareness that before the end of 1883 he will be forty. He knows that the average man's life expectancy is forty-seven years and a few months; that knowledge, in combination with the chest pains that plague him, with increasing severity, throughout the novel, creates in Gideon intimations of his own mortality. As a consequence, he is consumed with a question, which Jakes introduces in the prologue, "Lost." "*I may have only a few years left to set things in order. And once I'm gone, who will bear the burden of leading this family?*" (17; emphasis in original).

As always, Jakes links the destiny of the Kent family to the nation's destiny. Gideon, who has been a good steward of the heritage and responsibilities passed down to him by Jephtha, fears for the future. For, as the novel opens, none of the younger generation—neither Eleanor nor Will nor Carter—seem destined to take on that responsibility. Gideon feared that "family traditions would wither, the family's dedication to principle evaporate in the climate of materialism settling over America" (24). The plot lines encompassing the seven years of this novel are thus largely unified by Gideon's search for an answer to "Who will lead the family?"

As he has done in earlier novels, Jakes again makes use of multiple points of view—in this instance to assess Eleanor, Will, and Carter as potential family leaders. Gideon and Julia remain touchstones rather than participants in the action through most of the book. The reader, like Gideon and Julia, follows the lives of the younger generation in a search for who will lead. But Jakes does not make the path easy for any of the young people. They rebel against the stringent family expectations. They begin naive and must struggle against cynicism when they come face to face with bigotry, political corruption, and exploitative materialism. They search for their own identity with varying degrees of success. They all struggle with the legacy of the past as they try to define their future.

Carter, Julia's son by Louis Kent, had a golden smile and a silver tongue capable of charming almost anyone. He'd filled the hero/big brother role for Will, giving the shy younger boy confidence. However, at Harvard his career had been, at best, mediocre; his most significant accomplishment, making friends with Willie Hearst from California. Carter is conscious of the family motto—and of his failure, so far, to live up to it; for most of the rest of the book, his life will be an attempt to make a mark, but with goals of which most Kents could not approve. Carter heads west, having "freed" himself from family responsibilities. Before leaving the distraught Will, however, he makes him promise to "be somebody—and make sure everyone knows it" (166). The promise, of course, underlines Carter's own goals, too.

Carter finally arrives in San Francisco, where, by sheer luck, he saves the life of Buckley, the blind boss of the Democratic party, and thus gains entree to the political machine; his con-man tongue, his amorality, and his willingness to be tough when need be facilitate his rise. Warned by Willie Hearst that political reformers are going to bring down the Boss, Carter is only briefly forked by his dilemma: Buckley has befriended and trusted him for years—but Hearst has given him a chance to save his hide. He does what's best—for himself. Somewhat ashamed of himself, Carter sums up his philosophy: his stepbrother Will is the "decent one" in the family; Carter must be content being the "successful one" (782). His cynicism, however, demonstrates how far he's drifted, with America, into the amoral materialism that Gideon fears.

Eleanor, discovering how her mother had poisoned her feelings for her father, reconciled with Gideon just before she left with Leo Goldman and other actors in a road troupe. Early in *The Americans*, despite at least some opposition from both families, she and Leo Goldman marry. From that moment on, Eleanor too lives with the bigotry, the anti-Semitism that Leo has experienced much of his life. The Goldmans' marriage is not as idyllic as they (consummate actors) let others believe. Leo's adolescent assurance that he would become rich and famous has been dashed; he and Eleanor have tired of life on the road. But most important, after four and a half years, their marriage is sexually dysfunctional. Never once has Eleanor been able to overcome the horror of sex since she was gang raped by hoodlums sent by Thomas Courtleigh, her father's enemy. Although Gideon suspects what happened, and gently asks her about it, Eleanor's defense mechanism is to lock all memories of the rape behind her "secret door." She is unable to tell anyone, including Leo, what's wrong.

On tour, she and Leo are trapped in the Johnstown flood, in which he perishes, his body never found. His death is especially brutal, for amid the power of nature, it is the force of bigotry that really kills him. A vicious German traveler, outraged at their mixed marriage, knocks Leo into the flood waters because he is a Jew (529). Nearly insane from the horrors around her, Eleanor shrieks her loss to a total stranger, Rafe Martin; she purges her soul in comforting anonymity.

Eleanor's bitterness persists long after she returns home. There, raging against America and flirting with madness, Eleanor finally fights her way free to return to the stage, an act of incredible courage. She eventually marries Rafe Martin—the one person from whom she has no secrets. With his patience and understanding, she is finally able to open her secret door and, for the first time in her life, participate in mutually pleasurable lovemaking. Her resulting pregnancy assures the next generation of Kents.

As the book begins, Gideon sees Will as the most likely prospect to lead the family. However, he seems to lack any sense of direction. He knows only that he doesn't want to work at Kent and Son, the family publishing firm. And, in addition to his almost total lack of ambition, he is haunted by his mother's abuse, which has left him convinced he's a bungling incompetent. As a desperate last resort, Gideon sends him off to Dakota, to spend the summer before college on Theodore Roosevelt's ranch. There he becomes tougher and learns he can do things—ride hard, build a corral, brand cattle. A pivotal discovery is that he can stand blood. Astounded that he didn't "puke," one of the cowboys asks whether he has ever considered being a "sawbones" (241). And when one of the cowboys suffers a broken back during a stampede, another, part Cherokee, gentles his way to death with herbs and human compassion. This compassion becomes for Will the "symbol of the most meaningful skill a man could possess" (253).

Complicating Will's decision to be a doctor, however, is his promise to Carter that he would "be somebody" and "make sure everybody knows it." Thus he's torn between medicine as service to humanity and medicine as a means to wealth and social prominence. This dilemma is further exacerbated by two friends' sisters—Laura Pennel, a young, promiscuous society woman who traps Will into an engagement, and Jo Hastings, sweet but seething with resentment that she too cannot receive a medical education like her brother. The choice between the two young women intensifies Will's dilemma and underlies Gideon's eventual assessment that Will is, indeed, a worthy Kent.

Because of the novel's compelling central question, two narrative devices—the use of simultaneous events and the emphasis on the past—take on more significance than usual. There are numerous instances of simultaneity. Eleanor announces that she wants to be married in Boston "before the year is out" (111); and Ortega, the Portuguese sailor, wants to return to Boston to settle the score with Carter so he can "celebrate the holy Christmas season in good spirits" (112). This prepares for the jarring arrival of the police just as the wedding ceremony has been completed (140-41). Not only does this produce dramatic shock, but it initiates an upward swing in Eleanor's life with a corresponding decline in Carter's. Similarly, Jakes shocks the reader with simultaneous, though ironically disparate perceptions of Will's motives for entering Harvard. Will knows exactly what he wants from life: to own a mansion like Vanderbilt's, to become a prominent member of "Society," and to marry someone who can help him achieve these goals (295). Happy at Will's choice of a medical career, Gideon reflected that idealism had finally won out over the "less laudable characteristics" in Will—his best hope for family leadership (296)! Like all dramatic irony, this discrepancy is made all the more powerful because we know what Gideon does not. Yet another instance of simultaneity has Eleanor and Leo wait in Johnstown with liberal foreshadowing of disaster on the very night that Carter limps into San Francisco (456-57). Eleanor's life is, within hours, to descend into a maelstrom of floodwater, death, and near madness. Carter's fortunes have reached their nadir, and this night marks the beginning of his rise to success. Finally, in Newport, full of suspicions about his fiancée, Will seeks out the truth from the Casino ballboys with whom she has been promiscuous; early that same afternoon, Gideon insists that Eleanor face the truth about herself and choose life again over the refuge of madness (610). That parallel insistence on seeking and embracing truth leads to Eleanor's return to the stage and Will's decision to abandon the shallowness of Society for a life of service.

In most of the novels, Jakes uses the device of simultaneity as a means of establishing unity, a way to juggle multiple plots, a means of making transitions between plot lines. In *The Americans* all these purposes are still viable, but the technique accomplishes more. Because of the novel's controlling question—Who could lead the family?—the technique allows for necessary side-by-side comparison and assessment of Eleanor, Carter, and Will.

Similarly, the importance of the past is not a new element in *The Americans*. Throughout the Kent Family Chronicles, from the moment Lafayette gave Philip the sword, tradition, heritage, and the icons which recall the past have been precious. But here, the past takes on a special significance, and Jakes brings to it a wide variety of nuances.

Sometimes Jakes evokes the past (Gideon's memories of the Chicago fire and the subsequent bitter enmity with Thomas Courtleigh [105-6]) as a means of reminding the reader of events which had so scarred Eleanor as to prevent her sexual fulfillment with Leo. In a similar fashion, the evil, destructive influence of his mother Margaret's abuse haunts Will (69-73). More positively, Philip Kent is repeatedly invoked as a touchstone and role model. Will, facing the town bullies at the train station in Dakota, thought of the painting of Philip back home in Boston. Doing so, he felt "better, more confident" (208). Will uses Philip as justification of his goal to become one of America's elite: it was a "thoroughly Amer-

ican goal," he reminded himself. His ancestor, the French/English bastard who'd founded the Kent family had come to the colonies for the
same reasons—to "escape the limitations of his past and better himself"
(285). Will's interpretation of Philip's motives provides a telling contrast
between the traditions Gideon reveres—which include strong measures
of responsibility and service—and Will's current ambitions. But when
he visits the new Statue of Liberty with Drew and Jo, Will is reminded
that his family had been founded by a young European boy *yearning to
breathe free.* Unconsciously, the Emma Lazarus poem and its application
to his family moves Will toward his final decision: to serve, rather than
exploit.

Jakes constantly reminds us of the past. It is no surprise that as Will
grows more and more worthy of assuming the family leadership, Will
is the Kent who most frequently thinks of Philip. It is significant, too,
that Will, the boy who at the outset of the novel had rebelled against
family responsibility and values and, in so doing, had exasperated Gideon, begins to draw closer to his father. That Will has shifted to his
father, rather than Philip, as a role model not only demonstrates their
increasingly similar values, but works toward concluding the cycle of
Kent family novels.

Jakes also utilizes Eleanor's pregnancy to achieve this end. Not only
does it demonstrate that she's been healed of the trauma of her rape, but
it provides links to the past. In an earlier letter, her uncle Matt, the
expatriate painter, reminds Eleanor of her great-great-great-great-
grandmother, Marie Charboneau (421). Marie and Eleanor—both actresses, both strong women. Marie, who'd given birth to Philip, founder
of the dynasty, and Eleanor, pregnant now with the next generation of
Kents. The reference to Marie, less than a sentence halfway through the
book, demonstrates Jakes' efforts throughout to craft a *finis* to the Kent
Family Chronicles.

Jakes reinforces this finality in the epilogue, ". . . And Make a Mark."
Gideon is a few days short of his forty-eighth birthday. Reflecting on the
family mementos, "these symbols of the family's strength" (786), he can
think of nothing that is his own contribution. Yet this Christmas of 1890
the entire family will be together again. It is to the family that Julia calls
her husband's attention. Gideon's contribution, Julia insists, is three children who behave responsibly and care about more than their own self-
gratification, children who will carry the family into the next century
(790-91). As he and Julia walk out into the December night, to the harbor
where Philip had landed those many years ago, Gideon's doubts have

faded. Together they stare out to sea. Out there lay Europe, where the family had its beginnings. Here they'd contributed to the goodness and growth of their adopted country. As had Gideon. He was no longer necessary to the survival of the family—or the nation. There was a "touch of sadness in knowing that, but there was also a release, and peace" (792).

Thus, John Jakes allows Gideon to die, smiling, with Julia at his side. He's brought the Kents full circle. He's carefully crafted an end to their saga. And in that, Gideon may speak for Jakes: "There was a touch of sadness . . . but there was also a release, and peace."

CHARACTER DEVELOPMENT

Gideon's concern about who would step up to lead the family makes character a central consideration in *The Americans*. Neither Gideon nor Julia has to do much: they have already been established as ethical, responsible people in earlier books. They are near the statistical life expectancy for Americans in the 1880s. Consequently, Gideon's role is primarily to act as touchstone against which the younger Kents can be measured; Julia's role is to provide Gideon with support and strength.

As he usually does, Jakes reveals character through what an individual says and does and by comparing that to others' evaluations of him. In addition, he often makes use of foils—closely juxtaposed but dissimilar characters who provide, by their difference, insight into each other's essential traits. We can think of obvious pairs: the two Drs. Vlandingham, Jo Hastings and Laura Pennel, Carter and Will, Mrs. Grimaldi and Don Andreas Belsario. But, although a discussion of these foils could be fruitful, Jakes' dominant technique as he treats characters in this novel is to contrast static and developing characters. The assumption at the outset, if Gideon is right, is that one or more characters *must* develop, must change, for initially none is capable of leading the family.

Carter neither develops nor changes over the course of the novel. He chafes under discipline, or others' control—whether it be imposed by Harvard professors, Gideon, or Portuguese sailors in a bar brawl. Unlike Gideon, who goes to the docks for peace and contemplation, he goes for excitement and physical gratification. He loves waterfront dives because of their casual disregard of the law, in sharp contrast to the rules and regulations he'd hated at Harvard (29). Even barmaids like Josie recognize his rebelliousness. As does his friend Willie Hearst: "We both hate the unexpected . . . we like to hold the reins" (56). It's Willie who first suggests that Carter, with his silver tongue, may have a future in politics (57).

At the end of the book Carter is pretty much the same person he was at the beginning. Though he has succeeded in party politics in San Francisco, he rejects family duty and responsibility—and political duty and responsibility—as that "pious garbage" the Kent family has been "purveying for several generations" (776). He's learned how to buy votes, to give orders instead of taking them, to survive in a political jungle even if it means abandoning those who have befriended and trusted him. Politics, for Carter, is not service. He would have sneered at JFK's "ask not what your country can do for you; ask what you can do for your country." To Carter, Kent family idealism is "pure bullshit" (777).

And, despite Gideon's and especially Julia's wishful thinking to the contrary, he knows himself—and his goals. He still wants cheap success. He sees government officials as manipulators and exploiters—and includes himself in that pack. Politics is a "game" in which you "get all you can from the trough while convincing the rest of the hogs to be high-minded instead of hungry" (777). Not only is Carter a static character; he almost personifies the "drift to materialism" Gideon so fears.

In contrast, Eleanor's whole life has been one of dealing with change. From a relatively secure early childhood, she had to survive in an environment of her mother's worsening madness. Learning how Margaret poisoned her relationship with Gideon, she is able to become reconciled with him. Having chosen a career often deemed socially unacceptable, she succeeds on the stage. Having married Leo Goldman, she endures, with him, vicious anti-Semitism—endures and stands up against it. Eleanor is a powerful woman in the tradition of Jakes' powerful women. But she has one devastating, destructive flaw. Despite being an actress, she is still bound by Victorian proprieties. These, and the psychological trauma of her rape, make it impossible for her to be a real wife to Leo— and equally impossible for her to explain to him why. Thus she is doubly full of guilt after his death. The guilt plunges her into vitriolic anti-American statements—for all she had been raised to believe in seems shredded by the bigotry which caused his death. Paradoxically, it is only through making herself most vulnerable—telling Rafe Martin her most secret shames—that she gains the possibility of being healed. And only by willing herself to change, to summon the courage necessary to take up her professional life again, does she gain the opportunity to once again be whole. Her pregnancy with Rafe is proof of her wholeness—

for the first time in her adult life. The baby is also promise of the continuation of the Kents. Eleanor has summoned the strength and courage necessary to change. She is clearly a developing character. She can provide Gideon with hope for the family's future.

Will, too, had been grievously scarred by the dysfunctional family life with Margaret. But his wounds, unlike Eleanor's, remain hidden. The discovery of Margaret's diary, detailing her schemes to alienate Eleanor from Gideon, allowed for father-daughter reconciliation. But there is no such overt evidence of what she'd done to Will. Instead, it is seared into his soul: "You'll never amount to anything. . . . You'll be a bungler all your life" (72). The summer on Roosevelt's ranch helps to counter this. Under the tutelage of Christopher Tompkins and Lon Adam, he learns to *do* things. Moreover, Roosevelt contributes an ethical base, reinforcing Gideon's ideas. He responds sharply to Will's desire to make lots of money: Will must decide his priorities. Is personal wealth more important than principles? Making that decision, argues Roosevelt, determines the direction of a man's life and, more important, the "worth of it" (234).

Will listens to Roosevelt more patiently than he would have to his father. But he is far from accepting either man's beliefs. He does not recognize that he cannot do both, cannot have it all. Only after savoring the siren call of Society—and consequently seeing its duplicity, venality, and immorality, does he find himself and his true goal: practicing medicine with his friend Drew among the slum-bound immigrants who need him, and marrying the spunky Jo Hastings. Will finally destroys the specter of inadequacy bequeathed him by his mother when he operates on Jo, saving her life. He truly has changed and is now a man of whom Gideon can be proud.

Jakes emphasizes the route of Will's changes through the motif of the promise, for Will, even when without any sense of direction for his life, was an honorable young man who believed that promises must be kept. There's his promise to Carter, that he'll "be somebody" and "make sure everybody knows it" (165). The promise to Laura that he won't do any more "horse-doctoring"—that is, treat injured servants. His promise to Drew to come visit him in his slum infirmary is, of course, in direct conflict with his vow to Laura. Moreover, its result, the decision to practice where he's needed, violates the material goals implicit in his promise to Carter. A sense of filial responsibility is demonstrated when he promises himself never again to engage in violent discussion with Gideon for fear of aggravating his heart condition.

Increasingly, the impetus for Will's behavior is internal, until he can realize that his promise to Carter was the "wrong promise," for the "wrong purpose." He recognizes that as long as he has meaningful work and a woman he loves, his life is full. He has realized that he doesn't have to prove anything to anyone, except to himself (739).

Will is free. As is Eleanor who, with Rafe's love, has opened the secret door behind which she'd hidden her shame and repressed her horrors. Both Will and Eleanor have changed, have defined freedom for themselves, and with others. Only Carter remains unchanged. For him freedom is still what it was when he set out for the West—to be free of family duty and responsibility to others.

THEMATIC ISSUES

Most of *The Americans'* themes are suggested by Gideon in the prologue, "Lost." Central is the nation's "drift toward materialism." Now success matters more than integrity; appearance, more than substance. People's ambition is less to live in liberty than to be accepted by Society (18). Jakes integrates four other issues in his exposition of this drift to materialism: the increasing urbanization of America, and, with it, a changing significance of the West; increasing stratification of United States society; the polarization, among many, of responsibility and success, and a consequent diminution of noblesse oblige; and increasing immigration and the resulting need to redefine the word "American."

By framing his narrative between 1883 and 1890, Jakes chose a period of great demographic changes—and consequent changes in attitude. In 1890 the Bureau of the Census declared that there was no more free land (defined as less than two people per square mile), and thus the frontier as an escape valve was no more. In contrast to the freedom—for good and ill—we saw in the West of *The Warriors* and *The Lawless*, the West of *The Americans* has become settled, domesticated, regulated.

At much the same time, increasing industrialization drew workers to the cities. Moreover, after 1870, technologies such as the elevator allowed for new, vertical patterns of urban land use. And while the city was soaring upward, it was also extending outward, producing the familiar American pattern of central business core, close-in slum and working-class residential areas, and a ring of prosperous suburbs. In *The Titans* and *The Lawless* we saw something of this pattern, with the mansion of Thomas Courtleigh separated by miles from the tinderbox houses of the workers. Louis Kent's construction of Kentland was another manifestation of this pattern.

This stratification is all the more evident in *The Americans*. Carter's philosophy of wanting to give the orders, not take them, is a relatively benign illustration of this, as is his belief that success must be defined through material goods. Eleanor meets the polarizing effect of bigotry after her marriage to Leo Goldman. Perhaps most indicative of social stratification and its absurdities is that money, and especially new money, is not enough to gain access to Society. Gideon, for example, despite his fortune, is "unacceptable" because, as a publisher, he's "in trade." The insidious hierarchy is present even at Harvard, where connections rather than contributions were the criteria for admission to the "best" clubs.

All this would be un-American enough, but it is made worse by the exploitation of the very poor by the very rich, because of an amoral disregard for anything but material gain. Such behavior is most evident in the Pennels—with their Newport "cottage"—being majority owners in some of the most overpopulated, crumbling, disease-ridden New York City slum buildings. Will becomes increasingly aware of the dichotomy between the haves and the have-nots. At Newport, Will had seen the total disregard for servants as people. It is Will's insistence that he, a medical student, rather than one of the horse grooms, treat a servant's broken leg that is the basis for his first serious argument with Laura. When she demands that he must never again do any more "horse doctoring" (371), Will had trouble understanding the Pennels' system of values—until he realized that, to them, Jackson wasn't a human being, but merely a servant (362).

To the parasitic rich, the fact that many of the workers and slum dwellers are recent immigrants is yet another cause for unconcern. When Will tells Laura, during their final conversation, that he plans to practice in the slums that provide her family with much of their wealth, she accuses him of "turning into a radical like that father of yours" (748). Her hysteria rises: "You're going to squander your life among a lot of foreigners . . . a—lot—of—dirty foreigners, they—aren't—even—Americans." Will faced her, "Yes they are. Better ones than you" (748).

Will, thus, speaks for Jakes. For, while neither romanticizes the immigrants or demonizes the rich, both call to mind the meaning of America to the immigrant. The mother of the baby Will and Drew delivered at Castle Garden could only murmur, like an invocation, a blessing, "*Born in America.*" The meaning of the Emma Lazarus poem on the

Statue of Liberty becomes clear to the two friends. They understand, having seen Castle Garden, that what many take for granted is a miracle: America is a haven unlike any other country in the world (394). And we too remember, as, with Julia, we watch Gideon staring out to the Atlantic, to Europe, that, like the founder of the Kent family, all our ancestors were immigrants.

Despite America's problems, despite its materialism, its social stratification, its apparent loss of idealism, the wonder of America as haven and fresh start infuses *The Americans* as it does earlier books in the Kent Family Chronicles. Despite bleak moments, both Gideon and Jakes share hope for America's future.

ALTERNATE PERSPECTIVE: NEW HISTORICISM

As in previous Kent Family Chronicle novels, the family in *The Americans* is a metaphor for the nation. Thus Gideon's question, "Can the family survive?," can be extrapolated to: Can the United States survive? Having withstood the apocalyptic division of the Civil War, in the waning years of the nineteenth century the country faces equally powerful threats: a seemingly irrevocable drift to materialism; an increasingly diverse population and the ugly concomitant bigotry; a diminution of America as the land of opportunity as the contrasts between the haves and have-nots become increasingly obvious; and, with increasing power among the unprincipled rich, an apparent denial of the promises of "liberty and justice for all."

These social and economic issues which Jakes explores make *The Americans* appropriate for New Historical analysis. For, quite unlike the New Critics (see Chapter 8), New Historicists treat a work of literature not so much as a transcendent document worthy, in its own right, of analysis, but rather as a representation of historical forces. The New Historicist examines the social, cultural, and historical implications of the text and often reads the literary work to uncover ideologies which illustrate culture and even law.

The New Historicist would read *The Americans* as an examination of the contrast between early American idealism and late nineteenth century materialism, between the individual in control of his own destiny and the individual submerged in the mass. Jakes argues, as did the muckrakers, a need for social reform if America is to be true to its principles.

Coined by Theodore Roosevelt, the term "muckraker" alludes to a character in Bunyan's *Pilgrim's Progress*, a man, "muck rake in hand," who was so busy raking filth that he couldn't raise his eyes to look up at nobler things. The muckrakers were the product of two separate phenomena: the reform movement and an emerging school of journalists who saw their function to be to report almost scientifically the conditions and the ills of an industrial America. The muckrakers included novelists as well as journalists; their techniques often bridged the two genres. The journalists would often utilize case histories of specific individuals, giving their readers a face with which they could identify; moreover, they often set these people in dramatic situations and provided interview-generated dialogue. The novelists often borrowed techniques from the journalists, most specifically, research upon which to build fact-based plot lines, and the use of statistics. Wherever there were social ills, the muckrakers' goals were to dig them up for public inspection. Subjects included business and political corruption, the exploitation of child labor, the filth of the meat packing industry, and horrendous slum conditions.

Though Theodore Roosevelt felt that the muckrakers could go too far, he knew firsthand many of the conditions about which they wrote. As New York City police commissioner (1895-1897), he invited Jacob Riis, the journalist-reformer, to accompany him on unannounced checks on city enforcement of health and safety regulations. Both Roosevelt and Riis figure significantly in *The Americans* to awaken Will's social conscience. Nor is it accidental that Gideon is portrayed as one of the new breed of journalists; in the chapters describing the Johnstown flood, he rails against irresponsible newspapers which inflame public opinion with invented stories (537).

This insistence on accuracy reflects one of Jakes' most strongly held beliefs—in the power of the printed word. It is, thus, intriguing to see how he integrates some of the muckrakers' beliefs and techniques in *The Americans*.

Theodore Roosevelt explains to Will one evening why he must return to public life, much as he loves his ranch. As Samuel Gompers had shown him, there's too much in need of reform: sweatshops, dirty, lightless tenement buildings, antiquated laws governing wages, hours, and working conditions. Roosevelt knows a man must accept his obligations to society; the poor are often too weak to protect themselves, and some of the rich, if not opposed, will exploit those weaknesses (230-31). Roosevelt supports his argument with the case of a little girl, eight or nine years old, beaten and nearly starved to death, who was brought into a

New York City court and legally declared an animal so she could get help under the laws protecting abused dogs (231). It is probable that Jakes got this detail while researching New York slum conditions, quite probably from reading muckraking journalists. In any event, the girl is illustrative of the muckraking technique of using case histories. Another technique is the use of statistics. We learn, along with Will, that in some New York slums, people are packed at a density of 350,000 per square mile, that the infant mortality rate of the Bend is four or five times that of the rest of the city, that the slums create half a million beggars, dooming charities to failure. It is Jacob Riis, author of *How the Other Half Lives*, who initiates Will into these statistics of shame. Jakes has incorporated two actual reformers to shape Will's conscience.

In addition, he frequently uses juxtaposition, one of the muckrakers' favorite tools, for making a point. The more closely two dissimilar things, ideas, or people can be juxtaposed, the surer the author can be that his reader will come to the desired conclusion. Thus two quite different doctors are made brothers—the Vlandinghams. The elder, Clement, chose to live and practice in the slums, where people need him. To his patients, he's a good man, a Christian who treats his patients without asking for payment (645). Clement, whose name, incidentally, means merciful, boils the polluted water he must use to clean wounds, shows compassion to an Italian immigrant dying of colon cancer, and has the courage to stand up to the local don, exploiter of his own people. The younger Vlandingham, Cyrus, conducts his practice among New York's elite (287). He views Lister's practice of using carbolic acid to prevent infections as "nonsense"; he scorns doctors who value their Hippocratic oath more highly than their investment portfolios (291). He views his brother as "misguided," "foolish," lacking "intelligence or self-esteem" for having chosen "like a madman or a hack" to practice in the slums. Not only do the Vlandinghams illustrate the polarity between those willing to exist as Society's parasites and those willing to serve society, but they also echo the dichotomy between Will's values and those of Carter, revealed when they meet again in San Francisco.

A second major juxtaposition is that between Newport and the Bend. In Maison du Soleil, the Pennels' summer "cottage," built by local and imported labor, the entrance door cost "a mere fifty thousand" (584). Wall facings include marble, inlays of green Spanish leather stamped in gold, panels of Circassian walnut, and mosaics carefully crafted in Italy (585). The tub in Will's guest bathroom has four taps—two for fresh water from cisterns, two for salt water from the ocean. (One can't forget the need to boil water in New York City slums so it can be safely drunk.) Nine gardeners are at work outside, transplanting, weeding, sweating. A "simple midday meal" is six courses served by liveried footmen under crystal chandeliers. Servants or townspeople are referred to as "oafs" or "clods" or "creatures"; to the Pennels, ordinary people are little more than animals. Gideon warns Will about people like the Pennels. He unequivocally believes that such people are a disgrace to the country, the antithesis of everything the Kents—and the nation—stand for. Only nominally Americans, they are more like the "rotten nobility old Philip despised and fought" (569).

In contrast are the residents of the Bend. Mostly recent Italian immigrants (Jakes emphasizes this by including untranslated Italian dialogue), they live in squalor and are often exploited by countrymen like Don Andreas Belsario. They eke out an existence picking rags or working in the city dump. Others sell sticks of stove kindling; carrots and cabbages black with mold; long loaves of bread already stale and crumbly; and big fish with iridescent, slimy scales from pushcarts (638). Crammed into tenements, six to twenty residents per room, they take relief from blistering, fetid summer heat on fire escapes, "verandas of the poor." These "verandas" look down on muddy courtyards filled with bales of rags, as well as garbage and dung, both human and animal (646). Cockroaches fall off the walls. Disease is rampant—smallpox, venereal disease, tuberculosis. Not only is infant mortality high, but some simply abandon their babies, like the feeble, dirt-encrusted four- or five-week-old Mrs. Grimaldi took home, trying to give it a fighting chance.

The contrast to Newport could not be more pronounced. Will, trying to choose which Vlandingham will be his professional model, can hardly believe that Newport and this neighborhood are both part of America (661).

But they are. Will's search for the truth takes him to Marcus Pennel's office—a room that could have held a dinner table seating thirty people. The room's fixtures of brass and marble and walnut include a twelve by six-foot map of lower Manhattan, the lower East Side studded with bright red and blue pins, each representing one of the Pennels' slum properties. Marcus, sweating in his opulent office during the summer heat, wishes he were at Newport, away from the city whose exploited slum dwellers have made his family's cottage possible. The scene in the office is a microcosm of the juxtaposition between Newport and the Bend. And Marcus' sneer that nothing bothers his conscience except "failure to earn maximum profits from the family's slum holdings" (709-

11) encapsulates the behavior and attitudes the muckrakers worked to change. They are attitudes which are anathema to Gideon—and to Jakes.

It is this juxtaposition of Newport and the Bend, of exploiters and the exploited, that reaffirms Will's decision to practice medicine among those who need him. It reaffirms the Kent family values of service and responsibility. And, in the context of this last book of the American Bicentennial Series, it reaffirms Jefferson's beliefs. As Gideon had insisted to Will, "Jefferson said men are naturally divided by temperament into two classes. Those who fear and distrust ordinary people, and want to concentrate power in the hands of a small, select elite—and those who trust and cherish ordinary people, and think of them as the safest, if not always the wisest repository of power" (567). These people—Roosevelt and Riis, Chris Tompkins and Lon Adam, Jo and Drew Hastings, Mrs. Grimaldi and her son Tomaso, Gideon and Julia—and Will and Eleanor—*these* are the Americans.

PART III

NEW BEGINNINGS

10

North and South
(1982),
Love and War
(1984),
and *Heaven and Hell*
(1987)

John Jakes' second major series consists of three novels: *North and South*, *Love and War*, and *Heaven and Hell*. Unlike the books of the Kent Family Chronicles, those of the North and South series demand that they be discussed together. Totalling 2,658 pages in the Dell North and South paperback editions, these novels are united by goal, genesis, structure, and philosophical and intellectual underpinnings.

The plan for the Kent Family Chronicles was to bring the Kent family from colonial times up to 1976, but *The Americans*, the last of the series, stopped ninety-plus years short of that goal. In contrast, the plan for the series beginning with *North and South* was for three novels "about a group of Americans caught up in the storm of events before, during and after the Civil War" (*North and South*, "Afterword," 809). With *Heaven and Hell*, the series concludes, having achieved its announced goals.

Originally Jakes planned to write one novel about a single military family during the Civil War. But, as he was doing research at the Library of the United States Military Academy at West Point, he encountered case after case of cadets, brothers in arms at the Academy who, when the nation was rent asunder, resolved personal dilemmas about their fundamental loyalties—to state or to nation—and ended up opposing one another on the battlefield. This historical reality led Jakes to create *two* families—the Mains of South Carolina and the Hazards of Pennsylvania—friends who became opponents though never quite enemies.

Thus, as he did so frequently in the Kent Family Chronicles, Jakes uses family as metaphor for the nation. In the prologue to *North and South*, Jakes establishes the two families, one laboring, one aristocratic, one northern, one southern, both seeking freedom and a new start; both Americans. The entire series explores the causes and consequences of "the central experience of the still-unfolding story of our republic . . . the War Between the States" (*North and South*, 809), which set American against American.

The historical significance of the Civil War binds the three books together. Many historians believe that the Civil War links the entirety of the American experience in a way no other event does. Others feel that the war "marks our national coming of age," a time in which we learned more about ourselves than in all the years since the first colonists arrived (*North and South*, 809). Jakes presents these insights not in relatively brief segments, but as part of a one or two generation continuous revelation. Though the three North and South novels can each stand alone, it is their collective impact that reveals much about who we are as a nation.

Jakes from the outset was conscious of the series as a tightly linked, structural whole: an examination of American life before (*North and South*), during (*Love and War*), and after (*Heaven and Hell*) the Civil War. In structural terms, the series thus has a clear sense of beginning, middle, and end. These are played out by theme (dissolution and separation—*N&S*; change and slaughter—*L&W*; Reconstruction and possible reconciliation—*H&H*); by the historical reality of almost unending warfare during the period (the Mexican War—*N&S*, the Civil War itself—*L&W*, and the Indian Wars—*H&H*); and by the unfolding lives of the Mains and the Hazards.

Frequently asked which side he took on the Civil War, Jakes replied, "The side of those who suffered. The side of those who lost their lives in battle, and those who lost their lives more slowly, but no less surely, in bondage" (*North and South*, 810-11). This compassion for those who suffer further unites the three volumes of this series.

Finally, reflecting on the series, Jakes notes "the tragic paradox" controlling its forty-one year span (1842-1883): "The schism should not have happened, and it had to happen" (*North and South*, 811). This "tragic paradox" allows for an almost archetypal reading of the Civil War, the loss as a nation of innocence and idealism, the inevitability of personal—and national—dilemmas, and the almost Biblical opposition of good and evil made more complex by all the intervening shades of gray. These concepts are dramatized by continuing plot lines, characters, and themes from the first novel of the series to the last. Thus the discussion which follows will integrate all three works: *North and South, Love and War,* and *Heaven and Hell.*

PLOT DEVELOPMENT

When, in 1842, young George Hazard of Lehigh Station, Pennsylvania, intervenes to even the odds in a free-for-all fight between New York stevedores and the sixteen-year-old Orry Main from South Carolina, the seeds of friendship are planted which will bind their two families together for the next forty years. Both George and Orry have come to West Point because it provides the "best scientific education available in America" (*North and South,* 43). They survive summer encampment, learn to live a life regulated by the drum, yearn for food and home and leisure, and avoid dismissal for an excess number of demerits. Along the way, "common hopes and hardships forged a strong bond of affection" between them (*North and South,* 72).

George and Orry, upon graduation, are assigned to the infantry and sent to Mexico to participate in "Mr. Polk's war." There, Orry is hit by a shell which takes off his left hand and forearm; his longed-for military career at an end, he returns to Mont Royal, the Main family rice plantation near Charleston, South Carolina. George returns to Lehigh Valley and the family ironworks. To Lehigh he soon brings Constance Flynn, despite local prejudice against Irish Catholics. Until Constance's death, their marriage will be a happy, growing, supporting relationship. Orry, however, is not as lucky, for the woman he fell in love with during leave from West Point, Madeline Fabray, was, at the time of their meeting, on her way to marry another local planter, Justin LaMotte. Until LaMotte's death, Orry and Madeline carry on a guilt-ridden, passionate but platonic affair, for LaMotte was, at best, a cruel and abusive husband.

As he so frequently does, Jakes interweaves many other characters' lives with the central ones. Stanley Hazard, several years older than George, is, by comparison, ineffectual, unimaginative, and pusillanimous. His wife Isabel, however, has brass enough for both, propelling him into Republican politics when George supplants him in the family business. Following Simon Cameron to Washington, D.C., Stanley spends much of the Civil War in a series of jobs as a minor government functionary. With Isabel's goading and corrupt political connections, and despite the obvious conflict of interest, Stanley gets the contract for supplying shoddy shoes to *both* armies. Stanley and Isabel, while not illustrations of consummate evil, do illustrate the horde of profiteers who saw the war as a means to amass fortunes while others died.

Their sister Virgilia is a woman driven, an example of those of passionate beliefs incapable of admitting the possibility of compromise. An ardent abolitionist, she is unable to understand George's friendship with Orry, whose family owns slaves. During the Civil War, she too goes to Washington, and serves as a nurse. Although her single-minded devotion to her cause leads her to intentionally cause the death of a wounded Confederate soldier, Virgilia gradually begins to mellow, her hatred submerged in service. Becoming involved in a home for orphaned children of slaves, she replaces hatred of slaveholders, and, by extension, all southerners, with love of individual black children; her early vituperative oratory is replaced by loving care. And, after the war is over, she marries a Negro cavalryman; together they face outrage, even in the North, toward their mixed marriage.

Visits exchanged between the Mains and the Hazards at Newport and Mont Royal allow the younger generation to get to know each other, too. Orry's sisters, Ashton and Brett, are strikingly different. The former is a tease, "manipulating others while pretending to play the traditional feminine role" (*North and South*, 457). Even as a teenager, she saw her body as a weapon which she would willingly use to achieve what she wanted. Brett, in comparison, at fifteen demanded that Orry give her authority to help him run Mont Royal; she's responsible, intelligent, and concerned for others' welfare, willing, for example, to lance boils on slaves. Ashton clearly stated their contrast: "Those who mean to rise in the world don't waste time on the problems of niggers and white trash. They court the important people" (*North and South*, 458). Ashton sets her sights on Billy Hazard—not out of love but because of the family's wealth. Also at Mont Royal is Cousin Charles, orphaned when his parents went down in a shipwreck off Hatteras. Originally allowed to run wild on the plantation, Charles becomes something of a rebel. While still a boy, he objected to the plantation overseer's treatment of one of Mont Royal's slaves. He didn't understand why some men were free and others enslaved just because of their color. Though he believed such a system was "unjust, even barbaric," he also realized that it was "immutable and universal" (*North and South*, 84). He is, then, even as a boy, idealistic but not quixotic, traits which will intensify and deepen through his adult life. Finally taken in hand by Orry, Charles becomes more mature and responsible, and, like Billy Hazard—and George and Orry before them—gains admission to West Point. There Charles and Billy further cement the Main-Hazard friendship.

Billy's earlier rejection of Ashton for Brett set off a whole series of events which will contribute themes of jealousy, maliciousness, and revenge to the rest of the series. During a family visit by Orry, Ashton, and Brett to the Academy, Ashton's promiscuity first becomes apparent, beginning her penchant for collecting fly buttons from every man with whom she has had sex, a collection eventually numbering in the hundreds. Her wanton lovemaking with six or seven cadets resulted in pregnancy, which, because of her engagement to James Huntoon, had to be terminated. Her scheming with one of Brett's old suitors to kill Billy and Brett as they set out on their honeymoon is punished, irrevocably, by Orry, who expels Ashton forever from the plantation—and from the family (*North and South*, 761). Despite his firmness, Orry can't comprehend his sister's behavior. Charles, however, can: her common sense is consumed by a desire for power (*North and South*, 761). For the rest of the novels, Ashton is in pursuit of power, personal or political. Briefly, as her husband James takes positions of power in Richmond as part of the Confederate bureaucracy, she's satisfied. But he is far too ineffectual for her—both sexually and politically. Eventually she becomes involved with her lover in a plot to assassinate Jefferson Davis and then, as the South's military position worsens, to establish a new Confederacy in the Southwest. Surviving her lover—and the Confederacy—Ashton eventually amasses enough money to implement her plans for revenge on Orry (and by extension Madeline) for expelling her from Mont Royal.

In the meantime, many Mains and Hazards have been sucked into the maelstrom of the Civil War. Charles, who had resigned his army commission, joined Wade Hampton's Legion. A professional army man among gentlemen, a realist purged of romance, he fought at Bull Run and Antietam Creek and Gettysburg; he slept in the saddle, suffered from dysentery, picked off lice, and wrote letters—too many letters—to the families of fallen soldiers. He maintained his sanity with the love of a Virginia widow, Augusta Barclay, courageous enough to smuggle quinine for the Confederacy, to continue managing her farm as armies battled back and forth across it, and to break with Charles—who was determined to go down with the Confederacy, abandoning all else, including Augusta—without telling him she was pregnant with his child.

Billy, after recovering from the wounds received on the eve of his honeymoon, left his bride Brett at the Hazard house in Lehigh Station, and was assigned as an engineer to building and repairing bridges. Captured by Mosby's Rangers, he was sent to Libby Prison in Richmond, where, with other Union prisoners, he was the victim of the psychopathic Corporal Vesey, whose behavior violated all the rules of warfare. Billy survived six months of starvation, overcrowding, disease, brutality, and torture. He wrote in his secret journal that, after being required to obey any order, however demeaning, after having "dwelt a while in the soul of a shackled black man," he understands how the "enslaved negro" feels (*Love and War*, 732). His understanding is visceral, physical, powerful, quite different from his sister Virgilia's earlier abstractions.

Secret—and dangerous—communication between George and Orry, working in their respective capitals, initiated a plan for Billy's rescue. Orry forged papers for the prisoner's release; Charles carried them out, in the process killing the sadistic guard. The bonds of family—and the friendships forged at West Point—hold, despite the fundamental changes the war has wrought.

During most of the war George Hazard and Orry Main were at government jobs in Washington and Richmond, respectively. George, a major in ordnance, became disillusioned with the venality, corruption, and politicking—and "all the money being made from death and suffering" (*Love and War*, 658); he grew increasingly angry at profiteers like his brother Stanley, building fortunes on soldiers' misery. Nor could he condone the arrest and beating of critics of War Department policy, the so-called peace Democrats (*Love and War*, 506). With a great sense of relief, he left Washington's Byzantine politics to do honest work on the military railroads.

Orry, too, grew increasingly appalled at political machinations in Richmond, at plots to kill Jefferson Davis, at the existence of hell-holes like the Libby Prison. When it became clear that the fall of Richmond was imminent, he packed Madeline off to the Hazard home in Pennsylvania and returned to active duty. On the day before Christmas, while on patrol, he came across a gut-shot Union soldier. Overcoming his caution to help the man, he was shot; Orry died instantly, the top of his head blown away.

Cooper Main perhaps changed most. Before the war he'd often argued with his father, Tillet, over the evils of slavery. Estranged for philosophical reasons, he'd left the plantation to establish the Carolina Shipping Company in Charleston. His marine expertise meant that when the war broke out, he was tapped to contribute his services to the Confederate navy. Having designed blockade runners in England, he was returning to Charleston aboard a boat smuggling luxuries to a Confederacy in dire need of war materiel. The boat, incidentally owned by his sister Ashton and her lover-conspirator, exploded while evading Union ships blockading the harbor. Cooper's son Judah died, scalded. Cooper had learned, too well, the lesson that Orry and George knew, that the war gave the unscrupulous opportunity for vast profit while others died. From that moment, Cooper changed. Guilt-ridden and withdrawn, Cooper became more and more rigid and conservative. From a man who'd argued against slavery and who'd agreed to aid the Confederate navy solely out of love of his home state, he became, during Reconstruction, more rabid than early secessionists. Although he gave Orry's widow, Madeline, the opportunity to manage the plantation, he was adamantly opposed to the school she established to help prepare ex-slaves for a life of freedom. Not only did he fail to protect her from the depredations of the Ku Klux Klan, but ultimately he barred her from his Charleston home.

Madeline, who had spent the last years of the war at the Hazards' Lehigh Valley home, returned to the devastation of South Carolina, vowing that, as a memorial to Orry, she would rebuild the great house at Mont Royal, destroyed in an unholy uprising of freed slaves, army deserters, and rootless whites. Throughout *Heaven and Hell* her journal reveals the challenges which beset her. Her efforts are made far more difficult because, in Richmond, Ashton had spitefully revealed Madeline's past, a past she'd told Orry about before their marriage. For Madeline Fabray, from New Orleans, was "not French or Spanish but Octoroon. . . . Being one-eighth Negro, however light the skin, is exactly the same as being all Negro" (*North and South*, 691). Ashton's revelations about Madeline's past made life exceedingly difficult for her in the South of Reconstruction. Indeed, her heritage became one of the issues separating her from Cooper, providing yet another indication of how much he'd changed.

Charles Main, a burned-out veteran of the horrors of war, realized that amputating and cauterizing the love he and Augusta Barclay had shared was the worst mistake of his life. Arriving at her farm, he found it deserted. Remembering, finally, the name of an uncle, Jack Duncan, a brigadier in the Union army, he sought him out, making contact just before the older man left for a posting with the Plains cavalry. From Duncan, Charles learned that he was the father of a son, that Augusta had died soon after childbirth, and that he must choose whether to play a role in his son's life. To be nearer to the boy, Charles also opted for the West.

He lied to get into the cavalry; West Point officers who had served in the Confederacy were not acceptable. Having assumed the name Charles

May, he pretended to have no prior experience, until he ran into Captain Harry Venable, whom, back at West Point, Charles had repeatedly put on report. Working out his vengeance, Venable and a pack of others left Charles near death from a beating. He was nursed back to health by a trader, Wooden Foot, who proposed that Charles join up with his trading company. Not only did Wooden Foot teach Charles survival skills— reading sign, the rudiments of Indian languages and culture—but, gradually, he brought him back from the dark depths to which he'd sunk during the war and the darker ones after the news of Augusta's death. Thus, when a party of nine Cheyenne in full war regalia arrived to settle old grievances, Charles fought fiercely. By the time a lightning strike ignited a prairie fire, causing the Cheyenne to flee, Wooden Leg was dead and his retarded nephew was split from throat to groin, the cavity stuffed with the body of their border collie. It was Sharpsburg, it was Northern Virginia all over again. Charles left the killing field with one vow: to kill Cheyenne.

Once again under an assumed name, Charles August, and with the help of Brigadier Duncan and Col. Benjamin Grierson, he joined a unit of black troops, anathema to many officers. He molded them into an effective fighting force—their mission to protect the settlers, the travel routes, and the railroad construction crews. Again encountering Venable, Charles barely avoided imprisonment and a dishonorable discharge. Though out of the army, he maintained his vow to avenge Wooden Foot's death, and, despite the growing love he felt for Willa Parker, a young actress in St. Louis who abhorred the government policy toward the Indians as well as Charles' bloodthirstiness, he returned to the Plains, this time as a scout with Custer. He left his son with the Brigadier. However, the massacre at Washita, the attack on the village of Black Kettle, who had sued for peace, the slaughter of women and children and old men sickened him. He had been wrong in seeking revenge, he now believed. He didn't belong in South Carolina, or in the U.S. Army, carrying out federal policy. "There was no place for him in all the world" (*Heaven and Hell*, 562).

For all the Mains and Hazards, there is a single mad antagonist, Elkanah Bent, who has nursed hatred of both families ever since being expelled from West Point as a result of what he believed was entrapment by George and Orry. Never very competent, a failure at leadership, Bent nonetheless believes himself to be the American Napoleon, and through high political connections, always manages to avoid the discharge he deserves. We wonder for years about the source of his protection and his madness; only much later do we learn that both spring from his birth; he is the illegitimate son of Lincoln's wife's sister, conceived during an incestuous assault on her. Bent seems omnipresent, an enduring personification of absolute evil. His incompetent command nearly causes Orry and George to be killed in the incident in Mexico that results in the loss of Orry's arm; Bent is in Texas when Charles serves there, trying more than once to kill him during skirmishes with the Indians; the hatred had grown even more intense when Charles had rejected his homosexual advances. In New Orleans, seeing a portrait of Madeline's mother in Madame Conti's house, he deduced the connection with the Mains and filed it away as a future weapon. As George was beginning to make a peacetime success, Bent, by now quite mad, slit Constance's throat and left his name in blood on the bedroom mirror. (George fled to Europe, where he remained for years in a near-vegetative stupor, caring about nothing.) And, having learned of the existence of Charles' son Gus, he kidnaps the boy from Fort Leavenworth and heads for Indian Territory, planning to kill the boy and send him, piece by piece, to Charles. Only after Charles tracks him and hangs him are the families free of this insidious evil.

Only gradually do the two families heal from all the traumas they have suffered. And, as the families function as a metaphor for the country, their reunion at George's invitation to the Centennial Exposition in Philadelphia is symbolic of the coming together of the nation after the war. There the wonders of postwar America are displayed—technology and agriculture and arts; the new America is a force to be reckoned with in the modern world. And the families, whose friendship survived the war, come—from all over the country: Madeline from South Carolina (Cooper wasn't invited), Charles and Willa and Gus from their Texas ranch, Billy and Brett and their seven children from California, George's son William and his wife from Ohio, Patricia and her newspaper editor husband and their three children, and Virgilia and her husband, Scipio Brown.

All of them are aware, as was George when he emerged, Lazarus-like, healed from his great depression, of the depths they and their nation have escaped. All have known pain.

> *The pain . . . from understanding what we've lost. . . . from knowing how foolish we were. . . . from knowing how fragile and doomed the old ways were. . . . from knowing we can never be children again.*
> Losing innocence. Remembering heaven.
> That was the essence of hell. (*Heaven and Hell*, 712-13)

But they all knew, too, that they could only resume their lives, for there was nothing else to do. And so, no one is surprised, as the final act of re-union of North and South, Hazards and Mains, when George and his best friend Orry's widow, Madeline, plan to marry, to start a new life, as has the nation.

Jakes controls this incredibly complex plot, these forty-one years of American history, carefully. He uses historical events as a chronological framework. The Hazards and Mains, like hundreds of thousands of other ordinary Americans, were riven by great passions, did their duty, died horribly, were greedy and heroic and vicious and venal and loving and forgiving. Some were destroyed; some prospered; most simply survived and went on. Jakes lets his readers participate in unifying the plot when he shows the extraordinary similarity between North and South in Orry's and George's careers; when he underscores the parallels between Lincoln and Davis as they dealt with conniving underlings and electorates which condemned them; when he unifies what might be fragmentary narrative by devices such as Billy's journal in *Love and War* or Madeline's in *Heaven and Hell*; and when he has characters wake from nightmares—Orry's dream of the drum (*North and South*, 206), Lincoln's strange, doomed dreams, George's nightmares of the picnicking civilians' retreat from Manassas (*Love and War*, 310-11), Charles' nightmare of Sport's death and an inferno of fire and bayonets ripping his guts (*Heaven and Hell*, 15-16)—which, like a demented mosaic, are the collective metaphor for the nightmare of the Civil War.

Jakes unifies the narrative by questions such as that Madeline posed in her journal entry for April 1867: "I wonder if there is any end to the rancor caused by the war?" (*Heaven and Hell*, 300), or by his own underlying question: How, in the face of absolute evil, which truly exists, can good people endure? He unifies it by continuing all his major characters, save Orry—who lives, in a way, in Madeline's need to speak to him in her journal—from the beginning of *North and South* to the end of *Heaven and Hell*. He unifies it by the exploration of a series of themes, to be dealt with later, which are not exhausted in any one book. He unifies it with a whole series of chapter or book epigraphs, distilling those themes to an aphorism, the quotation itself linking his fictional characters who dramatize the idea to the historical figures who uttered the observation in the first place. And, architecturally, he unifies it with the epilogue to *Heaven and Hell*, where Charles and Billy, having brought *their* sons, Gus and G. W., to West Point in 1883, remember all that has happened—"so many births. . . . So many deaths. So important. So inconsequential" (*Heaven and Hell*, 773)—since the first Hazards and Mains met at the Plain above the Hudson in the summer of 1842.

CHARACTER DEVELOPMENT

A reader of John Jakes is aware that his plots are character-driven and that he frequently makes the central family a metaphor for the nation. Thus a discussion of character can effectively link discussions of plot and theme. Jakes notes this explicitly in the afterword to *Love and War*. After observing that the book is not intended to demonstrate that war is hell or to prove that slavery was our greatest national crime—though he believes both to be true—he states that the book, and the series, by extension, is meant to explicate the "greatest redefinition of America, in the shortest time, that we have ever experienced: the Civil War" (*Love and War*, 1089).

He chooses to convey this change, however, in a manner different from those of the military historians whom he has researched carefully. Jakes quotes the librarian-scholar Richard H. Shryock: "historians might . . . [better] picture reality and convey a sense of the costs [of the Civil War] if, in describing campaigns, they gave less space to tactics and more to . . . the camps and hospitals" (*Love and War*, 1080-81). This comment is, in many ways, a distillation of the philosophy underlying all Jakes' historical novels; it certainly constitutes his marching orders for the North and South books. It is the reason, as Jakes writes, that "there is less here about generals than about soldiers of lower rank tending their horses, losing company elections, getting ill, feeling homesick, reading tracts and pornography, scrounging food, sewing clothes, scratching lice" (*Love and War*, 1081). Thus, in these novels, although we see the darkly haunted Lincoln, the erratically egotistical Custer, and a host of other historical figures—J.E.B. Stuart and Louisa May Alcott, Sam Grant and Mathew Brady, Stonewall Jackson and Buffalo Bill Cody—the focus is on the "little people," real and fictional. These people, for the most part, do not claim even footnotes in history, but they are the people whose side Jakes takes: "the side of those who suffered" (*North and South*, 810).

To provide himself with a broad canvas for this portrayal, Jakes makes both of his fictional families fairly prolific. Gus, the son of Charles and Augusta Barclay, and Charles himself are the only only children. One generation of the Hazards includes Stanley, George, Virgilia, and Billy; the same generation of the Mains includes Orry, Cooper, Ashton, Brett, and Charles. Not only is this an honest rendering of mid-nineteenth century demographics, but this multiplicity of central characters and their plot lines allows Jakes to convey a spectrum of Civil War America. The number of people readers get to know increases geometrically as we meet all the people our nine central figures meet, casually or intimately. We meet some only briefly, as in vignettes. One such example is the nameless Union cavalryman who shoots Orry Main. In contrast, we know far more about Wooden Foot, who, at least momentarily, begins Charles' recovery from the horrors of the Civil War; consequently we share Charles' outrage at his death and we understand Charles' need to "kill Indians."

Jakes reveals his characters through a variety of techniques. The first of these is through their responses to crises or trauma. Ashton Main, though somewhat of an oversexed minx even before her rejection by Billy Hazard, responds to her thwarted first love with greater promiscuity and a desire for revenge which essentially neutralizes any principles she may originally have had, allowing her to engage in wartime profiteering, carry on an affair with Lamar Powell, be on the periphery of plans to assassinate Jefferson Davis, and attempt to wrest the family plantation from her brother's widow, Madeline, who has restored it from wartime ruin. Cooper's loss of his son Judah seems to be the central catalyst for his change from an idealistic young man to a bitter middle-aged one, unable or unwilling to accept his sister-in-law in his home or to protect her from the Ku Klux Klan. George, after Constance's slaughter by Bent, becomes almost aphasic, fleeing to isolate himself in Europe, where he sees no one, does nothing, and seems to care about nothing; his essential strength of character is evident in the fact that, for less clearly defined reasons, he once again takes control of his life and eventually brings the two extended families together at the Centennial Exposition, thus signaling a reunion, a bridging of the national schisms caused by the Civil War.

Jakes also reveals character by those beliefs and causes to which individuals dedicate their lives and loyalty. At times their intensity reaches fanatic proportions, especially in *North and South*, where characters illustrate and symbolize strongly held positions, honestly espoused by people of good faith, positions often idealistic, patriotic, or ethical, which so divided the country, casting it into the cauldron of civil war. Virgilia, for example, does bad things in a good cause; a harshly outspoken advocate of abolition, she runs roughshod over family and friends who do not share her beliefs; she is an advocate of the end justifying the means.

She, too, is one of those characters who change as, gradually, she learns that love of individual black children who need her care is more important than hate toward slaveholders. George and his best friend Orry believe passionately that, whatever their regional loyalties and duties, their friendship, their family, *must* survive the war. This faith is sorely tested, first by Orry's death and then by Constance's murder, but its strength is reaffirmed at the reunion of both families at the Centennial Exposition. The symbolism is obvious. As the Mains and Hazards are metaphors for the nation, bonds stretched and nearly sundered during the war are once again knit together. The families' friendship—and the nation—endure.

But, while Jakes presents the almost phoenix-like reemergence of America from Civil War ashes, he quite consciously tries to avoid the mythologizing tendencies to which many novelists, film makers, and Americans in general have succumbed. He writes:

> As a people, we all tend to be myth makers as the generations pass. Thus our icon version of Lincoln is forever the all-knowing, eternally calm idealist and humanitarian, rather than the doubt-ridden, depressive, and widely hated political pragmatist who was lifted to greatness by necessity and his own conscience. Our Lee is the eternally benign hero seated on Traveller, not a soldier whose ability was suspect, whose decisions were often questioned, and who received the scorn of many fellow Confederates. . . . We mythologize not only individuals but also the war itself. Perhaps . . . our . . . quite natural human tendency to prefer the glamorous to the gory [has] . . . put a patina on the war. To render it romantic. It was— for about ninety days. After that came horror. And the horror grew. (*Love and War*, 1083)

Although John Jakes is not a revisionist historian, he *is* a demythologizer. For perhaps his overarching theme—demonstrated by plot lines and character development—is the moral, political, physical, and emotional suffering that permeated the Civil War era.

THEMATIC ISSUES

While suffering may be an overarching theme for all three novels, each individual novel has its own controlling theme. For *North and South* it is disintegration, dislocation, and division. We see this in politics, as arguments over slavery, but, more especially, over states' rights, drive a wedge between North and South. We see it also in the cultural and economic differences between North and South. The South, an agrarian society in a world increasingly dominated by technology and manufacturing, is a region dangerously infused with the romance of Sir Walter Scott, using arrogance as a defense mechanism against a growing sense of inferiority. Cooper Main sums it up from the point of view of an enlightened Southerner: "We aren't attuned to the times" (*North and South*, 81). His father's strong objection—"Hold your tongue. Southerners don't speak against their homeland"—demonstrates another sort of rift increasingly evident in the novel—within individuals and families. "The son was caught and squeezed—between his own convictions and his eternal inability to change [his father's] mind" (*North and South*, 81).

Everywhere there are dilemmas and dichotomies: between well-meaning idealists and fanatics; between social classes, illustrated by the workers' hovels, the larger frame or brick residences of Lehigh Station's mercantile community, and the spectacular mountainside home of the Hazard family; between West Point graduates and non-Academy officers; and ultimately, tragically, between region and region. Such divisions continue through all three volumes.

The central theme of *Love and War* is change, the cataclysmic, earth-shattering change underscored by carnage and slaughter. We see the growing sense of despair on both sides as battle flags are bloodied, casualties mount, symbolized by growing mountains of amputated limbs at battlefield surgical stations, and thoughtful people reexamine their convictions. And the carnage continues into *Heaven and Hell*, though the scene of slaughter may have shifted to the West. There the psychological wounds of war continue to haunt the survivors, and, although there's the symbolic reconciliation of the families at the Centennial Exposition, the news of the Battle of the Little Big Horn interrupts the nation's celebration of healing and hope and calls attention, dramatically and ironically, to yet other schisms, wars, and antipathies which will require reconciliation.

Unifying Motifs

Recurring motifs also unify all three novels. The first of these is the United States Military Academy at West Point. First and foremost, West

Point is presented in 1842, and more so in 1883, as providing a rigorous education preparing young Americans for military leadership. It is a society stressing equality amid excellence; despite political connections which might result in a young man's appointment, he was admitted to the entering class only by his personal efforts at surviving summer encampment; he had to earn the right to be the lowest of the low, a plebe. West Point forged a band of brothers who shared more, as initiates and survivors of the system, than did most actual brothers. The friendship born between Orry and George at the Academy was thus more powerful than that between Stanley and George Hazard. This bond was further intensified by the Academy honor code, the result of which was that every cadet and graduate could depend on every other, could accept his word. The bonds hold even despite war. And so, one Academy man looked after another, as the Confederates Orry and Charles engineered the Yankee Billy's escape from Libby Prison. The extended family between Mains and Hazards had been created at the Academy; Billy's marriage to Brett only strengthened it. When Charles had first met Augusta in her role of quinine smuggler, he used this bond—and the code of honor—to prevent her capture by the Union Lieutenant Prevo. Having ordered Augusta to hide in the barn, Charles could assert, "I give you my word, there's no such person [as a female smuggler] inside this house. . . . My word as an officer and an Academy man." And Lieutenant Prevo accepts it: "Capt. Main, I accept your word and thank you for your gentlemanly co-operation" (*Love and War*, 166). Charles has punctiliously avoided lying; he speaks the truth with impeccable precision. We learn much later that Prevo knew exactly what was going on, but the code of officers and gentlemen, the bond between Academy graduates, prevented his calling Charles out.

The bond, of course, often brings friction between those who are and those who are not Academy graduates, the perhaps inevitable envy of the elite. In addition, nongraduates were even more likely to label southern graduates who chose to defend their states as traitors. This is especially evident in the arguments in Congress about closing the Academy, that "nest of traitors" (*Love and War*, 480ff.). Yet another illustration of this sense of betrayal is the insurmountable barrier erected against Academy graduates who had served the Confederacy being pardoned and allowed to enter the postwar army on the Plains. Charles had to lie, pretend total lack of experience, and assume false names to get in; and, when his true identity was discovered, he was dismissed, lucky to avoid imprisonment.

Finally, of course, the West Point motif provides structural unity to the series. In the epilogue to *Heaven and Hell* Charles and Billy take their sons Gus and G. W. to West Point in 1883; the epigraph for this section is the exact dialogue from Chapter 1 of *North and South* (42), when George and Orry met in 1842.

The second such motif, literally appropriate in a war in which cavalry played such an important role, was the horses. Jakes himself notes that he uses the horses as metaphor for the apocalyptic change in America (*Heaven and Hell*, 775). He cites two images. The first is that of a beautiful sunny meadow, across which five black horses gallop, "splendid coats shining, manes and tails streaming" (*Love and War*, 22). The second image is after the war as Charles goes west in search of his son. He rides the railroad, the iron horse (a hint of technology which will soon dominate warfare?). Because his attention was elsewhere, "he didn't see [outside the window] the . . . feasting buzzards disturbed by the train and swirling upward, away from the rotting remains of a black horse" (*Love and War*, 1078). In between, horse images relentlessly illustrate the inexorable change, the incredible slaughter that was the Civil War.

The matched horses of the Black Horse Cavalry had quickly become "an assortment of nags," the original horses "lost to disease, poor care . . . and enemy fire" (*Love and War*, 319). One of the most shocking passages is the discovery of a "scene of horror" which caused a battle-hardened veteran to throw up "all over his own shotgun, saddle, and surprised horse": a field in which 168-180 horses have been shot, their carcasses a "fantastic sculpture of fly-covered horses heaped upon one another" (*Love and War*, 819), left because "the Yanks must have decided a horse herd would slow down [their] retreat" (*Love and War*, 819). Charles reported on the scene to Wade Hampton: "I've shot injured horses but never foundering ones. To kill fine animals wantonly is even worse. It's a sin" (*Love and War*, 819). The implicit analogy with slaughtered soldiers is powerful.

It is intensified by the bond developed between horse and rider. Several times (*North and South*, 477; *Love and War*, 624) man and horse are referred to as a centaur, that perfectly fused mythological creature. Charles had developed a "strong and unexpected liking for the quirky little gray" (*Love and War* 159), Sport. Early in the novel he fed the gelding molasses for extra energy, rubbed him down with the softest blanket he could find, and brought him treats (160). Later, evading a much larger body of Union cavalry, Sport jumps a fallen tree trunk Charles hadn't seen. "At the top of the arc his heart nearly burst with love. He was

riding the strongest, bravest horse on God's earth" (*Love and War*, 328).
The bond between cavalryman and mount is as strong as the bond between West Point grads. When, during action in Texas, Charles' troop is
caught in an ice storm and the sergeant's horse breaks his leg, Charles
shoots him, for his rider cannot; afterward, "Sergeant Breedlove covered
his face with his hands and cried" (*North and South*, 569). So close is the
bond between Charles and Sport that often "the gray seemed nearly
ready to speak" (*Love and War*, 160). As the numbing effects of the war
make it more and more difficult for Charles to communicate with Augusta, she notes, "You still have Sport" (*Love and War*, 880). What was
originally only a man/mount relationship has become Charles' only
emotional outlet; having parted from Augusta, he has only Sport to love,
and so the horse's death, after heroically rescuing Charles despite his
own mortal wound, leaves Charles kneeling bareheaded by the animal,
wanting to cry—but unable, "purged, dead" inside (*Love and War*, 929).

Because of this extraordinarily tight bond, all references to the slaughter of horses serve as a metaphor for the slaughter of humans in this
war. The worsening conditions and the shortage of war material, especially hard on the South, are underscored by the horses' condition—
becoming ever more gaunt as feed is unavailable; moreover, absence
even of forage for the horses demonstrates war's ravaging of the coun-
tryside. The psychological stress of the war is demonstrated by the young
soldier pounding a wounded horse's head into a bloody mass during
the retreat from Manassas (*Love and War*, 201); it is a scene that haunts
Charles in recurring nightmares as he becomes more and more emotionally fragile (*Love and War*, 310). Horses also serve to illustrate changing
national policy. The vaunted Black Horse Cavalry that struck terror into
the North early in the war (*Love and War*, 199) is replaced, as a catalyst
for fear, by the black horsemen of the Fifth Massachusetts Colored Cavalry (*Love and War*, 986). The battle of the buffalo soldiers of the Seventh
Cavalry for respect among their army colleagues demonstrates the residual racism even after the war. And finally, Custer's order to slaughter
800 Cheyenne horses at Washita, after burning tents and food supplies
(*Heaven and Hell*, 552-57), demonstrates what many view as a policy of
genocide during the Indian wars.

Significantly, all of these horse references are linked to another image
of destruction, division, and devastation, presented early, in "Ashes of
April," the prologue to *Love and War*. One of George Hazard's reliable
workmen at the iron foundry had discovered his much younger cousin
making love to his wife. That infidelity ("a house divided against it-

self"?) resulted in a stabbing and a fire which consumed both the house and its inhabitants. The apocalyptic foreshadowing of all that will follow is evident in Jakes' description of the scene. Spectators and firefighters dash back and forth, silhouetted by the blaze. The fire's "red light" reflected on the metalwork of the "outmoded . . . pump engine and on the black coats of the four horses" (a suggestion of the Four Horsemen of the Apocalypse?), that had pulled the fire equipment to the site; they "pawed and snorted like fearsome animals from hell." To George the scene suggested nothing but hell. It "conjured strange specters. Not merely fire. Death. Suffering. Loss. And, in overpowering summation, war" (*Love and War*, 11-12).

These motifs reinforce a theme running through these three books: Jakes' certainty of the existence of absolute evil. He has written: "Somewhere [between 1960 and 1965] I came to the conclusion that, yes, absolute evil (in human form) does exist—with no redeeming 'causes,' excuses, or other ameliorating aspects. It may be relatively rare, but I believe it's with us. Look at the pathological Nazis for an obvious example" (letter, 9 July 1995).

It is probable that, in Jakes' philosophy, the killing soldiers do in time of war is not synonymous with "absolute evil." Their "evil"—for rarely can killing be considered absolute good—is ameliorated in part because it may produce, on balance, a greater benefit than would passivity or inaction. Additionally, most soldiers kill out of self-defense, because to refuse would be to violate a direct order, or to accomplish a governmental policy, not because they enjoy killing. It is true that such observations may be complicated by philosophical considerations of whether the end justifies the means and by the legal precedents set at the Nuremberg trials following World War II. Nonetheless, it is doubtful whether deaths resulting from battle—not from massacres—in these novels, even the emotionally wrenching death of Orry Main, are presented by Jakes as acts of absolute evil.

Other acts, however, seem tainted with evil. What of the political ambitions of Simon Cameron, Stanley Hazard, and George Armstrong Custer—all of whom, at least occasionally, violated conventional standards of ethics and morality? What of all those war profiteers who not only made fortunes during the war, but, worse, did so by providing shoddy shoes, sure to make life even more miserable for front-line soldiers—or shells, pitted and patched, sure to explode prematurely, causing absolutely purposeless, meaningless deaths? Ashton Main has a liberal dose of original sin, exaggerated by jealousy and revenge. Elkanah Bent, in his inexorable pursuit of any Main or Hazard who crosses his path, seems a likely candidate for one totally evil. He is sexually evil, not only making unwanted homosexual advances toward Charles, but also willing and able to cheat and abuse women. He is true to no cause save himself, and he is incapable of seeing himself truly, always believing that his destiny as the American Bonaparte has been thwarted by others, who thus deserve to die. Killing, for him, is not an unfortunate necessity in a larger cause; it is merely an expedient, often orgasmic, for his own advancement and satisfaction. Like Custer, he has no compunction about wreaking violence on women and children, and his sadomasochistic fantasy of sending Charles his son Gus, piece by piece, is an obvious example of consummate cruelty. The only ameliorating condition for Bent is probable insanity, a fact we recognize when we learn of his parentage (*Heaven and Hell*, 435-39). He is truly bent. Whether insanity excuses him or not, it does not dilute the absolute evil with which Elkanah Bent corrupts his world. In addition, though he is a minor character, Corporal Vesey, the guard at the Libby Prison who pokes Billy with a bayonet, stomps on his hand with hobnailed boots, intercepts his letters to loved ones, and tortures him by tying him to an artillery caisson which is then driven down a bumpy road, is the very incarnation of evil. Unlike Bent, he has no reason to treat Billy this way; he lacks the excuse of insanity. He richly deserves to die, shot in the stomach by Charles during the prison escape (*Love and War*, 787). But, to corroborate the existence of evil, Jakes does not make Vesey unique; he has a superior officer who condones his behavior, collaborates in his plans for the torture, and calls him an "exemplary soldier" (*Love and War*, 723).

Truly, evil, absolute evil, exists in the world Jakes portrays. Is there, then, in other characters, a sense of hope, of goodness, which might ameliorate this bleakness, let us overcome the destruction of a nation, forget Constance's gaping slit throat, get past the Washita massacre? Jakes provides us with Virgilia, able to grow from a harridan to a truly compassionate person. He shows us the healing effects of love between Willa and Charles. He shows us, at the Centennial Exposition, how technology can be harnessed for peace—though guns are still popular exhibits.

And he gives us two symbols. One is the laurel that grows on the mountain above the Hazard home. The laurel thrives where other plants die. "Mother always believed our family's like the laurel," says Billy to Brett, "and I expect yours is too. Strong enough, because there are a lot of us who love each other, to live through anything" (*North and South*,

806). The laurel is symbolic of the verities—love and friendship—which will outlast all change and allow people to endure (*Love and War*, 899-900). The other symbol is the crater of the meteorite that fell in the spring of '61, "like a harbinger of God's wrath" (*Love and War*, 762), poisoning the earth so that nothing could grow. The evening in 1876 when George proposes to Madeline, effectively reuniting the families in the hope that love can conquer all the evils they've lived through, he takes her to the edge of the crater. They saw a "deep emerald bowl in the mountain. . . . In the crater, on the sloping sides, the concave bottom, a carpet of summer grass caught the wind and moved gently, gently" (*Love and War*, 762-63). Enough time has passed. Healing has occurred. Evil has not been banished, but perhaps it has been vanquished, by love and nature, at least for awhile. Jakes' bleak recognition of absolute evil has been ameliorated, at least partially, by hope.

ALTERNATIVE READING: NEW HISTORICISM

New Historicism views literature as a representation of historical forces rather than simply as an autonomous bit of writing. (See also Chapter 9.) Stephen Greenblatt, one of the most prominent New Historicists, has argued that "great art is an extraordinarily sensitive register of the complex struggles and harmonies of culture. . . ." (Greenblatt, *Renaissance Self-Fashioning*, 5). He further argues that "the texts that traditionalists think of as our common cultural heritage [are] interesting not [because] they represent consensus, . . . but [because] they are the accumulated record of the most passionate conflicts" (Begley, 36).

Especially when one considers the concept of creation out of conflict, it is hard not to suggest the possibility of a New Historicist treatment of John Jakes' North and South series. Though its subject is the American Civil War, Jakes has clearly been influenced—as were all other Americans who lived through it—by the central historical event of the decades immediately preceding the publication of North and South—the war in Vietnam. Indeed, Jakes has noted that he had the Vietnam vet in mind when he created Charles Main (interview, 30 March 1995).

Jakes' comment on *Heaven and Hell* and the two novels which preceded it, that it was "meant first as a story, and only second as history," is clearly in tune with the New Historicists' belief that literature and history may mutually reflect and reciprocally influence each other. Moreover, Jakes' research techniques reinforce this in their catholicity: literature (Alcott, Whitman, Scott, Poe, and Crane, for example) is supplemented and interwoven with Negro folk songs, Civil War diaries, government documents, recipes, ladies' fashion books, and newspaper stories and advertisements. Literature thus becomes only one of many artifacts reflecting what sort of society America was.

Even more telling is the thesis underlying Book 1 of *Love and War*, "A Vision from Scott"—that the chivalric vision of warfare rampant in the South and drawn from literature was, if not a cause for rushing into battle, then at least the basis for unrealistic expectations of a short and victorious conflict. Just before their first skirmish with Union cavalry, Ambrose, Charles Main's friend, is singing in his monotone, "*O young Lochinvar is come out of the west*"; others join in: "*through all the wide border his steed was the best. . . . So faithful in love and so dauntless in war—there never was a knight like young Lochinvar.*" Jakes observes, through Charles, "How they loved their Scott," these Southerners. Men and women alike "worshipped Scott's chivalric vision" and read and reread everything he'd written "*to give it life. Maybe that odd devotion to old Sir Walter was one of the clues to this decidedly odd war*" (*Love and War*, 24; emphasis added). The observation is an extraordinarily apt description, too, of the mechanics of reciprocity, of "negotiation"—literature and history engaging in cross-fertilization—about which the New Historicists write. Yet another similarity is Jakes' desire not to continue to mythologize historical figures such as Lincoln and Lee. This rereading the character is consistent with the New Historicists' belief that "history itself is not a set of fixed, objective facts but, like the literature with which it interacts, [it is] a text which needs to be interpreted" (Abrams, 249).

Aside from critical theory, one may also see an extraordinary number of other similarities Jakes draws between 'Nam and the Civil War. In both, there was a disproportionate number of poor boys on the front lines. During the Civil War, this was partly the result of the practice of buying exemptions for a few hundred dollars; during the conflict in Vietnam, college deferments achieved much the same result. In Vietnam, this also resulted in a high number of blacks seeing combat. Black regiments didn't serve until relatively late in the Civil War; their very existence was frightening to many Americans, North as well as South. But the idea that black Americans could contribute their lives, perhaps to advance their collective position—to "be all you can be"—is another eerie similarity between the wars.

Both wars were the products of and catalysts for division within American public opinion. Both resulted in acrimonious debate, civil disobedience, even violence. Disagreement during the Civil War crossed regional boundaries. One could not assume, for example, that all Southerners favored states' rights or that all Northerners were abolitionists. Similarly, during Vietnam, antiwar protests, including burning draft cards, American flags, and even threatened self-immolation, were not limited to region or to political party. The objections to a foreign war based in part on the domino theory—the need to stop Communist expansion before it reached our shores, essentially a conservative Republican position—eventually brought down a Democratic president.

Further similarities between military actions separated by almost exactly a century are made clear by Jakes in the afterword to *Heaven and Hell*. "To me certain aspects of the Washita bear an eerie similarity to Vietnam. A frustrated Army, up against guerrilla fighters whose unconventional tactics it was too cumbersome to match, moved in and destroyed an entire village—men, women, and children—the theory being that even small boys might wield weapons against their enemies (some evidently did)" (*Heaven and Hell*, 778). The readers' recollection of recent history—the My Lais, the Vietnamese children offering GI's Coke doctored with ground glass—infuse our examination of a history a century distant.

Finally, in at least two aspects, Charles Main is remarkably similar to at least some Vietnam veterans. When, after the killing of women and children, after annihilating Black Kettle and other old Cheyennes, Custer orders the horses slaughtered, "Charles formed fists and beat the air and screamed then, really screamed, because it seemed the only way to get through. . . . 'Let them go. Let them go free. Stop the killing!' " Quickstepped to Custer's tent, Charles comes close to killing the Boy General—his motivation remarkably like that of soldiers in 'Nam who "fragged" officers by rolling grenades into their tents. Charles' "stinging eyes moved over the ruined village . . . the ashes . . . the hideous quivering mound of dead and dying horses. 'I had to kill a boy this morning [he tells Custer]. Not a man. A boy. I'll see him in nightmares till I die. I'll see this obscene place, too. I'm sick of this army. I'm sick of soldiers like you who work out their ambitions with human lives. I'm sick of the whole god-damn mess. Now either let me go or shoot me' "(*Heaven and Hell*, 560). The horrors of both wars—Vietnam, like the earlier one on the Plains—fracture command structure and shatter fragile psyches.

It is as he crosses the Washita River, away from the army, that Charles realizes that he is a hollow man, that "there was no place for him in all the world" (*Heaven and Hell*, 562). In this, and in many pages which follow, Charles demonstrates another similarity to Vietnam veterans who had to "struggle to come to terms with their experiences, to readjust to civilian life, and to reintegrate into American society" (Moss, 384). Their view, especially after 1967, that the war was both futile and wrong, made this adjustment all the more difficult. Thousands suffered from post traumatic stress disorder, long after the war. The clinical symptoms of PTSD included (1) drug and alcohol abuse, (2) recurring nightmares, (3) chronic depression, (4) psychic numbing, the inability to feel any strong emotion, (5) guilt feelings about their war actions or for having survived when buddies were killed, (6) the inability to experience intimacy, and (7) unpredictable outbursts of aggressive behavior (Moss, citing Veterans Administration studies of Vietnam era veterans, 384). Charles Main demonstrated, at one time or another, virtually every one of these symptoms.

The similarity is more than coincidental. It is further illustration of a New Historicist tenet: that the author, like the reader, is the product of all the conditions and ideological formations of his own era. Thus, such a critic would observe, it is inevitable that John Jakes would notice—and share with his readers—the remarkable parallels between Vietnam and the American Civil War.

11

California Gold
(1989)

Of the thirteen major novels for which John Jakes is best known, *California Gold* is the only one not part of a continuing family saga. Though the novel deals with three generations of the Chance family and, through other characters' family stories, over 150 years of California history, Jakes chose to focus rather than to extend the narrative. The book is, on the one hand, the story of James Macklin Chance and his almost Horatio Alger–like rise from abject poverty to nearly inconceivable wealth. It is, on the other hand, the story of California. If Mack Chance personifies success, California symbolizes hope.

John Jakes "wanted to write about California before [he] finished the *Kent Family Chronicles* or undertook the *North and South trilogy*" (*California Gold*, 747). For a decade, while Jakes completed those projects, California bubbled, like tar in the La Brea pits, under the surface, but potentially richer than imagination. *California Gold* is, in a way, the distillation of those two earlier series. For "California is quintessentially American. Yet it is also a universal symbol, exciting a universal appeal with the visions of sunshine and surf, palm trees and movie glamour, indolence and escape and renewal. California is the world's paradigm of hope and opportunity" (747). California is America's America.

PLOT DEVELOPMENT

James Macklin Chance knew poverty. The son of a Pennsylvania coal miner, Mack too had gone to the mines. When his father died in a mine accident, Mack buried him with the $25 settlement from the company, and, in 1886, set out to walk to California, accompanied by his Pa's only legacy, an emigrant's guide to California. The guide becomes a talisman in this book, as important as are the bottle of green tea, the sword, and the rope bracelet in the Kent Family Chronicles. It symbolizes hope, the chance to achieve a better life.

The trip is not easy, of course; walking from Pennsylvania to California sometimes takes on the dimensions of an odyssey, a quest. Mack is almost always hungry, despite stopping along the way to work for food. His toes poke through his shoes; he staggers through chest-high snowdrifts in the Sierra Nevada; he poisons his guts with alkali water; his clothes become stinking rags.

Stopping to drink at a river bisecting seemingly endless wheat fields, Mack is halted by a gunshot. Otto Hellman announces himself and what, to the Pennsylvania boy, is a bizarre concept. "You're on my land, drinking my water" (33). Hellman, the second largest landowner in California, has title to everything through which Mack has been traveling for the past twenty-eight miles. Despite his daughter Carla's pleas to be civil to a stranger, he refuses Mack a drink, instead demanding that the young lawyer accompanying them, Carla's suitor, Walter Fairbanks III, explain the common law doctrine of riparian rights: the rights to water belong to the man who owns the land through which it flows. The lawyer's arrogance and Hellman's truculence are only slightly offset by Carla's encouragement that he drink—probably based more on rebellion against her father than on any sense of responsibility or concern toward a traveler.

The incident is significant. It is Mack's first realization of the sharp schism between the haves and the have-nots in California. It introduces major antagonists to Mack throughout the novel. And it intensifies his motivation to succeed in this land of hope.

On his arrival in San Francisco from Oakland by ferry, Mack meets the final character central to his life and career, Nellie Ross, whom he "rescues" after she has plunged into San Francisco Bay from the deck of the ferry. A "sob sister" for the Hearst papers, she has flung herself overboard intentionally to gather material for an exposé of the Southern

Pacific's lack of concern for human life when such concern would conflict with profit. (Would the ferry turn back and save her, or maintain its schedule and let her drown?) Mack is immediately smitten with her—and remains so throughout the book.

A major strand of most of the rest of the book is Mack's poor-boy-makes-good rise, mostly from a willingness to work exceedingly hard, occasionally from luck, as when he rescues Jane Lathrop Stanford—Leland P.'s wife—from a runaway horse. In the Bay Area he delivers champagne, works at Stanford's Palo Alto racing stable, and, in competition with the Southern Pacific, co-owns a nickel ferry from Oakland to San Francisco with the Chinese Bao Kee. When, however, their boat is sunk, his partner beaten to death, and he himself worked over unmercifully with brass knuckles by a corrupt police detective, Mack leaves for the south, vowing not to return until he has achieved success. In and around Los Angeles, he gradually amasses a fortune in land booms, oil strikes, and citrus orchards.

When he returns triumphant in his yacht to San Francisco to build a mansion on Nob Hill, he is faced with more than business challenges. He cannot escape the power of the Southern Pacific. Throughout the novel Jakes portrays the railroad much as Frank Norris did in *The Octopus*; indeed, he specifically refers to the confrontation at Mussel Slough, in which wheat farmers were slaughtered by agents of the railroad. Mack himself had earlier seen the brutal lack of concern of the SP, a monopoly brooking no competition; it was probably the SP who ordered Bao Kee killed. And Nellie, writing for the Hearst newspapers, was part of the journalistic muckraking campaign against the SP. But nothing had availed; the railroad owned judges, railroad commissioners, and mayors. It was inevitable, thus, that the successful Mack would campaign actively for the Progressives who were trying to purge the political corruption and sever the connections between the Octopus, the railroad monopoly, and municipal and state officeholders.

The conflict turns personal, once again, for goons hired by the corrupt entrenched politicians attack Mack and his eight-year-old son Jim, severely maiming the boy, who would limp for the rest of his life.

Jakes structures the potentially episodic plot by repeatedly allowing and then dashing Mack's success and happiness. After virtually every peak, he is plunged into a valley of catastrophe, both becoming more pronounced as the novel progresses. Mack reaches "the promised land," only to have Hellman deny him water. He scrimps to buy the *Bay Beauty* with Bao Kee, only to hold his dying partner in his arms, blood and brains covering him. Having achieved legal title to San Solaro and learned the oil business from the ground up, he happily shows Nellie around his successful oil venture, only to have Carla appear on the scene, breathlessly exclaiming, "Darling, darling" (270). He pays off all the creditors his former partner Wyatt had bilked, only to have him turn up again, demanding his share of the profits (287). He succeeds prodigiously in business but cannot break through to his son, who, feeling unloved and abandoned, runs away from home on the eve of the 1906 earthquake, not to be found for years. The pattern seems to cast doubt on the California hope that Mack had inherited from his father. The dichotomy between rich and poor, seen in economic terms throughout the novel, is evident also between Mack's material success and emotional failures.

Jakes also connects plot lines through the device of love triangles, which, though they may stretch probability, achieve narrative economy and heighten the ironic conjunction of success and failure. Two of Mack's major antagonists, Wyatt Paul and Walter Fairbanks, are bound to him through Carla.

When Mack was, for all practical purposes, run out of San Francisco by the combined power of the SP and crooked policemen in the railroad's pocket, he sought a new start (continued hope) and fresh opportunity in Los Angeles. There, despite his reservations about the man's character and ethics, Chance became a 20 percent equity partner with Wyatt Paul in the San Solaro land development scheme. In a letter to Nellie he shared his ambivalence about the venture. He knows his partner is crooked, though charming. And though Mack wants to make a lot of money, he remembers his father's teaching: a man, to be successful, must act ethically (170).

This uneasy partnership is complicated when Carla, always in heat and usually bored with whatever man she is currently with, throws herself at Mack, for which Wyatt never forgives him. Indeed, much later, Wyatt almost succeeds in killing Mack—and Nellie—on their honeymoon.

Mack's relation with Walter Fairbanks III, however, never changes. From the first meeting by the river, they are enemies. When Mack, bested in that contest, asks the way to San Francisco, Fairbanks snarls, "We don't need penniless trash or inferior specimens like you in the City" (30). Though Carla once described Fairbanks as a "typical lawyer: no blood, no passion" (42), he *does* have the capacity to hate.

When Fairbanks becomes lawyer for the SP, he automatically becomes the enemy of Hearst, and thus of Nellie and Mack. This relationship is further exacerbated when the railroad gives him as his sole responsibility the defeat of the Progressives in the 1910 election. Moreover, while Carla was still married to Mack, she had an affair with Fairbanks, who, it is later revealed, is actually the father of Mack's only son, Jim.

Twice Jakes condenses the Fairbanks-Chance antagonism into metaphors of competition: the polo match in Riverside and the automobile race up the coast highway from Monterey. In both, Walter employs any methods, however unsportsmanlike, to win. It is probably inevitable that Fairbanks will hire Wyatt to kill Mack; their relationship is one that changes only to grow more poisonous with time.

Thus, though this novel seems filled with a cast of hundreds, the forces which drive the plot are essentially three antagonists (four counting the SP) and two strong women, in many ways foils for one another.

CHARACTER DEVELOPMENT

As with most of Jakes' fiction, plot in this novel is largely character-driven. Unlike the family sagas, however, we become caught up in Mack's character rather than sampling multiple points of view. It is true that we are occasionally given limited omniscient insight into Jim's mind, primarily because his vulnerability precludes his giving voice to his thoughts. In contrast, Carla acts out, and Nellie explains her positions. Some of the relatively minor characters are present almost exclusively to further our understanding of Mack.

On further reflection, however, one realizes that the minor characters also develop our understanding of California. For the novel has dual protagonists: Mack, whom we see growing, developing, and changing over a thirty-five-year period (1886-1921), and California itself, which develops from a utopian fantasy (1510) to the personification of modern America (1921). Jakes' development of both protagonists is controlled largely through the contrasting motivations set forth in Mack's letter to Nellie: a drive for great wealth versus the concomitant struggle to maintain integrity. Jakes uses juxtaposition and contrast to explicate the struggle between these goals. He does so by examining dream symbolism, by sharply contrasting the two women who sing very different siren songs to Mack, by asking what it means to be a Californian, and by linking Mack's past to his present through the motif of water.

The dream/nightmare with which Jakes opens *California Gold* goes far toward establishing the young Mack Chance. The world, for him, is threatening. Not only is nature portrayed as his antagonist in an uneven struggle (the blizzard, the physical hardships of his trek to California), but the stiff, frozen corpses of men hanged for labor agitation define Mack as an underdog in the conflict between rich and poor. The horror of this dream—as much as his Pa's legacy of hope—propels him west. The epitome of his poverty, fear, and vulnerability, this nightmare recurs throughout the novel. It is made manifest in Mack's conscious refrain, "Never be poor again. . . . Never be cold again. . . . Never be a nobody again." The nightmare also helps define California—or at least Mack's perception of it. While Pennsylvania is brutally unjust, cruelly demanding, "sunless," California is warm, golden, offering hope and opportunity. This perception intensifies Mack's shock and outrage each time he is denied opportunity. Born poor, he might have become as ruthless in pursuit of wealth as any of the multimillionaire capitalists who oppose him. Instead, he remembers his father's injunction to stand up for the underdog. That and his own early poverty explain his friendship with Bao Kee, his insistence on providing decent housing for his immigrant farmhands, his affinity for Diego Marquez, the activist priest who has to break with the church over labor reform. Mack would probably have been drawn to the anti-monopoly crusade of the Hearst chain even if Nellie were not writing for it.

Another dream illustrates the gulf between Mack, ever in search of wealth, and the already rich Californians. In this dream, he is sinking, drowning, in the clear cobalt water of a mountain lake. "He sank through *sunlit depths* in which dead things floated—drowned birds, foxes, a grizzly, a stag with a garland of dead wildflowers hanging from its antlers" (510; emphasis added; see the discussion of hope/despair under "Thematic Issues"). This dream terrifies him more than any he has had since that blizzard/corpse horror. He understands it perfectly. He realizes how close he'd come to sacrificing personal principles in a drive for wealth— and changes his mind about supporting the proposal to flood Hetch Hetchy as a reservoir for San Francisco. He chooses the forces of conservation rather than exploitation of nature. He is still in touch with natural beauty; he refuses to succumb to the merely expedient. He refuses to align himself with those who will provide gratuitous pain to the vulnerable. (It should be noted that in the novel, bad people harm the weak: animals [Fairbanks' destruction of the polo pony], children [Coglan's maiming of Jim], and women [the police beating up Margaret in the campaign against "French restaurants"].) Additionally, Jakes uses this nightmare to define the character of California in the late nineteenth century. It is no longer a bucolic Spanish-Indian backwater filled with natural beauty. The hundreds of thousands who have poured in since 1849, drawn by California's beauty and opportunity, have begun to destroy the very qualities that attracted them. Despite conservationists like John Muir, despite social reformers like Diego Marquez, despite the muckraking efforts of the Hearst chain, California is in danger of losing its soul.

As Jakes uses the two nightmares to help delineate Mack's character, so too he creates a polarity between Carla and Nellie. Both are in the tradition of Jakes' interest in strong women: "strong women make strong characters" (letter, 6/22/95). Neither could be called conventional. Mack meets both early in the book, and both continue to hold a degree of power over him.

Carla is outrageous, flaunting her appearance, her lack of convention, her sexuality. Constantly in search of a new thrill, she is almost constantly bored. Pampered by father, lovers, and husbands, she always wants more, though she is ill equipped to define precisely what it is she wants. She is almost always in heat, having relationships, sequentially or simultaneously, with Wyatt, Mack, and Walter. Little excites her more than to have men compete for her. She uses her body as tease, as challenge, as reward, as punishment. She sleeps with Fairbanks to get back at Mack. She endures the resulting pregnancy but wants nothing to do with her son; indeed, his birth is one of the stimuli causing her to leave Mack. She keeps Jim's parentage her secret, her weapon until she unleashes it, on separate occasions, to wound both men. Otto Hellman knew his daughter well when he warned Mack against getting involved with her.

While Carla wields her body, Nellie uses her mind. While Carla, with or without benefit of marriage, is a kept woman throughout her life, Nellie makes her own way. Indeed, it is her professional ambition that comes between her and Mack through most of the book. She is pleased with the mark she's making within the Hearst organization; she has the physical courage necessary to investigate unsanitary hospitals or unsafe ferries. She has the personal integrity to write about them, and the craftsmanship necessary to write well. She is successful in her own right, first as a reporter and then as a novelist. While Carla counts as her social equals wealthy landowners and the nabobs of the City, Nellie counts among her friends Willie Hearst with his crusading zeal, John Muir, equally fervent in his fight to preserve nature, and authors such as Ambrose Bierce, Edwin Markham, and Frank Norris. While Mack once wondered how many animals had to die to clothe Carla with her furs and decorative egret feathers, Nellie is comfortable in shirtwaists or, when camping, prospector's jeans. Carla drinks too much, and when she does, may break out in a sickly slick of perspiration; Nellie rarely drinks and is a capable outdoorswoman, raising a healthy sweat setting up a tent, hiking a trail, or climbing a mountain. Carla is an instigator, then a spectator; Nellie is a doer. Carla is a California reincarnation of Alicia, the bitch goddess of *The Bastard* and *The Rebels*; Nellie, more of a forest sprite.

Carla is a manifestation of much that is wrong with modern California—its superficiality, its materialism, its insistence on instant self-gratification. Nellie, a competent career woman, has roots in California's past and in its diversity. Part Russian, part Basque, she understands California's agricultural heritage and is committed to preserving the state's natural beauty. Thus it is not surprising that, while maintaining her own independence and integrity, she becomes the agent for Mack's change. Jakes demonstrates this in three separate camping trips they take together. After the last trip with Nellie, Mack understands the state's heritage, abandons his "wrongheaded" ideas about women, and can begin to temper his frenetic drive for wealth.

In defining Mack as a person and as a Californian, Jakes utilizes yet another contrast, one which simultaneously reveals the depth of the danger Mack escaped. Mack will always be an adopted Californian; in contrast, both Bao Kee and Walter Fairbanks are native Californians, then and now a rare breed. Bao Kee personifies the harsh heritage of the Chinese in California. He knows the dark side of *Kam Saan*, Gold Mountain, the name Cantonese miners, his father among them, gave to California. His father, a laborer during the gold rush and later a railroad construction worker, had been beaten to death; his mother, a picture bride, died, unable to deal with the hatred. Kee, who has survived as best he could, knows that the hardest job is staying alive (57). He's bitter—but resigned. Although Kee is a native Californian, he faces the cry of the bigots: "The Chinese must go!" He can't become a citizen. Nor can he own property (58). Mack experiences some of this racial hatred firsthand when he and Kee run afoul of the oyster pirates who shout, "This bay's for white men, you fucking dog on two legs." This experience shows the young Mack that the established nabobs "sure as hell don't like outsiders" (64).

Walter Fairbanks personifies all those who advocate exclusion. When he and Mack first met, he refused to give the young emigrant directions to San Francisco, instead calling Mack "penniless trash," an "inferior specimen," and "riff-raff." Fairbanks prides himself on having been born in California: "That makes me a native son—something you'll never be" (38).

Like Bao Kee, Fairbanks' heritage went back to the gold rush, but instead of actually mining (here Jakes establishes a polarity between those who actually work and those who exploit the workers), his ancestors "established a service to handle the dust and money of the miners" (86). Subsequent Fairbankses joined almost every anti-democratic movement in California history. They belonged to the Chivalry, the proslavery wing of the Democratic party, and campaigned for the Exclusion Act of 1882 to bar Chinese immigration. Fairbanks is proud of his membership in the Native Sons of the Golden West, "a private society of white males born in California"; of them, Nellie would only say, "I consider the Native Sons a bunch of prigs and bigots" (86-87).

Jakes not only tells us of the differences between these two native Californians; he also reveals them through their actions. Where Fairbanks' SP threw Mack into the Bay, Bao Kee fished him out. Where Bao Kee fed him, taught him about Chinese culture, and eventually became his partner, Fairbanks bought police to beat him up. While Bao Kee died in Mack's arms, thugs probably sent by the SP killed him.

The contrast emphasizes the "dark side to [Mack's] dream" of California. As the old Chumash Indian had warned him: "In California there are only two kinds. Those who take, and those they take from" (46). Mack was appalled at the implication that, once he had money, he would be one of the "takers." But the Indian gravely replied that, although Mack is a "good man," he too will be tempted by greed. "It is the only way. It is California" (45-46).

Mack almost succumbs to this danger. For, in competition with Fairbanks, with the SP, with all those who blocked his ambition, he had almost *become* his enemy.

The higher Mack climbs, the lower he falls. The fall is one of spirit as well as fortune. Mack, whose central quality for so long was vitality, feels dead inside. Life—even its accomplishments—is no longer fun. It is almost as if he's been infected with Carla's boredom.

Mack's personal nadir occurs on one of his San Joaquin Valley ranches near Fresno. Conservative ranchers, angry at Diego Marquez' efforts to organize farm labor, have gathered; police violence results, in large part because of Mack's reputation for championing the underdog. Exhausted by the drive down from San Francisco and by internal conflicts (his old friendship with Marquez vs. his dislike of harboring Wobblies), in pain from his arthritis, violently condemned by conservatives who think him too radical for providing decent housing for his laborers, Mack rests for a moment by his horse trough. At that precisely wrong moment, a young Hindustani immigrant introduces himself to Mack, announcing his determination and his ambitions, ones eerily similar to those of the young Mack a quarter century earlier. "I will be a Californian now" (712). Mukerji presses Mack for a job. On the roads just off the ranch, neighboring ranchers opposed to foreign labor and to Wobblies are gathering. The tension crackles. Stress lines appear. Mack denies the job, orders Mukerji out of sight, and flings the water dipper, for which the Hindustani had reached, into the dust. Only when Mukerji pleads, "Sir, not even a drink of water first?" does Mack see their parallels. Jakes has created an incident precisely analogous to that between the young Mack and Hellman. "You're on my land, drinking my water." Recognizing this, as in an epiphany, Mack is shocked and ashamed. *What the hell have I become? How is it that I've forgotten so much?"* (713). Mack is jarred back to his center; he is saved by his fundamental concern for people. "A human life is more important than money or land" (716).

How much Mack changes, how thoroughly he has sloughed off the dead skin of greed and uncaring ambition, is evident in the Coda. He and Nellie, finally his wife, are celebrating his son Jim's twenty-third birthday. Now reunited with his father, financial manager of Mack's companies, and an accomplished pilot (daring new frontiers), Jim receives a racing biplane for his present. Clearly the family enjoys its wealth. The hangar, though, catches the reader's eye. One remembers an earlier, driven Mack, determined to be somebody, to shove his success down the throats of those who had driven him from San Francisco. The successful Mack had almost literally branded every bit of his property with his initials—the JMC cartouche. Though no one dared question the "ceaseless replication of his identity on clothes and possessions" (408), Mack was clearly overcompensating for his early poverty. Lacking love, he had come close to succumbing to hubris.

Remembering such behavior, one is struck by the painted sign atop the hanger announcing its owner: CALROSS AVIATION. Mack's omnipresent initials have disappeared. His new company blends the names of his adopted state and his wife Nellie, who has showed him its best. It is Nellie, finally, and their reciprocal love, which has enabled Mack to soar once more.

The Coda is titled "El Dorado: 1911." Mack *is* the fabled king covered with gold. But now, amid family, able to love and to share, not just compete, he is, once again, untarnished.

THEMATIC ISSUES

As plot in *California Gold* is driven by character, so too does character serve to define theme. Jakes' portrayal of Mack and his adopted state suggests their complexity, including their contradictions. It is as if, at sunrise, one were to set a golden coin on end, its diameter on a north-south axis. One side of the coin would be sun-washed, golden, bright; the other, still in shade, would have no luster, its golden intaglio symbols obscured by gloom. Such opposing views of the same subject once again reveal a philosophically complex author. Jakes is both idealist and realist; occasional bleakness infuses his usual optimism. Both hope and despair permeate this novel. The tension between them is resolved in favor of hope—possible, however, only if human decency, rather than greed, triumphs.

On the one hand, Jakes presents the historical/mythical California, a land of hope and opportunity. The land of the earliest Argonauts whose letters sparked the boom of the gold rush, the land of quick fortunes, easily gained. A land larger than life, a land of hyperbole. A land of fresh starts, of opportunity for those willing to work, to dare, to chance. A land that rewards those brave/persistent/daring/creative enough to reach it. A land dreamed of since the start of recorded travel: warm, sunny, exotic, nurturing, promising, rewarding. The *peaks* of Mack Chance's career illustrate this California.

Jakes also presents this California by the device he often uses to state themes, the epigraph. He cites the earliest reference to the name California, from *Las Sergás de Esplandián* by Garcí Ordóñez de Montalvo, published in Seville in 1510: "Know ye that on the right hand of the Indies there is an island called *California*, very close to the Earthly Paradise." He quotes from James D. Houston's *Californians*: "I don't think of California as a place, you see. It is a certain kind of opportunity." And, from Henry David Thoreau: "Eastward I go only by force; westward I go free."

On the final page of the novel, Jakes lets Mack fly the new racing biplane. As the plane is "suddenly airborne" against the panorama of California, his wife, son, and best friend watch. Before Mack took off,

Nellie had recognized the look on her husband's face: the joy of facing a new challenge. His best friend saw it too: "He's goin' prospectin." As did his son, Jim: "He'll never stop" (746). Earthbound, they watch the plane shrink to a dot over the blue Pacific. "Flying due west." The spirit that is Mack, that is California, is indomitable, always looking for new opportunities. The point is reinforced by Jakes' final quotation, this time from an actual guidebook, Peck's 1837 *New Guide to the West*: "The real Eldorado is still further on."

But it should be remembered that the phrase "Gone West" during most of the period of the American frontier was a euphemism for "Died." Not all succeeded, to write glowing letters back home; many, probably most, simply disappeared or were defeated, lapsing into oblivion. The *valleys* of Mack's career attest to this possibility, even for the most successful. For others, the exploited rather than the exploiters, California life could be a miserable existence. A whole succession of immigrants—Chinese, Japanese, Indians—faced the vitriol of racial prejudice. Little people, moral midgets, took pleasure in subjecting *their* subordinates to scorn, physical brutality, or death. Common laborers, even on enlightened ranches like Mack's, could be terrified by overseers like Tarbox. No matter how hard they labored, most would not succeed. And many of those who had succeeded, often by using the labors of others, became oblivious to, scornful of, or vicious toward those they'd used. Fairbanks and the Big Four of the Southern Pacific—Huntington, Crocker, Hopkins, and Stanford—portray this group.

Nature was exploited as well. What, in Native American belief, was given by God for all men to share became, in Otto Hellman's words, "*my* land, *my* water." Development brought money, but also the desecration of the natural environment: the derricks pumping in the once sleepy Los Angeles, Wyatt's projected development with the stratagem of tying oranges to cactuses to lure purchasers. John Muir saw the danger: "Stay out of this place if ye can't treat it with respect. Any fool can cut a tree, but it takes the Almighty years to make one to replace it" (114).

Mack sees both the possibilities and their consequences. He remembered Southern California as he'd first seen it in 1888-89: a dusty, rural frontier. He knew that flooding Hetch Hetchy could water the entire Central Valley, creating an agricultural Eden while destroying a site of exquisite beauty. He was simultaneously exhilarated and saddened by the technology thrusting California farther and farther away from that "lost part of memory" (623).

Part of Jakes' take on this assault on nature is indicated in his "Final Thoughts," a rather wistful commentary on the novel and the state that inspired it. "There is a particular sadness in looking at present-day California, and then reading the descriptions of its clean, pristine beauties in works such as Nordhoff's from the late nineteenth century. If California is quintessentially America, it is also the exemplar of the quintessential American ruin—the destruction of a place of God-given beauty" (755).

Jakes' description of California in the novel is not a Chamber of Commerce promo. Despite the opportunities, he (and we) remains aware of the old Chumash Indian's warning: "In California there are only two kinds. Those who take, and those they take from" (46). We remember, too, that Mack's father, despite his memories of California, was a *failed* Argonaut. And, as Nellie pointed out, his particular guidebook, and its author, T. Fowler Haines, were false: the author had never been west; the book was merely the product of an avaricious publishing industry capitalizing on a fad.

The theme, then, if Mack is to be taken as a paradigm, is that society, and we as individuals, must somehow maintain a balance between ambition and social responsibility. Throughout the book Jakes has been careful to distance Mack from the exploiters. He recoils from his most damning behavior, the incident when he refused Mukerji water. One critic who thoroughly panned the novel (Carolyn See, "John Jakes: Cold No More, Poor No More," *Washington Post Book World*, 9/17/89), has called John Jakes "a nice man"; she somehow manages to give this phrase a pejorative connotation. What she misses is that the resolution of the conflict between two contradictory themes *is precisely* that of a principled, "nice" man who argues that ultimately human decency will?/*must* triumph over human depravity.

ALTERNATIVE READING: A MARXIST INTERPRETATION

A Marxist critic would probably question whether one *can* "maintain a balance between ambition and social responsibility." Marxism, a philosophy of history and political reform, sprang from the *Communist Manifesto* (1848) of Karl Marx (1818-1883). Marx sought to prove that "capitalism carried within itself the seeds of its own decay and that revolution was inevitable" (Elliott and Summerskill, 224). Among the revolutionary ideas advocated in the *Manifesto* were the expropriation of landed property and the use of rent from land to cover state expenditures; a high and progressively graded income tax; the abolition of the right of inheritance; the nationalization of transport; and the duty of all to work (Elliott and Summerskill, 224). The *Manifesto* concluded that these goals could only be achieved by a violent overthrow of the existing social order. Rather than viewing a text as a product of individual creativity, many Marxist critics examine a work as a product of an ideology particular to a specific historical period. They judge it on its portrayal of social actions and class struggle.

Certainly the California of *California Gold* is a paradise for the capitalist, a hell for most workers. A few achieve incredible riches; most toil on, doomed to lifelong poverty. The separation of the classes is made all the more onerous by the fact that the rich control, indeed own—or can buy— most public officials: police, railroad commissioners, judges. Thus law, presumably the blindfolded goddess, is suborned by men of property.

Too few own most of the land, and since the days of the missions, always have. For example, Otto Hellman's land is measured not in acres but in square miles. Fairbanks explains that of those who need water but who are denied it by Hellman's riparian rights, those "who won't pay . . . [are] perfectly free to let their crops go without water" (36). Hellman soundly condemns Assemblyman Wright, who has introduced water reform legislation, as nothing but a "thieving radical, him and his water districts with everybody owning a piece—it's communistic. He's trying to rob a man of his God-given right to the fruits of his labor and property" (36).

His fear of political and economic reform is clear. Reformers are often called "Communists," using a scare tactic that works even today. Moreover, the assumption that the right to exploit nature is God-given should shock all fair-minded readers. To argue, further, that he is being robbed of the fruits of his labor is patently absurd. Neither Hellman, nor Fairbanks, nor Leland P. Stanford performs his "duty to work." Moreover, their control of many of the members of the State Assembly will defeat any reform, including proposals to tax their exorbitant wealth fairly and progressively.

Fairbanks is a clear argument for the abolition of the right of inheritance. Never having *really* worked, having inherited his fortune from his father's generation (and even they did no manual labor, choosing, instead, to handle the miners' gold dust and money), he is an arrogant, racist, snobbish bigot.

Moreover, Fairbanks is a lawyer for the SP, the Octopus, the railroad monopoly controlling all rates through California and thereby squeezing the small, honest shippers, as is seen in Frank Norris' book *The Octopus*, which Nellie recommends to Mack. And while it is true that members of the Big Four do practice philanthropy—the most noticeable example being the Leland P. Stanford, Jr. University—it is less out of "love of the people" than as an expiation of guilt.

In contrast to such capitalists, few workers own property and some, like the Chinese, are forbidden to do so. They are denied basic American rights, like freedom of speech; they are intimidated by foremen like Tarbox; and when they dare to challenge those with money and power, as does Bao Kee, they are beaten to death.

Those like Diego Marquez who advocate humane labor conditions are labeled "radicals" and "Communists" and are rousted from their pulpits and soapboxes by bullying police henchmen of the big landowners. California is not the "model frontier democracy of popular myth." California has "never been a harmonious, homogeneous, middle-class society. . . . Some succeeded economically; some failed. Some acquired power, others did not. Some were oppressors, some were oppressed. . . . Society in California has been as hierarchical, and the chasm between the poor and the rich as great, as in any other American region" (Rice, Bullough, and Orsi, 6).

Thus, if we examine the proposition at the beginning of this chapter—"If Mack Chance personifies success, California symbolizes hope"—we must again raise objections. We cannot ignore the racism, snobbery, political corruption, hypocritical utopias, or excesses of capitalism. And, to be fair, Jakes does not.

Moreover, among the very rich, Mack seems to be redeemed *because of* his rise from abject poverty through hard personal labor and physical sacrifice. Unlike most landowners, he provides decent quarters for his farm laborers. He remembers his father's injunction to stand up for the underdog. But he comes perilously close to losing his soul to capitalism. Only a titan like Mack could pull back from the precipice and regain his center, his integrity.

Although we cannot ask that he become a saint and give all his wealth to the poor, our final image of him is as an incredibly rich man, rich enough to give his son the expensive birthday toy of a racing biplane. It is as if, having re-espoused his social consciousness, he is rewarded by success and happiness and love—and even greater wealth. Even though Jakes mentions, and thus suggests that the reader examine, *The Octopus*,

Edwin Markham's "The Man with the Hoe," and Jack London, who "knew everything important about the writings of Darwin, Huxley, Spencer, Karl Marx too" (426), the novel's resolution is too facile. While class conflict, bigotry, and political corruption exist, the Marxist critic would argue, one cannot be placated by the happiness of one rich individual.

12

Homeland
(1993)

With *Homeland*, John Jakes inaugurates yet another epic undertaking. This time his narrative goal is to bring the story of America into the twentieth century, to reveal the United States in its role as a global power during what some historians have called "the American century." Thus, while focusing on American themes, Jakes must set his characters on a world stage to a greater degree than in any novel since *The Bastard*. *Homeland* focuses on a single family of German immigrants from 1890 to 1900, "a decade in which a naive young giant flexed its muscles and began to understand and use its enormous strength" (Author's Note). Successive volumes will follow the Crown family through the cataclysmic wars and social changes of the twentieth century.

In *Homeland* Jakes turns to a theme central to American history—immigration. Like the pivotal events of earlier works (the founding of a nation in the early Kent Family Chronicles, the exploration of "America's America" in *California Gold*, and the seemingly inevitable tragedy of the Civil War in the North and South series), immigration is one of a handful of catalysts making America what it is today. Immigration has deep personal meaning to Jakes, for his own grandfather, William Carl Retz, to whom he dedicates the book, lived the immigrant experience. Moreover, Jakes wrote *Homeland* with a sense of mission. Despite political polls in the spring of 1992 which noted that "60 per cent of those polled think America is a nation in decline" ("Afterword," 1181), Jakes writes with hope, mixed with realistic misgiving. In his afterword he muses, "Perhaps it is folly to write a novel about hope in a time of profound national confusion, even despair. But I try to mirror the realities of the past that I explore. . . . At the time of this story, people were swept along on a tide of hope. America symbolized virtually limitless opportunity. . . . Hope brought my grandfather [and many others] to America. . . . Some went home, disillusioned. But more stayed; many more. Hope was in the air" (1181-82). To personify such hope, Jakes founds yet another epic dynasty, the Crowns. They join the Kents (the Kent Family Chronicles), the Mains and Hazards (the North and South series), and the Chances (*California Gold*) as Jakes begins yet another family saga in his larger commitment to telling the saga of America.

PLOT DEVELOPMENT

Homeland and the cycle of novels which will follow begin at the point where the Kent Family Chronicles conclude, 1891. When we meet the protagonist, Pauli Kroner (Paul Crown), he is a thirteen-year-old dreamer trapped in poverty in Berlin; by novel's end, he lives his dreams, having acquired a profession, a family, and a country through a Horatio Alger–like combination of luck and pluck.

The almost 1,200-page novel is divided into ten parts, organized in a structure reminiscent of a five act play: exposition, complication, rising action, climax, and denouement. Although the novel is effectively unified through character and theme, each "act" exposes the protagonist—and the country he will eventually call home—to a specific congeries of conflicts.

Parts 1 ("Berlin") and 2 ("Steerage") establish Pauli Kroner's motivation for emigration and detail the hardships of the crossing and arrival in America. The Germany of 1891 had abandoned many of the revolutionary democratic principles of the "Men of '48" who had struggled toward a unified constitutional government and who had fled abroad—many to America—when the landed class, the Junkers, returned to power. In 1871, following the defeat of France in the Franco-Prussian War, the new German empire was proclaimed, ushering in the Age of Bismarck and the First Reich.

For those opposed to this nationalistic, militaristic Germany, there were two choices: bare survival in appalling poverty, or emigration. Pauli's Uncle Josef chose emigration, leaving Aalen in 1857 for Cincinnati, heavily populated by German countrymen. His Aunt Lotte raised Pauli after his mother's death, but when it became clear that she would soon die of tuberculosis, Lotte made arrangements to send the boy to his uncle in America, the land of opportunity. Aunt Lotte was well aware of the symbolism of Pauli's journey, a rite of passage—literally: "You're going to be an American, and you must be a good one, never forgetting you have changed your old country for a new one" (43).

The crossing, for poor immigrants like Pauli, was a nightmare. Stuffed below decks into holds crammed with iron-framed bunks stacked five high and three across, among Poles, Romanians, Austrians, and Russians as well as Germans, Pauli endured being fumigated, learned not to gag at the odors of unwashed bodies, overflowing toilet troughs, and sour vomit, dodged predatory youths bent on stealing his money belt containing—more precious than money—his letter from Uncle Joseph agreeing to be his sponsor; and made friends with a young Polish Jew, Herschel Wolinski, whose gift for music teased marches, folk songs, even "Marching Through Georgia," from his concertina.

Arrival at the newly opened Ellis Island was not the end of the immigrants' ordeal, however. Still facing them were the batteries of physical examinations, the confirmation of sponsorship, and, ashore, unscrupulous labor contractors enlisting new immigrants at slave wages. Herschel, however, did not get so far, for, as his mother reached the dreaded "eye man," she was denied admission because of trachoma. Though Herschel could not deny his promise that his family would stick together, no matter what, and thus joined them to be shipped back to Europe, he vowed to Pauli, "We will meet in this country one day. I am going to be an American" (85).

Parts III "Chicago," and IV "Julie," explore the coming-of-age motif. "Chicago" juxtaposes themes of love and nurturing with those of adolescent rebellion and striving for independence. Having arrived half-frozen at his Uncle Joseph's luxurious Chicago house, Paul is nursed back to health by his Aunt Ilsa. Jakes uses the fragrant warmth of a German-American household at Christmastime to suggest the close family into which Paul is accepted. However, tensions exist. Uncle Joe, whose military service during the Civil War has intensified his German insistence on order, cannot deal with the rebellion of his son Joe Junior, who, reflecting the growing dichotomy in America between labor and capital, chooses the workers' cause against his father, a self-made rich brewer; his flirtation with socialism and anarchy during the Pullman strike eventually results in another man's sabotage of his father's brewery. When Joe Junior is, in effect, disowned and sets off to wander America, Paul must choose between loyalty to his aunt and uncle, who have taken him in and treated him like a son, or to his cousin, who has become like a brother.

During much of this same period, Paul has fallen in love with Julie, daughter of Mason "Pork" Vanderhoff, who has made his fortune in meat packing. Unfortunately, imagined slights, overheard insults, and long-standing antagonisms have hardened into bitter and implacable hatred between the Crowns and the Vanderhoffs. The Paul-Julie relationship is thus doomed to clandestine meetings at skating rinks and notes left under secret stones—an upper-class Chicago version of the Romeo and Juliet theme.

Parts 5, 6, and 7, "Pullman," "Levee," and "Flickers," portray the American dream—and its sordid antithesis. While there are millionaires, there are also their employees, striking for decent wages and working conditions. While there are pampered women like Julie's mother who can wallow in their neurasthenia, there are others—laundry workers, farmwives, and madams—who know little but hard work. While there are flawed but fundamentally kind people like Wexford Rooney, who teaches Paul the fundamentals of photography, and Colonel Shadow, who shares his dreams of motion pictures with his young apprentice, there are psychopathic predators like Jimmy Daws who will do anything to satisfy their cravings. We see this dichotomy in American society through Paul, on his own in Chicago, and through Joe Junior, wandering Jack London/Tom Joad–like across the American West. It is during these three sections of the novel, too, that we watch Paul grow from the kid who can't draw but who wants to capture visual images to an accomplished photographer and a pioneer in motion pictures.

Parts 8 and 9, "Tampa" and "War," bring Uncle Joe and Paul once again into close proximity in the Florida staging areas and the Cuban war zones of the Spanish-American War. Joe seeks out a commission and goes to Cuba as general; he has multiple motivations: a desire to return to the military, which, despite its horrors, had been, during the Civil War, the single most formative influence on his life; a need to resolve a midlife crisis in which his previous faith in order, work, and family is being tested; and a desire to reaffirm, in the face of increasingly vocal German-American Bundists' posturing, his allegiance to his adopted country. Paul is there—along with actual pioneer filmmakers like Albert E. Smith and Billy Bitzer (cameraman for *Birth of a Nation*) and journalists like Stephen Crane and William Harding Davis—to report the war to Americans redefining their nation's role in world politics. Only when Paul is seriously wounded do he and his uncle become aware of each other's presence and reach a kind of reconciliation.

Part 10, "Homecoming," interweaves the novel's major plot lines. The Crown family moves toward further reconciliation after Paul and Joe's reunion in Cuba. Ilsa and Joe achieve greater equality in family decisions; Joe Junior returns home, at first almost unrecognizable from the hard life he's experienced; and both parents are more willing to accept their children's right to adult independence and their own goals. Julie, who has experienced the horrors of an arranged marriage to a brutal, sexually depraved, manipulative, unfaithful scion of a Chicago department store family, is freed when he is killed by one of his mistresses. Julie returns to Chicago just in time for the triumphant premier of Paul's film, *Conquest of the San Juan Hill*, and the lovers are finally reunited. Happily married, professionally successful, Paul becomes an American citizen on December 31, 1900, the cusp of a new century. At the party celebrating Paul's citizenship, a strolling accordionist played German folk songs, ragtime, and "The Stars and Stripes Forever," heard everywhere those days. "Sousa's melody summed up America's mood of strength, optimism, growing importance in global affairs" (1147).

Clearly, John Jakes continues in *Homeland* the technique of interweaving many linked plot lines presented from multiple points of view. But, quite different from any novel since *The Bastard*, Jakes here focuses on a single character. Paul, like Philip, is more than the protagonist; both men are the immigrant progenitors of new American families; both, having *chosen* to come to America, create an epic race or people; both personify the character and the fortunes of the United States. In contrast to the North and South series, in which the multiple subplots were themselves a metaphor for the polyphonic unraveling and tentative reuniting of America, we follow the plot lines of *Homeland* because they collectively explicate and complicate Paul's goals. Colonel Shadow and Wexford Rooney are, admittedly, interesting characters, but they are relevant specifically to develop Paul's photographic skills. And, while following Julie allows us yet another illustration of Jakes' strong woman motif and, incidentally, provides us with another wonderful villain in her husband, Elstree, we really care about her because we want a happy conclusion to the Romeo and Juliet motif.

Additionally, alternating point of view chapter by chapter in this book is more organically linked to structure than in any other Jakes book. For example, "Berlin" alternates between Paul and Lotte, establishing motives for seeking "a better road"—emigration or suicide. "Steerage" alternates between Paul, Joe Crown, and Herschel Wolinski, contrasting failure and success in immigration, while "Levee," from the points of view of Paul, Joe, Jimmy Daws, and Rosie, establishes the American dream and its sordid underbelly.

Jakes weaves these multiple plot lines and points of view into a unified narrative tapestry. He does this subtly throughout, mostly in his treatment of theme. But two instances are more overt. Late in Part 10 "Homecoming," Jakes engineers a reunion between Paul and his friend and comrade from the crossing, Herschel Wolinski, the boy so full of music he could make his concertina sing, the boy shipped back to Europe from the very shadow of the Statue of Liberty. In New York on business, Paul stops to listen to the musical hit of the season, "Ragtime Rose," by Harry Poland. Perhaps too coincidentally, also in the crowd of listeners is a vaguely familiar man, immensely enjoying the piano rendition of the song—his song. For, as Paul soon realizes, the familiar man is Herschel, now returned, now an American with his new name, now successful, like Paul, in his own dream of homeland and profession. As a second overt unifying technique, Jakes brackets Paul's search for a home with sentences emphasizing that theme. Starting the novel, as he often does, *in medias res*, Jakes writes: "[The boy Pauli] thought, WHERE'S MY HOME? IT ISN'T HERE" (3). At the very end, now a world traveled, sought-after movie maker, an American citizen, a happy husband, Paul stands on the catwalk atop the Statue of Liberty, filming a documentary. The immigrants below would replay his own quest. Their arrival provided confirmation, if any were needed, of the rightness of his own immigration, his choice of America. Watching them below, he knew "he was home" (1174).

CHARACTER DEVELOPMENT

The plot in most Jakes novels is character-driven. So it is in *Homeland*, as all events, as well as all other characters, contribute directly or indirectly to fleshing out the protagonist, Paul Crown. However, there is a greater conciseness in *Homeland* than in some earlier Jakes novels. The arrival of Buffalo Bill's Wild West Show in Berlin early in the novel illustrates this compression. As the eighteen-car train pulled into the Berlin freight yards—frontiersmen firing pistols, stagecoaches fleeing from gaudily painted howling Indians, the white-hatted Cody himself astride his rearing stallion—it was the embodiment of the American West which had already, however improbably, captured the German imagination through the novels of Karl May. (See Chapter 2.) The show epitomized America, especially the West, as a fresh start, a land of new chances. It inevitably drew the poor who dreamed of a better life. It drew Pauli. Jakes uses the scene to convey character—of individuals and of nations—to introduce minor characters who will recur throughout the book, and to set the stage for conflict between Germany and the United States, a conflict that will dominate later books in the series.

Although Pauli desperately wants to see the show, he refuses to allow his friend Tonio's father to pay his way: "That's charity, I don't take charity" (23). Thus Jakes sketches character traits which will ultimately let Pauli succeed: independence, a willingness to earn what he dreams of, an insistence on personal responsibility. Having raced across railroad tracks to the scene of the unloading, Pauli settles down to sketch the "magnificently heroic" Cody. As always, Pauli is disappointed at the difference between what his eyes, brain, and heart see and what his clumsy fingers draw, a disappointment reinforced by the seedily sinister journalist, Mikhail Rhukov, who observes, "That's terrible" (26). (Incidentally, Pauli's inability to draw makes photography a natural choice for his visual expression.) Rhukov will, from this point on, be an intermittently appearing figure, generally providing commentary on and a touchstone for Paul's personal and career decisions. Moreover, in this first meeting, he puts a different spin on Cody's extraordinary efficiency in unloading his show from the boxcars. "Amazing people, these Americans," he observed. "They're going to own the earth, I think" (27). Thus Jakes foreshadows America's maturation into a world power.

Rhukov and Pauli are not alone in watching Cody's show unload. Also at the station are six German army officers, assiduously taking notes on how elements of the show are unloaded in the correct order for the parade, thus reducing chaos and demonstrating efficiency. The German officers seem to sneer at the careful planning, surprised that Americans are "capable of such clear thought," and laugh, "Perhaps Büffel Bill is German" (29). The arrogant superiority, later to be manifested in the idea of the master race, is already evident. As is their purpose. When observing that the train had arrived six and a half minutes late, the brigadier snorted, "That would never do for artillery arriving in the field" (29). Jakes clearly foreshadows *blitzkrieg*. The saber-scarred Lieutenant Von Rike introduced in this scene will, like Rhukov, appear in cameos throughout the novel—watching American embarkation for Cuba, pumping General Crown (895-96), and photographing, along with Major Shiba of Japan, American preparation for battle.

As Jakes thus prepares for subsequent novels, he simultaneously provides Pauli with multiple motivations for emigration: to go to America, where there is hope, freedom, and opportunity, but, equally important, to leave his German homeland, a land becoming increasingly sinister. Von Rike and his colleagues demonstrate the might makes right philosophy when smashing the Kodak belonging to some tourists who, innocently capturing the Wild West Show unloading, may also be capturing Germany's preparation for war. Equally disturbing to Paul was his farewell to his friend Tonio, slightly retarded and deformed, who has been separated from his classmates and sent to a special school. Pauli hadn't liked the doctor's explanation: "It's the only way to keep up standards. It's the new German way" (9). The reader recognizes the ironic beginning, during the First Reich, of what, during the Third Reich, will become the Final Solution. Pauli can't foresee the future, but he doesn't much like what he sees of the "new German way." The boy reflects, "Perhaps that was why he had such a strong interest in the country to which his uncle had emigrated years ago" (9). Jakes thus foreshadows future German-American conflicts while providing Pauli with motivation to leave Germany.

Uncle Joe Crown provides a parallel to Pauli's experiences. He not only offers a haven and a first home for Paul in America, but, through his obvious richness, he demonstrates the validity of the American Dream: a poor immigrant who works hard *can* succeed. He serves as a role model, a father figure; but when his parental demands seem too confining, he serves as catalyst for Paul to seek his goals for himself and thus unwittingly initiates the growing-up process. Uncle Joe also demonstrates the dilemma of all immigrants: whether to renounce one homeland for another. Old Valter, who shepherded Paul through the immigration process on Ellis Island, expressed the decision metaphorically: "Germania our mother—Columbia our bride" (76). As a young man grows up, he makes his own life; though he may look backward, he can't go home again.

Uncle Joe twice affirms that mature choice by serving in the United States Army—once during the Civil War and again in Cuba—as well as by rebuffing the German nationalism expressed by Bundists like Oskar Hexhammer, publisher of the *Chicago Deutsche Zeitung*. Here, too, Jakes prepares for the conflicts of future books. Joe Crown's every deed shows him to be German by birth, temperament, and culture, American in politics, loyalty, and allegiance. Jakes offers Joe as a prior parallel to Paul's experience, thus underscoring the ongoing significance of immigration on American demographics.

Jakes also uses two other devices to underscore character. The first, the use of objects which become symbolic icons, is a technique familiar to readers of his earlier books. Here the tourists' Kodak, smashed by Von Rike, but carried by Paul as a talisman aboard the immigrant ship, represents what will be for Paul his ruling passion, his professional identity. Similarly, the globe bought for him by the rich old lady whom he'd defended from a thief (6-8, 20-22) symbolizes both his dream (23) and his success (1133). Other such objects include the paper flag of the revolution of 1848 (41), aligning Paul on the side of freedom and against military repression, and, of course, the stereopticon card of the Statue of Liberty (41, 1133). In a similar way, Uncle Joe's shaving mug (114, 270-73) served to remind him of a personal epiphany, the realization of the utter horror of the Civil War, transforming him in some "mystical way"; his wound, the "flowing blood, washed out the deepest part of his Germanness, . . . baptized him as an American, forever" (273).

Finally, character—and the transformation of identity through immigration and acculturation—is suggested through names. Pauli Kroner, like his Uncle Josef before him, changed his surname to Crown, its American equivalent. The boy Pauli becomes Paul to everyone except Aunt Ilsa, who mothered and nurtured him. Paul felt the sting of prejudice and bigotry; his pejorative nickname, "Heine," reminded him that not all Americans liked foreigners. His ultimate nickname, "Dutch," first applied by his mentor Wexford Rooney (524), also suggested his German origins—but revealed others' respect for his professionalism. It became his signature name—once he had gained full self-assurance. In a parallel fashion, his old friend Herschel Wolinski is now called Harry Poland, an *American* who doesn't forget his roots. Dutch and Harry, like Philip Kent before them (*The Bastard*), have been baptized as new men, having come to America.

THEMATIC ISSUES

In this most tightly constructed of Jakes books, all thematic elements reinforce each other. Jakes argues for maintaining personal and professional integrity (Paul is disillusioned by Shadow's willingness to fake documentary photography on the premise that the audience doesn't know any better). He juxtaposes a perversion of religion (Jimmy Daws strangling his victims with the chain from his religious medal) to the religion of service and love (Aunt Ilsa's unconditional nurturing of her family). He reprises through Uncle Joe the searing impact the Civil War had on the American soul. And he presents the irony of the diminution of opportunity in the post-frontier West—always before a symbol of fresh starts—in the very decade of the largest influx of European immigrants to American shores. Most important, however, is the search for and definition of *homeland*.

Jakes introduces the theme of homeland in the very first sentence; the quest continues to the last sentence. The protagonist's search for a home he can call his own is, thus, the central unifying element of the novel. Early in the novel, at the railhead where Buffalo Bill's show is unloading, Rhukov asks Pauli, "Where's your home?," to which the thirteen-year-old replies, "I don't know" (31). This is, however, not the plaintive wail of a little lost boy, for Paul already has plenty of street smarts. It is, instead, a realization, partly emotional and partly intellectual, that where he *is* is not home.

Throughout the novel there are many places which are "not-home." Certainly it's not the cramped Berlin apartment of his Aunt Lotte, dying of TB and supporting them with temporary liaisons with traveling salesmen. Even more certainly it is not Germany, increasingly dominated by a brutal military clique. Increasingly divided loyalties make his Uncle Joe's home inhospitable; finally he is, literally, thrown out on the streets for challenging his uncle's demands for unquestioning obedience. Haven though it is, his squalid cellar room at Shadow's is not home. Frustrated, Paul bleakly wonders whether home—for him—is simply "the place where I am at the moment" (835). Increasingly, he tries to harden his heart, set aside his dream of home. By the time he spends a night with Luisa in Tampa, he responds cynically to her question about his home. The hotel room is his home. Any place with a door, a window, a light, and a bed is "home enough for me" (971). They both know that's a lie. He protests too much. Saying good-bye, she utters a benediction: "Be safe in Cuba, and *go home safely afterward*" (971; emphasis added). As he's ready to ship out for Cuba, he seems to have reached a decision, one which will shield his heart from pain. Rather than return to America after the war, he was through with that "stupid child's dream. He hadn't any *home*" (990). Instead, he would follow his profession wherever it led. Having made that decision, he tore the stereopticon card of New York harbor and the Statue of Liberty in half, rejecting its symbolism.

Years earlier, as they entered New York harbor, Old Valter had told Paul, "Germania our mother—Columbia our bride" (76). The dual meaning is clear: one's place of birth is an accident, but one's nation is a matter of choice. Similarly, though one has no choice about his relatives, one does about his closest friend, his mate. It is not surprising, then, that almost simultaneously with falling in love with Julie, Paul is beset by dilemmas about his loyalties within his uncle's household. Increasingly, home for Paul is where Julie is. And when she is forced by her parents to marry Elstree, a vital element of Paul's search for home has been wrenched from him. Paul's subsequent rejection of America is less for Joe Junior's ideological reasons or Rhukov's cynicism than for his inability to have Julie. He tells his uncle, "I lost the one thing in America I wanted most. The one person" (1067).

And so he plans to leave—immediately after his greatest professional triumph, the premier of his film. At that moment, Paul seems destined to accept the despair and defeat personified by the Baker of Wuppertal, one of two exceedingly important minor characters in the novel.

The Baker is a Tiresias-like prophet of doom, foreshadowing the "dirt," "despair," "the truth behind the illusion you've created for yourself" (53). As Paul is setting out for America, the Baker is returning to Germany, a disillusioned, bitter failure, a man old beyond his years. Repeatedly throughout the book, Jakes uses the Baker as a cautionary figure warning that America is not El Dorado. But balancing him is Ott (Othello Person), a black corporal whom Paul meets in the staging area for the Cuban invasion. Despite the bigotry and prejudice he's faced, Ott believes that " 'Merica" might be a "wagon with one bad wheel," but it "carries a lot of folks farther than they ever thought they could go" (1054). Ott is a realist: "Ain't no place on earth won't disappoint you sometimes," but he pleads with Paul not to "run off" and leave America to the "mean ones" (1077). "Be an American," Ott exhorts (1053).

The dichotomy is clearly drawn. The Baker of Wuppertal versus Ott Person. Rejection of America versus affirmation of its possibilities. Disillusioned cynicism versus realistic commitment. Paul, despite his reconciliation with Uncle Joe, despite his professional success, is drawn almost equally in opposing directions, in need of a catalyst for decision. Years earlier, his benefactor, the old woman who gave him the globe, had hoped that, if Pauli's true home wasn't Berlin, he'd find it somewhere. She assured him that when he did find home, he'd know. Some unexpected sign would tell him (22). Quite appropriately, for Paul there are two signs. Julie, freed by Elstree's death, shows up at Paul's film premier (1120). But, even after his happy marriage to Julie, he still needed a sign to "banish the deep and haunting questions of childhood . . . to show him where he truly belonged" (1134). That final sign came when, at Ellis Island to film a documentary on immigration, Paul befriended an old German, tired and confused. Their bond was strong; they were countrymen, both from the same region. To the German, however, Paul was "My first American." Sensing Paul's ambivalence, the old man apologized: "I'm sorry I took you for an American" (1169).

The moment was, for Paul, an epiphany. The old man's quest mirrored—and validated—his own. There—at last—was the sign. "But I am, " he said, waving the old man on toward the inspectors. It was this incident with the old German which resolved Paul's doubts about his identity, the place he belonged. It was his sign that his place was here with Julie, in America, where men were "free to do good, and free to do evil, but free" (1173). And so, as he climbs the Statue of Liberty to get a dramatic cinematographic point of view, he has swung away from the Baker's doubt and toward Ott's affirmation. He is bound to his two loves, for Julie and for America. "He was home" (1174).

ALTERNATIVE PERSPECTIVE: THE COMING-OF-AGE NOVEL

Although *Homeland* could be approached from a variety of critical perspectives—Marxist, feminist, or New Historical criticism, for example— it might best be explored as a coming-of-age novel. The literary term for this kind of novel is *bildungsroman*, translated literally, a "novel of formation" or a "novel of education." Given Pauli Kroner's German origin, it is not inappropriate to use that critical term. The genre originated in German folktales of the dunce who goes out in the world in search of adventure and learns wisdom the hard way. The first novelistic treatment of the genre was J. W. von Goethe's *Wilhelm Meister's Apprenticeship* (1795-96), an account of the travels and adventures of a young man who learns that life itself is an apprenticeship. Twentieth century coming-of-age novels include James Joyce's *Portrait of the Artist as a Young Man* (1914-15), Willa Cather's *My Antonia* (1918), and J. D. Salinger's *Catcher in the Rye* (1951). These share the *bildungsroman*'s central feature: the protagonist's rite of passage from childhood to adulthood, often involving physical or psychological trauma; these experiences result in maturity, awareness of his identity and his place in the world. Jakes adapts these conventions and makes them his own.

For *Homeland* is a novel of a young German immigrant testing himself—against the elements, against corrupt and venal individuals, against prejudice and misunderstanding—and emerging, finally, perhaps bereft of some of his original naive dreams, but with a sure sense of self. The German street waif becomes a resourceful pioneer in the American motion picture industry; the abandoned and outcast youth finds selfassurance and personal integrity and, eventually, reconciliation and love; the boy with dreams becomes the man of accomplishment; the European man-without-a-country becomes, with conviction and affirmation, an American.

Bildungsroman is an appropriate label for this novel, for it is a comingof-age story not only of the protagonist, but, in a very real sense, of his adopted country, the United States. Though set from 1890 to 1900, the novel spans, through flashbacks and recollections, the time from the American Civil War in a country in disarray, a country divided against itself, politically schizophrenic, to a country which is the victor in the Spanish-American War, at the cusp not only of a new century but also of a new national role. America in 1900 had also come of age. Now a world power, the United States had outgrown its frontier adolescence and was poised on the edge of national maturity, capable, if it wished, of wielding military, political, and economic power far beyond its borders.

It had hope, of course, but hope mixed with assurance that it could now take its place as an adult in the family of nations. What the future might hold, in specific terms, was unclear, but few doubted that the next hundred years might legitimately be called "the American Century." America, like Paul Crown, had come of age. *Homeland* narrates the parallel rites of passage.

Finally, *Homeland* is a coming-of-age novel for John Jakes, for it is his best novel. In it he demonstrates his most mature techniques to date. His use of recurring images and motifs ("home," the camera, the Statue of Liberty, the "sign," and Herschel Wolinski) consciously and effectively unifies the novel. Without losing any of the panoramic effect observed in previous novels, the multiple point of view here is more organically linked to theme than ever before. Necessary historical exposition is more integrated into characters' thoughts and therefore does not interrupt narrative as it does in some Kent Family Chronicles. (See here Joe Crown's reflections during planning for the Columbian Exposition [pp. 110-14]). Because of this integration, exposition helps establish character.

Jakes also integrates themes he has addressed in other novels. The Revolutionary War of *The Bastard* and *The Rebels* is ideologically similar to the Boer War, which Paul covers (1137ff.). For Joe Crown, the Civil War was a more formative event than was his own immigration. And Joe Junior wandered the American West, which permeated *The Furies*, *The Lawless*, and *Heaven and Hell*; the difference, however, is that its connotation is no longer the land of opportunity. As we see these earlier themes addressed, we also see Jakes uniting the canon of his major works. He creates an intertwined world, rather like Faulkner's Yoknapatawpha County. A private Paul meets among the Rough Riders is from Texas, where he worked as a cowhand on a huge ranch called Main Chance (1026; see *Heaven and Hell*). In his western peregrinations Joe Junior picks navel oranges on the estate of a J. M. Chance near Riverside, California (799; see *California Gold*). And Joe Crown's tenant farmer on his South Carolina property is Orpheus LaMotte, who was born in 1855 and, after Appomattox, had taken the last name of his master on an Ashley River plantation named Resolute (552; see the North and South series).

In many ways, this is Jakes' most personal book. He is confident enough to reveal far more of himself than ever before. Elements of his biography are interwoven into the novel: Jakes' familiarity with advertising is passed on to Joe Crown (102-3); his early, and continuing, love of motion pictures takes life in Colonel Shadow and all the other movie pioneers, real and fictional, portrayed here; Joe Crown "loved the Low Country of Carolina" (554), and Wexford Rooney's personal tragedy (576-80) occurred on Port Royal Sound between Hilton Head Island (Jakes' current home) and the mainland. Jakes' passionate support of public libraries is demonstrated in Joe Junior's haunting libraries as he wandered from place to place (798) and in Julie's visit to Andrew Carnegie, patron of libraries, who served as her guide in philanthropy (1131).

Moreover, German friends on Hilton Head reunited Jakes with his "long-lost family" in Germany, including a cousin, Thomas Rätz in Aalen, and thus "planted the seed for this story" (1179). Jakes dedicates *Homeland* to his grandfather, William Carl Retz, who emigrated from Germany about 1870. And, in the novel, Uncle Joe and Aunt Lotte's mother's maiden name was Gertrud Retz (15-16). These very personal connections to the experiences of Pauli Kroner/Paul Crown infuse _Homeland_.

Once again, as he did in his previous historical family sagas, Jakes has returned to American themes and values. And though he finished the novel in 1992, "a time of profound national confusion, even despair," he chooses to write of an earlier time when "America symbolized virtually limitless opportunity," when "no problem was unconquerable. . . . Hope was in the air."

Jakes leaves the reader of _Homeland_ with his final, very personal benediction: "I hope Americans will be able to say that again someday" ("Afterword," 1182).

Bibliography

WORKS BY JOHN JAKES

Note: Some page citations are not to the original edition; when this is the case, the edition used is noted in brackets following the original bibliographic citation.

The Americans. New York: Jove Books, 1980.
The Asylum World. New York: Paperback Library, 1969.
The Bastard. New York: Pyramid Books, 1974. [New York: Jove Books, 1977.]
The Best of John Jakes. Edited by Martin H. Greenberg and Joseph D. Olander. New York: Daw Books, 1977.
The Best Western Short Stories of John Jakes. Edited by Bill Pronzini and Martin H. Greenberg. Athens: Ohio University Press, 1991.
Black in Time. New York: Paperback Library, 1970.
Brak the Barbarian. New York: Avon Books, 1968.
Brak the Barbarian vs. the Mark of the Demons. New York: Paperback Library, 1969.
Brak the Barbarian vs. the Sorceress. New York: Paperback Library, 1969.
Brak the Barbarian: When the Idols Walked. New York: Pocket Books, 1978.
"California Gold." *Cosmopolitan*, September 1989, 271, 306-22.
California Gold. New York: Random House, 1989. [New York: Ballantine Books, 1990.]
Conquest of the Planet of the Apes. New York: Award Books, 1972.
"Cultivating the Literary Habit." *Writer* 107 (July 1994): 5-6.
The Devil Has Four Faces. Thomas Bouregy and Co., 1958.

Dracula, Baby (lyrics; book revision, uncredited). Chicago: Dramatic Publishing, 1970.

Famous Firsts in Sports. New York: G. P. Putnam's Sons, 1967.

The Fortunes of Brak. New York: Dell Books, 1980.

The Furies. New York: Pyramid Books, 1976. [New York: Jove Books, 1978.]

G. I. Girls. Derby, Conn.: Monarch Books, 1963.

Great War Correspondents. New York: G. P. Putnam's Sons, 1967.

Great Women Reporters. New York: G. P. Putnam's Sons, 1969.

Heaven and Hell. New York: Harcourt Brace Jovanovich, 1987. [New York: Dell, 1988.]

"The Historical Family Saga." *Writer* 92 (November 1979): 9-12ff.

Homeland. New York: Doubleday, 1993. [New York: Bantam, 1994.]

The Hybrid. New York: Paperback Library, 1969.

"If I Don't Like It, I Don't Blurb It." *Wall Street Journal*, 20 February 1991, A15.

The Impostor. New York: Thomas Bouregy and Co., 1959.

In the Big Country. Edited by Bill Pronzini and Martin H. Greenberg. New York: Bantam Books, 1993.

Johnny Havoc. New York: Belmont Books, 1960.

Johnny Havoc and the Doll Who Had "It." New York: Belmont Books, 1963.

Johnny Havoc Meets Zelda. New York: Belmont Books, 1962.

The Last Magicians. New York: Signet/New American Library, 1969.

The Lawless. New York: Jove Books, 1978.

"The Longest Walk." *Ladies Home Journal*, August 1985, 157-64.

"Love and War." *Ladies Home Journal*, November 1984, 111ff.

Love and War. New York: Harcourt Brace Jovanovich, 1984. [New York: Dell, 1988.]

Making It Big. New York: Belmont Books, 1968.

The Man from Cannae. Rev., enlarged edition. Los Angeles: Pinnacle Books, 1977. Originally published as *Traitor's Legion* by Jay Scotland, 1963.

Mask of Chaos. New York: Ace Books, 1970.

Master of the Dark Gate. New York: Lancer Books, 1970.

Mention My Name in Atlantis. New York: Daw Books, 1972.

"Mercy at Gettysburg." *U.S.A. Today Magazine*, 1 July 1994; 10-11.

Mohawk: The Life of Joseph Brant. New York: Crowell-Collier, 1969.

Monte Cristo #99. New York: Modern Library Editions, 1970.

New Trails: 23 Original Stories of the West. Edited by John Jakes and Martin H. Greenberg. New York: Doubleday, 1994.

A Night for Treason. New York: Thomas Bouregy and Co., 1956.

North and South. New York: Harcourt Brace Jovanovich, 1982. [New York: Dell, HBJ, 1988.]

On Wheels. New York: Paperback Library, 1973.

The Planet Wizard. New York: Ace Books, 1969.

The Rebels. New York: Pyramid Books, 1975. [New York: Jove Books, 1978.]

The Secrets of Stardeep. Philadelphia: Westminster Press, 1969.

The Seekers. New York: Pyramid Books, 1975. [New York: Jove Books, 1978.]

Six-Gun Planet. New York: Paperback Library, 1970.

Stranger with Roses. Chicago: Dramatic Publishing, 1972.

Susanna of the Alamo: A True Story. San Diego: Gulliver Books/Harcourt Brace Jovanovich, 1986.

The Texans Ride North. Philadelphia: John C. Winston, 1952.

"There's Always a Book—Or Is There?" *Parade Magazine,* 13 March 1994, 12-13.

"Three Essentials for a Successful Writing Career." *Writer* 94 (July 1981): n.p.

Time Gate. Philadelphia: Westminster Press, 1972.

Tiros: Weather Eye in Space. New York: Julian Messner, 1966.

The Titans. New York: Pyramid Books, 1976. [New York: Jove Books, 1978.]

"To Be a Writer: What Does It Take?" *Writer* 100 (January 1987): 9-11.

Tonight We Steal the Stars. New York: Ace Books, 1969.

The Warriors. New York: Pyramid Books, 1977. [New York: Jove Books, 1980.]

Wear a Fast Gun. New York: Arcadia House, 1956.

"What? A Successful Media Campaign Without TV Spots and Phil Donahue?" *TV Guide*, 2 November 1985, 12-15.

When the Star Kings Die. New York: Ace Books, 1967.

Witch of the Dark Gate. New York: Lancer Books, 1972.

Writing as Alan Payne

This'll Slay You. New York: Ace Books, 1958.

Writing as Rachel Ann Payne

Ghostwind. New York: Paperback Library, 1966.

Writing as Jay Scotland

Arena. New York: Ace Books, 1963.

I, Barbarian. New York: Avon Books, 1959.

The Seventh Man. New York: Thomas Bouregy and Co., 1958.

Sir Scoundrel. New York: Ace Books, 1962.

Strike the Black Flag. New York: Ace Books, 1961.

Traitor's Legion. New York: Ace Books, 1963.

The Veils of Salome. New York: Avon Books, 1962.

WORKS ABOUT JOHN JAKES

General Information

Allis, Tim. "The Spoils of War: 'North and South' Brought Three Couples Together." *People Weekly*, 28 February 1994: 76-78.

Ashby, Franklin. "The Making of 'North and South': They Had to Shoot Around
the Mercedes-Benzes—But Finding Okra for Liz Was Even Tougher." *TV
Guide*, 2 November 1985, 4-8.

Bachrach, Judy. "15 Million Paperbacks Later . . ." *Washington Post*, 20 April 1977,
B1, B2.

Begley, Adam. "The Tempest around Stephen Greenblatt." *New York Times Magazine*, 28 March 1993, 36.

"Best-Selling Author to Speak at USC System Commencement." *USC Times* [Co-
lumbia, S.C.], 10 December 1993, 1.

Brannon, Barbara, and Vanessa Farr. "John Jakes: The People's Author." Exhibition catalogue. Columbia: University of South Carolina, 1993.

Chepesiuk, Ron. "Writers at Work: How Libraries Shape the Muse." *American
Libraries* 25 (December 1994): 984-87.

Czura, Gwen. "Up Close and Personal with John Jakes." *Island Events*, December
1994, 12ff.

Dahlin, Robert. "John Jakes." *Publishers Weekly* 226 (30 November 1984): 99-100.

———. "The Making of a Best Selling Series: Jakes' Pyramid Novels for the
American Bicentennial." *Publishers Weekly* 209 (5 April 1976): 59-60.

Dakers, Beryl. Interview. "Art's the Thing." May 1989. South Carolina Educational Television, Columbia.

Downing, Bob. "A Trip to the Past with John Jakes." *Times-Picayune* (New Orleans), 4 March 1982, 3:11.

Farr, Sharon. "Dayton and Beyond." WDTN. Dayton, Ohio. February 1994.

Feldman, Gayle. "Love Me Not? A Second Look at Some Books Whose Time
Had Not Come." *Publishers Weekly* 241 (7 March 1994): S9-S12.

Greenblatt, Stephen. *Renaissance Self-Fashioning: From More to Shakespeare*. Chicago: University of Chicago Press.

Hanscom, Leslie. "Paper Tiger." *Detroit News*, 12 February 1982, 1B.

Hawkins, Robert. *The Kent Family Chronicles Encyclopedia*. New York: Bantam
Books, 1979.

"Interview with Kettering, Ohio, Author John Jakes." *Gem City Saver Bicentennial
Issue*. Dayton, Ohio: Gem City Savings Association, 1976.

"Jakes' Manuscripts on Display at USC." *The State* [Columbia, S.C.], 5 December
1993, 5F.

Jarvis, Jeff. [Television program reviews.] *TV Guide*, 26 February 1994, 55.

"John Jakes Spins Out Paperback Best-Sellers on the Bicentennial." *People Weekly*, 12 April 1976, 25.

Just, Patty. Interview. "South Carolina Writers' Circle." 5 June 1993. South Carolina Educational Television, Florence, South Carolina.

Kelley, George. In James Vinson, ed. *Twentieth Century Western Writers.* New York: Macmillan, 1982, 349-51.

King, Larry. Interview. 22 February 1983. Mutual Radio.

———. "The Larry King Show." Mutual Radio, 8 September 1989.

Kinsella, Bridget. "Jakes Contest Seeks the American Experience." *Publishers Weekly* 240 (17 May 1993): 27-28.

Koris, Sally. "For One John Jakes, the Bicentennial Seems Perennial." *Wall Street Journal*, 9 June 1977, 1ff.

"Kup's Show." National Public Radio, WTTW, Chicago, 18 February 1983.

Magnus, Edie. Interview. *CBS This Morning.* 28 June 1993. New York.

Maryles, Daisy. "The Sky's the Limit: Soaring Numbers Fueled by Superstore Expansion." *Publishers Weekly* 241 (7 March 1994): S3-S8.

Mitgang, Herbert. "Behind the Best Sellers." *New York Times Book Review*, 30 April 1978, 74.

Moore, Gene. Interview. *By-Line*. 29 April 1980. Educational Television Network. Atlanta.

O'Connor, John J. "John Jakes' 'Heaven and Hell.' " *New York Times*, 25 February 1994, B8, B14.

Olendorf, Donna, ed. *Bestsellers 89: Books and Authors in the News.* Vol. 4. Detroit: Gale, 1990.

Osgood, Charles. Interview. *CBS Evening News.* 1 April 1978. New York.

" 'The People's Author' Speaks—and English Students Listen." *Publishers Weekly* 241 (10 January 1994): 7.

Phelan, Charlotte. "Covering Old American Ground in Jakes' Streaking Roller Coaster." *Houston Post*, 14 March 1982, 26AA.

Polking, Kirk. "John Jakes Has a Fever. A Writing Fever." *Writer's Digest*, 57 January 1977, 22-23.

Rosenberg, Howard. Review of ABC's miniseries "North and South, Book II." *Los Angeles Times*, 2 May 1986, VI:20.

Ross, Jean W. Interview. In *Contemporary Authors* (New Revision Series). Vol. 10. Detroit: Gale, 1983, 244-46.

Ross, Michelle. "Book Critic Michelle Ross Looks at More Summer Reading." *CNN Morning News.* Cable News Network, 13 August 1993. Show #383, Segment 3.

Salvatore, Nick, and Ann Sullivan. "From Bastard to American: The Legitimization of a Fictional Family." *Radical History Review* 26 (1982): 140-50.

Schindehette, S. "Bedrooms and Battlefields Fill John Jakes' Sagas of the Old South." *People Weekly*, 12 November 1984, 63-67.

Seibel, Deborah Starr. "Heaven and Hell Stops in Between: The One-Time Miniseries Queen Knows What It Means to Be a Survivor." *TV Guide*, 26 February 1994, 24-26.

Shales, Tom. "Ask Not for Whom the Belle Tolls." *Washington Post*, 26 February 1994, D1, D5.

Skotnes, Pearl. Interview. "All About Books." 14 October 1989. Pacifica Radio KPFK. Los Angeles.

Starr, William W. "Jakes Donating Papers to USC." *The State* [Columbia, S.C.], 13 June 1993, 4F.

Strickland, Bill. "Keep the Words Coming." *Writer's Digest* 71 (February 1991): 26-33.

Suplee, Curt. "The 50-Novel, Multimillion Dollar Saga of John Jakes." *Washington Post Book World*, 28 February, L1f.

Sweeting, Paul. "A View from Abridge." *Publishers Weekly* 223 (22 April 1988): 53-57.

"Take Two." Cable News Network. Atlanta, 1 March 1982.

"Thomas Cooper Exhibit Gives Insight into Jakes' Novels." *USC Times* [Columbia, S.C.], 10 December 1993, 8.

Today Show. National Broadcasting Corporation. New York, 2 February 1982.

———. National Broadcasting Corporation. New York, 5 November 1987.

———. National Broadcasting Corporation. New York, 5 September 1989.

Walters, Ray. "Paperback Talk." *New York Times Book Review*, 7 October 1979, 41-42.

Washington Post Book World, 7 March 1976, 10.

Wholey, Dennis. "America: Personal Conversations with Dennis Wholey." Interview by Public Broadcasting Corporation, Washington, D.C., 16 July 1993.

Winchell, Mark Royden. In *Leslie Fiedler*. Boston: Twayne, 1985, 94.

Yoke, Carl B. In James Vinson, ed., *Twentieth Century Western Writers*. New York: Macmillan, 1982, 409-11.

Biographical Information

Contemporary Authors. New Revision Series 10. Detroit: Gale, 1983, s.v. "Jakes, John."

Contemporary Literary Criticism 29. Detroit: Gale, 1984, s.v. "Jakes, John."

Dictionary of Literary Biography Yearbook 1983. Detroit: Gale, 1984, s.v. "Jakes, John."

http://julmara.ce.chalmers.se/sfarchive/authorlist.

Something About the Author 62. Detroit: Gale, 1989, s.v. "Jakes, John."

Unpublished Sources

Jakes, John. Interviews with the author.
———. Letters to the author. 29 September 1994, 22 June 1995, 9 July 1995, 18 July 1995, 5 August 1995, 16 August 1995, 19 August 1995.
———. Publisher's biography.
———. "Words to Write By." Videotape of a lecture presented at the Atlanta Historical Society, 1987.

REVIEWS AND CRITICISM

A Night for Treason (1956)

West Coast Review of Books 8 (April 1982): 45.

The Devil Has Four Faces (1958)

West Coast Review of Books 8 (Fall 1982): 51.

Johnny Havoc (1960)

Rogers, Michael. *Library Journal* 116 (1 February 1991): 109.

Tiros: Weather Eye in Space (1966)

Best Sellers 26 (1 January 1967): 368.
Fortier, Oride. *Library Journal* 91 (15 October 1966): 5252.
Kirkus Reviews 34 (15 August 1966): 843.
Science Books and Films 2 (March 1967): 278.

Famous Firsts in Sports (1967)

Agree, Rose. *Instructor* 77 (August/September 1967): 207.
Kirkus Reviews 35 (15 February 1967): 205.
Library Journal 92 (15 May 1967): 2042.

Brak the Barbarian (1968)

Bookwest 1 (October 1977): 34.
Voice of Youth Advocates 4 (October 1981): 62.

Great War Correspondents (1968)

Kirkus Reviews 35 (1 December 1967): 1429.

Great Women Reporters (1969)

Cart, Michael. *Library Journal* 94 (15 February 1969): 885.

Mohawk (1969)

Kirkus Reviews 37 (1 July 1969): 676.

Secrets of Stardeep (1969)

Henniker-Heaton, Peter J. "Still Racing to the Moon." *Christian Science Monitor*,
        6 November 1969, B7.
Kennerly, Sarah Law. *Library Journal* 94 (15 December 1969): 4619.
Kirkus Reviews 37 (15 October 1969): 1123.
Russ, Lavinia. *Publishers Weekly* 196 (20 October 1969): 61.

Mention My Name in Atlantis (1972)

Lottman, Eileen. *Publishers Weekly* 202 (4 September 1972): 52.

Time Gate (1972)

Kirkus Reviews 40 (15 February 1972): 192-93.
Kliatt 12 (Spring 1978): 12.
Winnikoff, JoEllen. *Library Journal* 97 (15 May 1972): 1922.

The Bastard (1974)

Brod, Doug. *Entertainment Weekly*, 17 January 1992, 66.
Fein, Michael. *Library Journal* 118 (1 June 1993): 164.
Lamphier, Susan B. *Library Journal* 118 (1 June 1993): 208.
Turner, Alice K. *Publishers Weekly* 206 (2 September 1974): 71.

The Rebels (1975)

Diltz-Siler, Barbara. *Booklist* 90 (July 1994): 1965.
Stuttaford, Genevieve. *Publishers Weekly* 207 (3 February 1976): 76.

The Seekers (1975)

Stuttaford, Genevieve. *Publishers Weekly* 207 (16 June 1975): 83.

The Best of John Jakes (1977)

Miller, Dan. *Booklist* 74 (1 September 1977): 23.
Stuttaford, Genevieve. *Publishers Weekly* 213 (2 May 1977): 67.

The Warriors (1977)

Cook, Bruce. "They Went Thataway." *Washington Post Book World*, 3 April 1977,
    E3.
New York Times Book Review, 3 April 1977, 53.
Stuttaford, Genevieve. *Publishers Weekly* 207 (14 February 1977): 81-82.
Zajchowski, Carol. *Library Journal* 102 (1 May 1977): 1043-44.

The Lawless (1978)

Booklist 74 (15 May 1978): 1476.
Stuttaford, Genevieve. *Publishers Weekly* 213 (27 February 1978): 154.

The Americans (1980)

Hinkemeyer, Joan. *Library Journal* 107 (15 February 1980): 528.
Lodge, Salla A. *Publishers Weekly* 216 (24 December 1979): 56.

The Fortunes of Brak (1980)

Lodge, Sally A. *Publishers Weekly* 216 (3 December 1979): 49.

North and South (1982)

Adler, Anne G. *Library Journal* 107 (15 February 1982): 473.
Altinel, Savkar. *Times Literary Supplement*, 20 August 1982, 910.
Bannon, Barbara. *Publishers Weekly* 220 (18 December 1981): 59.
————. *Publishers Weekly* 222 (17 December 1982): 73.
Best Sellers 42 (April 1982): 8.
Brosnahan, John. *Booklist* 78 (15 January 1982): 618.
Dillin, Gay Andrews. "Popular Civil War Saga." *Christian Science Monitor,* 7 April 1982, 17.
Drake, Anstiss. "John Jakes Fires His Big Guns on Fort Sumter." *Chicago Tribune Book World*, 21 February 1982, 7:1-2.
Kirkus Reviews 49 (15 December 1981): 1540-41.
Kliatt 17 (Spring 1983): 8.
McDowell, Edwin. "Historical Accuracy." *New York Times Book Review*, 17 January 1982, 34.
Sales, Grover. "A Slave to Popular Success." *Los Angeles Times Book Review*, 21 March 1982, 8.
Watkins, Mel. *New York Times Book Review,* 7 March 1982, 24.
West Coast Review of Books 8 (April 1982): 39.
Yardley, Jonathan. "Antebellum Up to the Bar, Boys: John Jakes' Epic Novel of Pre-Civil War America." *Washington Post*, 3 February 1982, B1, B8.

Love and War (1984)

Abrams, Gary. "Blue and Gray Beget Bigness." *Los Angeles Times Book Review*, 2 December 1984, 8.
Best Sellers 44 (January 1985): 367.
Brosnahan, John. *Booklist* 81 (1 September 1984): 3.

Kirkus Reviews 52 (15 August 1984): 769.

Lamphier, Susan B. *Library Journal* 119 (15 October 1994): 102.

Piehl, Kathy. *Library Journal* 89 (1 November 1984): 2079-80.

Steinberg, Sybil. *Publishers Weekly* 226 (28 September 1984): 98.

Susanna of the Alamo (1986)

Bulletin of the Center for Children's Books, June 1986, 186-87.

Children's Book Review Service 14 (July 1986): 42

Croper, Ilene. *Booklist* 82 (15 June 1986): 1540-41.

Dingus, Anne. *Texas Monthly* 18 (January 1990): 132.

Loomis, Christine. *Parents Magazine*, November 1986, 72.

McConnell, Ruth M. *School Library Journal* 32 (August 1986): 93-94.

New York Times Book Review, 27 April 1986, 25.

Odell, Joshua. "Jakes and Bacon Create an HBJ Children's Book." *Publishers Weekly* 228 (18 October 1985): 29.

Publishers Weekly 237 (28 September 1990): 106.

Robak, Diane. *Publishers Weekly* 229 (25 April 1986): 78.

Sebesta, Sam Leaton. *Reading Teacher* 40 (January 1987): 460.

Sidley, Jeanette L. *Social Education* 51 (April/May 1987): 292.

Heaven and Hell (1987)

Brosnahan, John. *Booklist* 84 (15 September 1987): 90-91.

Perez-Stable, Maria A. *Library Journal* 112 (15 November 1987): 90.

Sabiston, Pat. *Atlanta Journal and Constitution*, 22 November 1987, J11.

Smith, Wendy. *New York Times Book Review*, 8 November 1987, 26.

Stabiner, Karen. *Los Angeles Times Book Review*, 27 September 1987, 11.

Steinberg, Sybil. *Publishers Weekly* 232 (18 September 1987): 161.

———. *Publishers Weekly* 234 (29 July 1988): 228.

California Gold (1989)

Abeel, Erica. *New Woman* 19 (September 1989): 32.

Books 3 (January 1990): 17.

Graham, S. Keith. "John Jakes' 'Gold' Rich in Momentum." *Atlanta Journal and Constitution*, 24 September 1989, L11.

Langlois, Karen S. *Western American Literature* 25 (Winter 1991): 371-72.

Morgan, Janet. *Library Journal* 116 (1 October 1991): 156.

O'Briant, Don. "Chills, Spills as King, Reagan Top Authors Booking It in Fall." *Atlanta Journal and Constitution,* 10 September 1989, L1, L4.

Pellecchia, Michael. *New York Times Book Review,* October 1989, 24.

Rawlinson, Nora. *Library Journal* 114 (15 April 1989): 60.

See, Carolyn. "John Jakes: Cold No More, Poor No More." *Washington Post Book World,* 17 September 1989, 3ff.

Stabiner, Karen. "Storytellers: New in September." *Los Angeles Times Book Review,* 20 August 1989, 5.

Steinberg, Sybil. *Publishers Weekly* 236 (28 July 1989): 204.

———. *Publishers Weekly* 237 (7 September 1990): 82.

Venant, Elizabeth. "The Modest Midas." *Los Angeles Times Book Review,* 18 September 1989, V1, 6.

Weingartner, Steve. *Booklist* 85 (August 1989): 1922.

West Coast Review of Books 15 (1989): 18.

The Best Western Stories of John Jakes (1991)

Jordan, Robert. *Library Journal* 116 (15 February 1991): 221.

Klaschus, Candace. *Western American Literature* 27 (Spring 1992): 90.

Kliatt 25 (September 1991): 32.

University Press Book News 3 (December 1991): 41.

Homeland (1993)

Blades, John. "Home-Brew." *Chicago Tribune,* 12 July 1993, 5:1-2.

Blaes, Shirley B. *School Library Journal* 40 (January 1994): 144-45.

Browne, Gretchen. *Library Journal* 118 (1 November 1993): 166.

Collins, Joe. *Booklist* 89 (1 May 1993): 21.

Cook, Bruce. "High Life and Low Dives." *Washington Post Sunday Magazine,* 18 July 1993, 1.

Donahue, Deirdre. "John Jakes, Spinning Stories from America's Heritage." *USA Today,* 3 August 1993, D3.

Hajari, Nisjid. "Bratwurst and Bathos: 'Homeland' Is More Miniseries Script than Novel." *Entertainment Weekly,* 16 July 1993, 51.

McCray, Nancy. *Booklist* 90 (15 January 1994): 953-54.

Rachlin, Jill. *People Weekly,* 26 July 1993, 28.

Ross, Michelle. "Saga Master Launches a New American Drama." *Christian Science Monitor,* 15 August 1993, 14.

Steinberg, Sybil. *Publishers Weekly* 240 (10 May 1993): 48-49.

Wilson, Frank. "Coming to America: John Jakes Traces the Progress of a Plucky German Immigrant." *New York Times Book Review*, 22 August 1993, 14.
Zinsser, John. *Publishers Weekly* 240 (5 July 1993): 34.

In the Big Country: The Best Western Stories of John Jakes (1993)

Browne, Gretchen. *Library Journal* 119 (15 November 1994): 106.
Kliatt 27 (May 1993): 21.

New Trails: 23 Original Stories of the West (1994)

Jordan, Robert. *Library Journal* 119 (1 October 1994): 117.
Lukowsky, Wes. *Booklist* 91 (15 October 1994): 403.
Steinberg, Sybil S. *Publishers Weekly* 241 (3 October 1994): 53.
Williams, Hart. *Washington Post Book World*, 8 January 1995, 8.

OTHER SECONDARY SOURCES

Abrams, M. H. *A Glossary of Literary Terms*. 6th ed. New York: Harcourt Brace, 1993.
Davis, Robert Murray. "The Frontiers of Genre: Science Fiction Westerns." *Science Fiction Studies* 12 (March 1985): 33-41.
Drowns, Anne. "Editorial Judgment or Censorship? The Case of American Psycho." *Writer* 104 (May 1991) 20-23.
Elliot, Florence, and Michael Summerskill. *A Dictionary of Politics*, Rev. Ed. Harmondsworth, Middlesex, G.B.: Penguin Books, Ltd., 1961.
Foner, Eric, and John A. Garraty, eds. *The Reader's Companion to American History*. Boston: Houghton Mifflin, 1991.
Holliday, J.S. *The World Rushed In: The California Gold Rush Experience: An Eyewitness Account of a Nation Heading West*. New York: Simon and Schuster, 1981.
Merriam-Webster's Encyclopedia of Literature. Springfield, Mass: Merriam-Webster, 1995.
Moss, George Donelson. *Vietnam: An American Ordeal*. 2nd ed. Englewood Cliffs, N.J.: Prentice-Hall, 1994.
Rice, Richard B., William A. Bullough, and Richard J. Orsi. *The Elusive Eden: A New History of California*. New York: Alfred A. Knopf, 1988.

Index

120, 174–77, through concrete
detail, 117–20; character-driven
plots, 26, 37, 39, 64, 173; character
motivation, 5, 15, 25; characters,
illustrative of themes, 40; closing
plot lines, 54, 127, 132–33;
continuing plot lines, 54, 146;
epigraphs, use of, 12, 40, 57–58, 96,
154, 160, 179; exposition, methods
of, 12, 33, 53–54, 131; first person
point of view, 26; juxtaposition, 17,
24, 41, 77, 102, 122, 140–42, 173;
manipulation of time, 26; multiple
plot lines, 26, 52, 66, 102; multiple
points of view, 26, 52, 86, 112, 127,
189–90; omniscient point of view,
26; opening plot lines, 54; point of
view, general, 68, 83, 99, 101, 173;
point of view of a woman, 17;
simultaneity, 12, 113, 130–31;
violence, use of, 15, 18, 19–20, 25–
26

—Works: *The Americans*, 20, 127–42,
145; *Arena*, 18; *The Bastard*, 3, 4, 21,
31–49, 51, 54, 55, 60, 63, 76, 79, 86,
127, 176, 185, 189, 193, 198; *Black in
Time*, 13; Brak the Barbarian series,
26; *California Gold*, 7, 9, 21, 169–84,
185, 198; *Conquest of the Planet of the
Apes*, 8; *The Devil Has Four Faces*,
12, 13; *The Furies*, 3, 13, 20, 52, 63–
80, 127, 198; *Gonzaga's Woman*, 12;
Great War Correspondents, 13; *Heaven
and Hell*, 9, 20, 21, 197, 198;
Homeland, 9, 12, 21, 185–99; *The
Hybrid*, 13; *I, Barbarian*, 7, 15–16; *The
Impostor*, 12, 13; *In the Big Country*,
14; Johnny Havoc series, 13, 26;
Kent Family Chronicles, 7, 8–9, 11,
25, 29–30, 145, 169, 185, 186, 197;
King's Crusader, 4, 14–15, 26; *The
Lawless*, 20, 111–25, 127, 136, 197;
Love and War, 9, 17; *The Man from

Cannae, 14, 17; "Manitow and
Ironhand," 19, 23–24; *Master of the
Dark Gate*, 16; *New Trails*, 19; *A
Night for Treason*, 12, 13; *North and
South*, 4, 9, 21, 81; North and South
series, 145–67, 169, 185, 189, 198;
Pardon Me, Is This Planet Taken?, 13;
The Planet Wizard, 12, 13; *The Rebels*,
3, 19, 21, 25, 34, 51–61, 63, 76, 127,
176, 198; *The Secrets of Stardeep*, 12;
The Seekers, 3, 20, 52, 54, 63–80, 127;
The Seventh Man, 12; *Six-Gun Planet*,
19–20; *Strike the Black Flag*, 18–19;
Susanna of the Alamo, 7, 13; *The
Texans Ride North*, 12, 14, 19; *Time
Gate*, 12; *Tiros, Weather Eye in Space*,
6; *The Titans*, 25, 75, 81–96, 136;
Tonight We Steal the Stars, 12, 16;
The Warriors, 20, 25, 81, 97–110, 114,
127; *Wear a Fast Gun*, 19; *When the
Star Kings Die*, 12, 13

Jealousy, 149
Jefferson, Thomas, 76, 142
Jeopardy!, 14
Johnson, Barbara, 108
Johnstown flood, 129, 139
Journalism, journalists, 13, 82, 91, 114,
139–42, 170–71
Journals, 151, 154
Joyce, James, 196

Kennedy, John Fitzgerald, 134
Kent and Son, 57, 64, 66, 72, 73, 74, 98
Kent Family Chronicles, 31, 117, 127
Kent family leadership, 65, 68, 107,
127–28, 131, 133
Kent family, as symbol for nation, 36,
56–57, 60, 72, 75, 83, 84, 85, 86, 128,
138, 141
Kentland, 32, 33, 99
Killing, 33–35, 70, 152, 162–63
King, Stephen, 10
Know Nothings, 71

About the Author

MARY ELLEN JONES is Director of American Studies and Associate Professor of English at Wittenberg University in Springfield, Ohio. She is author of *The American Frontier* (1994), *Seeds of Change: Readings on Cultural Exchange after 1492* (1993), and *Christopher Columbus and His Legacy* (1992).